All the Ghosts
Dance Free

T0273460

All the Ghosts Dance Free

A Memoir

Terry Cameron Baldwin

SHE WRITES PRES

Copyright ©2015 by Terry Baldwin

All rights reserved. No part of this publication may be reproduced, distributed, or transmitted in any form or by any means, including photocopying, recording, digital scanning, or other electronic or mechanical methods, without the prior written permission of the publisher, except in the case of brief quotations embodied in critical reviews and certain other noncommercial uses permitted by copyright law. For permission requests, please address She Writes Press.

Published 2015
Printed in the United States of America
ISBN: 978-1-63152-822-4
Library of Congress Control Number: 2015938665

For information, address:
She Writes Press
1563 Solano Ave #546
Berkeley, CA 94707

She Writes Press is a division of SparkPoint Studio, LLC.

For Deb, Mike and Edna
Whose early departures marked my life with loss

And to Gangaji
Who reminded me there is no one to be,
nowhere to go, and nothing to lose

Book One

Daddy's Girl

⌐

*Security is mostly a superstition. It does not exist
in nature, nor do the children of men experience it.
Avoiding danger is no safer in the long run than outright
exposure. Life is either a daring adventure or nothing.*

Helen Keller

Dad sharing his love of flight
Photo credit: Kitty Gray

One

THE DAILY BREEZE NEWS
Serving the South Bay Communities
in Los Angeles County

South Bay Yesterday

Children could pull lobster pots in the morning before school, peer at ships entering the port via telescope, check a nearby chart that would help them identify the shipping line, or they could swim in a large pool separated from the ocean by a rock groin. Adults could tie up boats to the long concrete pier, enjoy a cocktail in a glass-enclosed bar open to the sky, and dine in the elegant Garden Room before retiring to a brightly painted beach cottage for the night.

The world was my favorite color, and the sound of the sea was background music for my early years. I grew up on the California coastline, when tide pools teemed with life, in a cove bracketed by rounded promontories that to me were whales facing out to sea, their wide mouths spewing foam at the water's edge. These watchful sentries loomed large, and they defined my protected part of the vast, rhythmic world.

Those blue-white days on the beach were mine, and there was salty freedom in each breath. The sun caught in glistening tubes as

3

waves rolled in, surrounded me in lacy froth, then dragged the skittering, clicking pebbles over hardened sand as the water folded back into itself. The constant surging of the sea left treasure in its wake, and I scanned the ground for softened spirals, bits of glass, and scurrying life forms. Seaweed made hieroglyphics in the sand. I bent over rock-trapped pools that cupped orange stars, spiked purple urchins, and anemones I stuck my finger into, to feel it pulled and sucked until I jerked it back with a scream, adding my voice to the occasional seagull's cry.

Seaside explorations took place under the casual surveillance of mothers attending to their tans like religious devotees. Painted toenails made indentations in wet sand and cigarettes were stubbed out in the nacre of abalone shells. Young, graceful, and athletic, the women surveyed the scene with satisfaction, never imagining the earth split into fissures. White sails darted in the distance, wind-propelled over the white-capped waves, over the huge creatures that lived down deep.

I was in love with the ocean, rocks, seashells, and my piano, which stood in the living room in front of a glass wall. Through the window I looked at the sea while I stretched my fingers across smooth keys and experimented with sound. I knew the water's moods, and watched for signs of change—the way it gathered and darkened before a storm, when rain stippled the rare gray water in our mild Mediterranean climate. Sometimes, after the rain, a full arc of color hooped over Catalina Island, an arm resting its weight on the horizon.

Long before, our cove had been a smuggler's hideaway, and also a whaling cove, and though it is horrible to think that my best memories took place on the site of such carnage, we *did* excavate vertebrae from the cliff side. During the whales' seasonal migrations, we tracked the spumes of pods traversing the sea below the house.

Two

THE DAILY BREEZE NEWS
Serving the South Bay Communities
in Los Angeles County

South Bay Yesterday
Residents of all ages indulged in parties on the south-facing
beach that boasts a warmer and drier microclimate than areas
just a few miles away.

That was the private, gated Portuguese Bend Club in what
is now Rancho Palos Verdes on the Palos Verdes Peninsula.
From the outset in 1948, the project cultivated an exclusive
atmosphere. World War II GI pin-up Betty Grable attended
the opening. Performing seals played in the pool during a 1950
Labor Day party that also featured a luau cooked by a chef
flown in from Hawaii.

Our house looked nice in the *LA Times Home Section* as Dad's reputation as an architect grew. We lived inside the gate on the road that
sloped downhill to the clubhouse and dock and then switched back
along our beach. When Dad cleared lots for construction he brought
home rattles from the snakes killed, and I kept a noisy collection in
a shoe box.

Dad and I walked the dock on Saturdays. I perched on top of his shoulders and bobbed and weaved with his movements through the bright, buoyant day. The old man was always there, draped in nets he repaired in front of his tackle shed. He looked up from his work, squinted, then grinned, tipped his navy cap with the silver anchor stitched in front, and said, "Good Day, Captain Jack. I see you have your best girl out."

Dad swung me down off his shoulders, and I swayed on the grainy planks and said, "Hello."

It looked like there was rope under the skin of the old man's hands. They were bumpy and moved without stopping while he talked to Dad. I watched as he twisted twine into shapes that looked like letters or numbers or musical notes, and then, without looking, laced the rope in, out, and around, gave it a quick tug, and looped the finished knot through my fingers—hung it from my hand like an ornament from a tree branch.

"Would you like to learn to do that?" he asked.

"Oh, yes," I said as Dad hoisted me up again, the knot in free fall.

"Bye, Old Salt," Dad said, waving, and we ambled on down the dock, my hands locked under his chin, my chin on top of his head. Dad said our friend had lived his whole life on the sea. I imagined myself without a house, a floating island.

Boats full of friends came and went. They waved to us and we waved back. They arrived, secured their vessels fore and aft, making figure eights around iron cleats. Later they cast off and drifted away. We watched them get smaller, still waving, until they were wisps of white in a sapphire sea, and then Dad and I moved farther on down the dock.

Seagulls surrounded the end of the dock, wheeling high over fishermen with baited lines in the water, high over tubs of live catch swimming in circles, high over the albacore smokehouse, hoping to spot an easy bite. They flapped their wings and picked up speed; they cruised, and let the currents take them.

"Look at the birds, baby."

"I see the birds, Daddy."

Dad and I, our eyes trained on the vastness overhead: cottage cheese clouds, soaring birds, and a cobalt blue sky.

Three

THE DAILY BREEZE NEWS
Serving the South Bay Communities
in Los Angeles County

South Bay Yesterday

Some homeowners built so close to the ocean that surf would crash against windows during storms. Amenities included access to a yacht club formed in 1948 and a clubhouse with a lounge that boasted a spectacular view of Catalina Island. Recreational activities that included tennis, volleyball, sailing and waterskiing were a community focus. It was possible to fish from some of the homes.

It was an era of swimming and dinghy races, Friday night movies and formal Sunday dinners. In 1949 the club's two-day Independence Day celebration had a fireworks display second in size only to the annual American Legion version held at the LA Coliseum.

While my mother, Kitty, had my sister growing inside her, my care fell to my father, Jack. Dad was happiest when he moved fast, raced sports cars, flew airplanes. Everybody said he was a guy who got a big kick out of life. He played a game where he let my stroller pick up speed as it rolled downhill, then "ran like hell" to catch up before it hit the traffic.

Dad also liked to throw me up in the air and catch me outside on the patio. Up I'd go, the world somersaulting around my trajectory, and down I'd come, screaming with pleasure as those hands caught me in a giant tickle. One time they didn't, and I fell to the concrete. But I didn't break anything.

When I was two, Mother and Dad and I sat high in the crowded bleachers at a car race. I squeezed between Dad's knees, his hands under my arms; my feet brushed the seat in front of him. The air was busy with flags, the loudspeaker's crackle, burning rubber, men yelling, "Get your hotdogs, ice cold Coca Cola, Bud-weiser!"

"Do we want anything, Kitty?" Dad asked. His eyes never left the cars circling the track.

"It's a little early, Jack," Mother said, smoothing fabric over the mound at her middle.

Tires screeched. Engines whined in acceleration, groaned when the goggled drivers down-shifted into a turn. Cars banked to our left and roared closer. Dad let go. He jumped to his feet. He forgot I was there. I slid through the bleachers, airborne. My parents watched as I cleared the crossbars and landed in the dirt.

They scrambled down the bleachers, Mother lagging behind,

"Just GO, Jack," she said, waving him on. She leaned on the railing as she made her way down the concrete steps. "You can get there faster," she yelled, "just GO!"

Dad sprinted down the steps and knelt next to where I lay with the breath knocked out of me. His smiling face loomed into view. "Now that wasn't so bad was it?"

Wide-eyed, I shook my head "No."

"The checkered flag is up, folks." The announcer's voice echoed over the airwaves.

The bleachers rumbled overhead. Fans stamped their feet and cheered.

"She's alright, Kitty," Dad said as Mother caught up to us.

He lifted me, and pressed me to his chest, and we were on the move again. Over his shoulder, I saw Mother's look of surprise.

"For Christ's sake, Jack," she said, "where are you going now?"

"We can catch the finish if we're quick, Kitty, COME ON!"

Dad and I drove to the hospital to pick up my mother and sister, Carol, two weeks after her birth. That's how long moms lolled and languished in the hospital before going home in the forties. Carol had the longest eyelashes I'd ever seen and her skin felt like velvet. Mother said Carol had double tear ducts—that was why her cheeks got extra wet and her lashes clumped together when she cried. With the thumbs tucked in, her little fists looked like baby mollusks. Mother put her on my lap, facing out so I could wrap my arms around her and inhale her pansy smell. It was novel to be two, and unnerving to have my world change overnight; I stuttered for a while.

Carol grew round and blond; I, tall and thin, and my curls darkened to brunette. In 1946, when I was born, infant care was tightly regulated. Mother sat in a chair outside the closed door to my room and cried, waiting for the right time to respond to my wails. Two years later, Dr. Benjamin Spock said to pick babies up when they cry and to feed them on demand, so Mother fed Carol her bottle as they rocked back and forth in our new chair. Once, when Carol was sleeping in her crib and Mother was resting in the chair, I tried to climb up on her lap. She started, and said, "Oh no, this chair is just for babies, and you're a big girl now."

Four

THE DAILY BREEZE NEWS
Serving the South Bay Communities
in Los Angeles County

South Bay Yesterday

Frank Vanderlip was the first of several visionaries who planned to develop Portuguese Bend as early as 1914.

'I found myself reminded vividly of the Sorrentine Peninsula and the Amalfi Drive. Yet the most exciting part of my vision was that this gorgeous scene was not a piece of Italy at all but was here in America, an unspoiled sheet of paper to be written on with loving care.'

The Depression scotched Frank Vanderlip's planned project for Portuguese Bend, but he built a mansion named "Villa Narcissa" where he kept an aviary which included six peacocks, a gift from Lucky Baldwin, a prominent investor, businessman, and friend. Mr. Vanderlip was visiting Mr. Baldwin's estate in Arcadia when he admired the flock Baldwin had imported from India in 1897. Baldwin sent over six to "liven up" Villa Narcissa.

I made up stories about mermaids losing their tails, and crabs stranded without protective covering. When I walked the dock I

10

visited the fishermen, peered into tubs at trapped creatures, and ate smoked albacore from paper cones. The Old Salt taught me to tie knots as rubber-suited men with webbed feet brought up abalone. Piles of blue-pearl shells littered the dock.

Carol and I practiced strokes and dives in the pool at the club while Jack and Kitty sat behind the glass. We waved and hoped they watched us—hoped they weren't arguing.

For shopping trips in town, I dressed up, purse in hand, and heeled at Mother's side. Carol, however, crawled under clothes racks, got lost, and burst into strangers' dressing rooms.

At home our dolls lined up for play. Black cloth dolls brought back from Haiti displayed an "anything goes" fashion sense. Features stitched in yarn suggested their good moods. They grinned alongside porcelain dolls wearing ruffled gowns that reached to their ankles, where silver-buckled shoes poked out. I cut shapes in colored felt—stars, moons, and flowers—made holes in the middle, and pulled one, two, or three at a time over the dolls' heads, molding them around their now framed faces. My hats completed their eclectic look. Our dolls were ready for the world.

Mother encouraged me to identify with an assortment of Terry Lee dolls, even though my middle name was Lynn, not Lee. I didn't like them as much after we toured the factory in Apple Valley, where the dolls were made. It was creepy walking through rooms with naked, headless torsos, boxes of limbs, and bald heads without faces. It made me feel funny, like when I saw something I wasn't supposed to see. Like the day I found my cat covered with ants, and I showed Dad, and he said a rattlesnake had gotten her, and she was dead. He picked her up by a back paw and she didn't bend, and when he threw her over the cliff, she was stiff as a boomerang, but she never came back.

Mother taught me to read. Stringing the sounds of symbols together into something I recognized was thrilling. My favorite book was *The Boxcar Children*, a story of orphans, happy scavengers banded together in an abandoned boxcar. Then they found their kind, wealthy grandfather, and he adopted them, and moved the boxcar, now a playhouse, onto the grounds of his mansion, where they lived happily ever after.

⌐

The first day of kindergarten arrived in nearby Malaga Cove. The classroom looked cheerful; morning sun shone through windows that lined the far wall. My teacher approached, shiny, apple-red lipstick parted in a welcoming smile: "Hello, my name is Mrs. Maddox. Welcome to kindergarten. I'm your teacher this year." She took my outstretched hand in hers and I said, "My name is Terry Gray, and I'm excited to be here. I will need extra help with my numbers, but I've been reading with Mother's help for two years, and English is my very favorite subject." I stopped and took a breath, expectant. Mrs. Maddox studied me a moment, then smiled. "Honey," she said, "It's time for you to go out and play."

Carol seemed strong but she was allergic to cats and dogs and things that grew. That wasn't the worst part. On Fourth of July when Carol was four, she couldn't catch a breath. An ambulance rushed her to the hospital for an emergency tracheotomy—a slash to the throat to clear her airway. Carol had asthma.

When Carol woke up we brought her home but she stayed quiet. The bandages came off, and she covered the scar on her throat with her hand. After that Mother said I should watch out for her, and I did. I kept my hand on her shoulder now that I knew what could happen. Even a bee sting was serious. She didn't pull away from me. Carol was no longer fearless.

⌐

They made a movie on our beach with swim star Esther Williams and her real-life husband, Fernando Lamas. The school bus dropped us off at the club where we watched them film scenes—the same ones for days. Esther Williams pulled on a bathing cap and flounced into the surf, over and over. She grabbed the cap and put it on backwards. Someone yelled, "CUT!" then, "ACTION!" She grabbed the cap again and pulled it on and the strap broke loose. Another "CUT!"

We had to be quiet when we laughed. Microphones on poles

picked up sound. One day the makeup crew waved us over to their trailer and invited us kids inside. Paints and wigs and putty, palette knives, brushes, and powder puffs filled the shelves. They asked us if we wanted to play a joke on our parents, and of course we did. We walked home with bruises, black eyes, and splinted bones, pretending the school bus had crashed through the railing and rolled all the way downhill to the beach. Our parents screamed when they saw us at a distance, and we tried not to laugh for as long as we could.

Five

THE DAILY BREEZE NEWS
Serving the South Bay Communities
in Los Angeles County

South Bay Yesterday

Miye Ishibashi sold strawberries on the side of the road and her husband, Mas, farmed Rancho Palos Verdes for over fifty years, with the exception of the Internment Years.

In 1951, The Wayfarer's Chapel, also known as "the Glass Church," was completed, and dedicated to the eighteenth Century mystic, Swedenborg. Frank Lloyd Wright's son, Lloyd Wright, designed the church made of glass which became a popular tourist destination and wedding site. Anaïs Nin composed a poem for its twenty-fifth anniversary.

The playground was a minefield of hidden codes. I monitored the girls' shifting allegiances, but boys proved more predictable. They gave me bouquets and love notes, and jewelry I had to return to alarmed mothers.

Sometimes I went to a friend's house after school. Her father, a geologist, kept specimens in crude wooden sheds in their backyard. I wandered through the labyrinth of minerals in the dusty light. The sheds had no windows. Spaces between slats admitted pale shafts, and in the shadows, the uncut rocks and polished stones were self-illuminated worlds.

One day Nancy Ishibashi's family invited the class to pick strawberries, peas, and flowers in the fields at the top of the cliff. They sold what they grew in a roadside stand at a bend in the winding main road. Nancy, like everyone in our class, was born in 1946, the first year of the baby boom after World War II. Her older brother, Satoshi, went to the internment camps with their parents Miye and Mas, but Nancy was born after they came home. Many Japanese families didn't return after their imprisonment in Arizona or North Dakota—after the bombs their adopted country dropped on their native land. That stretch of coastline wouldn't have been the same without the fields of strawberries, peas, and flowers. Mas and Miye would have been missed.

A church made of glass sat on a hill on the other side of the highway. The transparent walls of the chapel were clean and modern, the ceiling a clear lens to blue sky. The chapel hosted many weddings—my own included, later in its opulent future, when the leafed-out limbs of mature trees surrounded the glass walls and ceiling.

I was attuned to how things were made, and whether they harmonized with their environment. Dad admired Frank Lloyd Wright, and the homes he designed were distinctive and blended with their setting. He sat on the Art Jury, and decided what could be built in our area. In Palos Verdes, homes with identical red tile roofs sat a minimum of a half acre apart, sharing space with horse farms and eucalyptus groves. There was a lot of emphasis upon taste—on defining good or bad, beautiful or ugly, natural or synthetic. We drove into Los Angeles and I couldn't believe what I saw from the back seat. Why were so many old cars on the road? I called a development of tract homes "wretched little hovels," and Dad and Mother laughed—especially Dad, who was pleased that I had absorbed his aesthetics.

A loose web of freeways connected vast expanses of open land in southern California. Citrus groves perfumed the air. Oil derricks dotted the landscape, bobbing like strange animals drinking from the earth. We visited my mother's parents, Herb and Marie, in a pink stucco house in a Downey residential neighborhood. Grandma grew showy stalks of gladiolas, Grandpa's favorite flower, and Grandpa kept horses corralled in back. My mother said Grandpa quit drinking when she refused to let him hold me when I was born, but Grandma still had "crying jags" and when Dad and Grandpa left to check on the horses, they came back a lot happier than when they left.

I was afraid of the horses. When the rodeo came to town, Grandpa and Grandma wore long-sleeved shirts with curlicue piping and mother-of-pearl buttons, and matching Stetsons, to promenade around the ring. At home we brushed the horses, fed them carrots and sugar cubes, and laid down fresh hay. Grandpa showed me how to flatten my hand to avoid their big square teeth when I offered food. I closed my eyes, felt the wet tickle, and tried not to show my feelings. Horses smelled fear.

Grandma's altars glowed red with candles. She stood before pictures of suffering Christ and sad Mary, and fingered a rosary with pale blue beads on a silver chain. I knelt by her bed and asked for everyone to be healthy before I climbed under the white chenille bedspread to nap.

Six

THE DAILY BREEZE NEWS
Serving the South Bay Communities
in Los Angeles County

South Bay Yesterday

Then the land began to shift and slide. The Portuguese Bend landslide was part of an ancient Altamira event, an ice age feature more than 2,000,000 years old. The slide remained dormant until an extension of Crenshaw Boulevard cut into a layer of diatomaceous clay, destabilizing the area. In the beginning stages of construction, they placed 160,000 cubic yards of road fill at the head of the ancient landslide.

A literal erosion of the idyllic enclave's lifestyle began when the two-hundred-acre slide began its inexorable march to the sea. In two years the earth slipped 40' seaward and 10' vertically. More than one hundred homes, including fifty within the Club, were destroyed, as was the pool and clubhouse.

My first grade class sat cross-legged on the patterned carpet. The topic: "How do we get answers to our questions?" Hands flew up offering conventional suggestions like:

"Ask mommy and daddy."

"Ask a librarian."

"Ask a policeman."

Yes, yes, yes: validation.

Until I raised my hand and added what was obvious to me: "Or, you can sit and get the answer inside yourself." In the scary SILENCE that ensued, I knew I'd made a mistake, and I vowed never to speak in that way again.

Dad was supposed to pick me up at school, but he was busy working and forgot. The police picked me up walking along the highway and brought me home. In class, I raised my hand to go to the bathroom, and my teacher followed me into the lavatory. She called Mother and suggested a checkup. The doctor said I was fine, maybe I had a small bladder, or it could be a nervous habit. Dad said, "Nervous? Nervous about what?"

Mother said I was high-strung, and compared me to the notes on the piano where the tightest strings stretched. I took piano lessons and played in recitals. Mother sewed a long, blue-and-white dotted Swiss dress with puffed sleeves, an empire waist, and a blue velvet sash. She brushed my dark curls, applied lipstick, and showed me how to press my lips on a tissue. I made a whole sheet of surprised-looking O's while she retrieved a headband covered with tight blue rosebuds.

In second grade I played a Bach étude for my school.

‿⁀

Mother often rounded us up for Palm Springs weekends. The "Playground of the Stars" had a dry climate, good for Carol's asthma. Sometimes Dad came. Sometimes it was better he stayed home. They bought a second house; Dad would commute. Jack and Kitty exchanged scary smiles with their teeth clamped tight, their voices too low for me to hear.

My parents were an attractive mismatch. Good partners on the dance floor, they jitterbugged in Sunday marathons during the war years. Kitty entered a beauty contest straight out of high school, and placed second to Donna Reed; she was convinced it was fixed, already bitter. She married a man who served after the Pearl Harbor attack. Dad, a flyboy with poor eyesight, designed aircraft at North American Aviation, where he met Kitty. After an aborted pregnancy—a big brother I missed—and while her first husband fought, Mother annulled her first marriage. At Forest Lawn, a popular cemetery with a chapel, Jack and Kitty tied the knot.

"Your arms opened wide and closed me inside, you took my lips, you took my love, so tenderly."

Ten years later, whether Mother knew what Dad was doing or not, when Kitty stepped out, the knot unraveled.

Mother was absent, Dad morose. The piano was a solace, and not only to me. Dad sat beside me on the hard bench and asked me to play the popular love song "Tenderly," recorded by Sarah Vaughan and Nat King Cole. The words were implied in the simple notes and chord structures I'd mastered.

"The tide rushes in, plants a kiss on the shore, then rolls out to sea and the sea is very still once more."

I longed for stillness, for a cleansing calm. The family tumbled in something tidal, and I drowned in my father's sorrow. My parents parried, jabbed with looks, raked flesh with sarcasm. When one advanced the other retreated, eroding the middle ground they both felt slide away. They threatened across the chasm to take their need elsewhere; they led with pride until it was too late to recant goodbye.

The sea advanced and withdrew in the dark. Dad's arms folded over the top of the piano, his head cradled. Tears fell on the glossy black-and-white keys, slippery beneath my fingers. I played until he sobbed, and we clung to each other in the dissonance of fading chords. Dad straightened, and said, "It's late. Let's get you to bed."

Carol slept undisturbed in her matching twin bed. Dad kissed me goodnight, and I closed my eyes and settled. He was there when the car hit the house. Mother was home. She pulled in too fast, overshot the carport, and hit the exterior wall, hard. I woke up crying. What thundered inside the house? Why did the room shake me awake?

"It's okay… it's okay. Everything is all right," Dad said.

I looked at my Mother—framed in the doorway, one hand on her hip, the other steadying herself against the jamb. "That's right, Jack, tell her everything is all right," she slurred, and disappeared from sight.

A second crash broke the silence. A vase full of marbles, swept off a table, shattered. Marbles coursed across the cork-tiled floor from one end of the room to the other, hit the far wall, and pooled in the corner closest to the sea, as surf crashed against rocks in blackness below.

Seven

THE DAILY BREEZE NEWS
Serving the South Bay Communities in Los Angeles County

South Bay Yesterday

An article by Point Vicente Interpretive Center docent, Sue Kersey, observed that divorce rates rose. Some took the slide in stride.

"It just didn't seem to be anything to be frightened of; it didn't seem tragic," resident Kaaren Hoffman remembered.

"I know we had a wonderful crack going through the living room that was about 6" wide. We used to drop rocks down it and you could never hear where they landed. It was actually just an ideal place to grow up. The sea was marvelous. The marine life was exceptional. It was a small community so everyone knew everyone."

Kaaren lived there from age 8-15, until the landslide caused the roof of her family's home to collapse. Club members displayed a degree of black humor about the loss of their treasured little empire. The clubhouse's closure was reportedly marked with a bittersweet party dubbed "The Last Days of Pompeii," with guests dressed in togas.

We were slow to notice new cracks in sidewalks and walls. One started on the bottom of the pool at the club, and it grew every day. People said, "Don't worry. It's just the land settling." Then it was inside houses, and there were open seams. Floors sat at different elevations from room to room, and people said, "Come on over. You've got to see this."

I remembered the toga party, though all the theme parties ran together. Dad in a straw hula skirt, a bra filled with oranges, dancing barefoot in a wig made from a mop; my Aunt Sally, famous for her big bust, wearing a cardboard box covered with hand prints and the words, "Community Chest." My mother in head-to-toe black body makeup, a plunging purple satin blouse, and gold high-heeled sandals, a garter peeking out through a deep slit in her tight black skirt. Halloweens at home with tunnels built across the patio that we made our guests crawl through, hung with slimy strings, and skeletons with bulging green grape eyes. Gatsby parties held at the club where women wore silk-fringed flapper dresses, men in straw boaters and striped suits. African safari parties, and toga parties, gilt wreaths in coiffed hair, bare legs and sandaled feet.

Portuguese Bend Club endured, but there were no more parties in the crumbled clubhouse, and no more holidays at our house. The pool was drained, the dock abandoned, my family broken. Carol and I became visitors where once we had belonged.

We put down tentative new roots in shallow, shifting sand.

Jack and Kitty Gray

Book Two

Living As Sisters

~

I like it when a flower or a little tuft of grass grows through a crack in the concrete. It's so fucking heroic.

George Carlin

Four generations: my Mother, Aunt, Cousin,
Grandmother and Great-Grandmother

Photo credit: Studio portrait 1946

One

Palm Springs

Mother, at thirty-one, lost the security of marriage, and became a single parent looking for work and "fun in the sun." Dad, at thirty-four, bought his first red Jaguar roadster, cut his house in half, and moved it to the top of a 250-foot cliff. Dad's new next-door neighbor, Clark Chittig, was quoted in THE DAILY BREEZE article saying, "The fishing isn't as good as it used to be; the abalone are gone, but the weather has always been very nice here and I don't want to live anywhere else."

I didn't either, but we three girls lived in Palm Springs now, Mother's idea of heaven. Mom wanted a new start on the life she might have had if her marriage had never happened. Gone were the ocean, the cool breezes, the watery worlds and, though it was not addressed, Dad was gone too. The loss was wrenching. I appeared to handle it better than Carol did. I learned to camouflage my pain, to carry an air of melancholy rather than grieve, and to be private, and to perform when I felt vulnerable. I grew immune to my own emotions, and good at assessing what others needed.

But the loss of my Father was foundational. I awoke one night and went to mother's room, upset. "I MISS Dad," I sobbed, ready to throw myself into her arms. Instead, I froze. I didn't know what Mother was feeling that night. She showed me her anger, hissing, "If you miss him so much, why don't you go live with him?" I knew that wasn't an option, and so did she. I backed out of her bedroom. There would be no more emotional displays. This was where I was now.

It was hot in the summer—fry-an-egg-on-the-sidewalk hot; run-barefoot-across-scorching-sand-to-a-spot-of-shade hot; blocks-of-ice-in-the-swimming-pool hot; roll-into-the-water-in-the-middle-of-the-night-and-fall-back-to-sleep-in-a-wet-bathing-suit hot. HOT. My feet grew calloused. My nose and shoulders flaked. "It's a dry heat. You'll get used to it," Mother said, "You look cute in a bathing suit. You know you love it here."

I never got used to it. It was thick, overpowering, and energy-stealing. Any thought or action took place in the cool early morning when I could function—before heat wrapped itself around me, got me in a choke hold, and held on tight.

Mom and Carol and I ran errands and window-shopped. We parked and I brought up the rear, sleepwalked toward the bank that resembled a Greek temple. White columns rose to the sky, lifted our gaze and dwarfed us. We pushed the glass revolving door and entered, hit by a wall of frigid air. I perked up, felt optimistic, able to speak, buoyed in my chance of surviving August. I even smiled at Mom and Carol, who I noticed had contracted into half their size, arms wrapped around their shivering bodies.

"Let's go," Mother said, urgent.

"*Oh, no,*" I thought.

"Let's go, NOW," she said.

She cycled through the revolving door, and I marched after her into the hot white blanket of a summer day. Carol and Mother were relieved; I, a wilted zombie, was blinded by the glare. I climbed into the back seat, trying not to touch the burning leather upholstery.

Downtown, machines lining the tops of buildings sprayed those who braved the sidewalk with a watery mist. Shoppers staggered, refreshed for a moment by the humid cloud. The windows displayed a glitzy glamour. I squinted at feathered boas in colors no bird wore, glittery gold and silvery baubles, rhinestone and sequin-sprinkled clothes that flashed on mannequins who smiled in the brazen heat. I wondered if I'd survive the temperature, the artifice, or the garish good cheer.

Odd things swept through, insect invasions, worms, very biblical, underscoring our recent expulsion from Eden. Whatever was descending at the moment piled up in the sparse shade under parked cars. When we climbed into Mother's Ford Fairlane sedan, we were careful to sidestep the bodies in our flimsy flip-flops. The car's tires either crunched or squished over their piled up carcasses as we backed out of our parking space.

Mother sat Carol and me down on the white leather couch in the living room of our new house. She admitted Dad was gone, and suggested we "live as sisters now." We were an all-female offshoot of our formerly nuclear family, wobbly like a table with one short or missing leg. Carol and I prepared to wobble into a new school, Carol in first grade, I in third. Mother dressed for work and, wobbly, feigned enthusiasm for her new start. We needed time to round off the missing corner—to become a stable tripod, to forget the solid feeling of four, to be just three.

Two

Palm Springs

Within a few months Dad had already met and moved in with Casey and her children, Debbie and Roger. Our first meeting proved awkward. Casey waited in the bar of a restaurant while Dad picked Carol and me up for dinner. We walked into the darkened lounge with Dad, and he guided us to our table while our eyes adjusted to the low light. The bartender set a fresh martini on the table in front of the glamorous stranger with feathered, platinum-streaked, black hair. He picked up her empty glass, winked at her, and walked back to the bar. He seemed like he was showing off.

Dad introduced Casey. We took turns shaking her hand, and then we sat down in tufted club chairs. A waitress took our order, and when she was gone we looked around the table, unsure how to begin, or who was auditioning for what. We were all nervous—except for Dad, who was normal, as always. Carol pretended to dance under the table, unable to keep her legs still. Her shoes kicked the chair and tapped against each other. Casey had warm black eyes that looked straight into mine; I felt seen, sized-up. Her voice stretched out the way some actresses' voices did when they were making the simplest things sound important.

"I'm sooo happy to meet you. I have two children close to your age who want to meet you too," she said, and she took a damp drag from her Benson & Hedges cigarette, staining its tip a frosted burnt-orange.

"Really?" I asked. "Do you have any pictures?"

"Nooo, no, no, I don't." She exhaled through her nose in two vibrating streams like a dragon, and reached for Dad's hand. They turned toward each other making a closed circle and kissed. Carol and I looked at each other with round eyes under raised eyebrows and stifled a giggle. Casey turned back to us and continued, "But we hope you'll visit us soon."

I nodded, said, "We'll have to ask Mother, I guess, but that sounds nice."

"OOH, don't worry. Your faaather can handle that." She crushed her cigarette out in an ashtray, and said, "Good then, it's settled. I'll reserve your flight."

Carol and I smiled and nodded a lot; we all got through it. When we were finished eating, Dad stood, and we excused ourselves, shaking hands again with Casey who again waited in the bar for Dad while he drove us home in the roadster.

I wasn't sure how I felt about this new and powerful presence in my life. I did cruel imitations of Casey eating French fries with a fork when we went home to make Mother feel better. Casey was theatrical where Mother was cool, affectionate where Mother was reserved, stylish where Mother was a conventional beauty. But they both liked the same type of man: the bad boy, the fly boy, the one with that mischievous promise of fun in his eyes. In love, they both became risk takers, high-stakes gamblers with nothing to lose.

Portuguese Bend Club

We visited Portuguese Bend Club. Dad picked us up at LAX; it was so good to see him waiting at our arrival gate. We couldn't hug him enough. When we got to Portuguese Bend, we went through the gate like we always did. The guard waved his hand and raised the bar. We turned left, instead of right, and entered a short cul-de-sac. Dad used a remote, and we turned into the garage of the second house on the right. He gathered our belongings and we followed him to the front gate.

Dad pulled the gate open with a bronze seagull-shaped handle, and we stepped onto a landing over a swimming pool. He pointed out a door to our left. "Here's my new office, girls."

He opened the door and we looked past him at two drafting tables lined up in front of the window.

"Looks nice, Dad. You can see the swimming pool," I said.

"That's right. I can see everything. I can see the ocean through the house. Come on, let's go inside. Debbie and Roger are eager to meet you."

We followed Dad down the stairs that made a bridge over the pool, and across the decking to the open sliding glass door, and Dad opened the screen.

"Hellooo," Casey greeted us, her arms opened wide. "Well, come on in." She backed up out of the doorway and we followed her inside.

"OH, this is," I said, looking out through the wall of glass at the blue world I remembered, "so beautiful." I walked straight ahead to another open screened door.

Dad said, "Keep your sweaters on then. I'll show you this first." He slid the screen open onto a deck that lined the length of the house, which extended beyond the cliff's edge. The sun sprayed rays as it sank to the horizon, and cast colored wands across the sea. I stopped and leaned against the middle bar of the railing.

Dad swept his arm across my shoulders. "I'll show you the circle."

I fell in behind Carol, and we walked single file to the end of the deck and down a flight to a railed circle, a solid disc surrounded by glistening ice plant, sprinkled with white daisies. We stood in the circle and watched the remaining sun set until its color and warmth faded—until the daisies withdrew their petals for night. Strategically placed lights on a timer lit up the rocks and surf below. The circle was a magic vantage point for sunrise and sunset, for whale watching; and I would soon learn that it was always the perfect place for solitude.

We headed up to the house and followed Dad across the deck. He slid the screen door open.

"Daddy, hi!"

We went in. Two children sat at the bar.

"Daddy, hi," the boy repeated. The girl just stared.

"Hello, everyone. Terry and Carol, this is Debbie and Roger."

Dad walked over to Casey, who was half reclined by the wrought iron fireplace at the end of the living room. She held up a wine glass to Dad and they toasted. Casey lounged across a lanai cushion, heaped with pillows that stretched from the fireplace to the glass wall on the ocean side of the room. Dad joined her. The opposing wall was paneled in walnut, lined with books punctuated by paintings and sculpture. Dean Martin sang "That's Amore" in the background.

Debbie looked bored. Roger was talking fast to Carol who looked like she might cry.

"Want to see the playroom?" Debbie asked. "Okay," I said, and Carol and Roger came too. We walked down a hall past the open door to the master bedroom, past Debbie and Roger's rooms, and the bathroom with the sauna that we would share. The hall continued to the playroom where another sliding glass door led onto the patio and pool on the left. A pool table occupied the middle of the room and couches lined the perimeter. Two of them were made up into beds and our suitcases sat beside them. A third door led outside from the playroom back up to street level, the two-car garage, and Dad's office.

"See," said Roger, "we have our own entrance." I nodded. Sliding panels were open to both Debbie and Roger's rooms, and I could see his bunk beds and her frilly twin.

"I think I'll go back," I said.

"Me too," said Carol.

"Why? It's better here," Debbie said.

"They'll probably call us soon," said Carol. "I'm hungry."

"Oh yeah? Okay, go ahead. You'll see," Debbie said.

Carol and I padded back down the hall to the kitchen, the physical center of the house, the seam where it had been split in two for transport from the beach to the cliff top. The bar stools were empty, pushed away from the bar that bordered the kitchen. I could hear low voices in Dad and Casey's bedroom through an open space between the rooms at the ceiling.

I wandered across soft beige wall-to-wall carpet and fell into a couch in the living room. Carol followed. We were tired and overwhelmed from our first flight and all of the changes confused and upset us. I could still hear Roger calling our Dad "Daddy" when we walked in from the circle.

Over the fireplace was a sand casting of a stylized sun and sandpiper, created by the new family. It covered half of the back wall; four handprints autographed the piece. The couches were deep, and they curled around a walnut coffee table inlaid with beveled glass. It was heaped with books and studded with silver candlesticks, cut crystal ashtrays, a decanter, a tall vase packed with blood-red roses, and crystal bowls of crisp daisies. A carved wooden chess set sat on a table by the window. The room, shrouded in the combined scent of roses and gin, burning tapers and cigarette smoke, perfume, fog and fire, was warm, sumptuous, and fully occupied. I felt adrift in Dad's new house, unsure of my place in his new life.

Casey came out of her bedroom and sat with Carol and me on the living room couch. She looked into our eyes, saw the tears, and didn't pretend them away. She said, "Each of us has a new life now. It's all strange and different, but we hope it's exciting also, to have new family." Then she listened.

"We're happy to have new family, but we don't live here any more, and we miss Dad," I said. Carol nodded; double tear ducts spilled salted tears.

"I know it must be hard," she said.

Dad approached warily to see if the storm he sensed had passed. "Are we all set now?" he asked, hopeful.

Casey reached for him, pulled him down onto the wide couch beside her. We all smiled at him. Dad didn't want to talk about feelings; he just wanted us to be happy for him. So we tried to get used to everything new. Casey was something very new: her exaggerated gestures, her southern manners, her Spanish fire.

We liked Debbie and Roger. Roger was sweet and goofy and his blue eyes had red rims—"granulated eyelids," he said. I liked to run the palm of my hand over his blond brush cut; it was prickly and made us both laugh. Debbie had brown eyes and light brown hair she wore in a ducktail. Her mouth was curvy and she had a beauty mark high on her left cheek.

I was seven, the oldest and tallest. Roger was six. Carol and Debbie were both five, but Debbie seemed older, much older. The next night, without meaning to, we lined ourselves up at the bar according to age. I sat on the far end closest to the door that opened onto the deck. Roger sat between Carol and me. Debbie, last, the most reluctant to show up at all, took her place on the other end. Dad and Casey occupied two stools on the kitchen side of the bar.

"Okay," Dad began, "we want you to know a few things. First of all, don't expect us to be like other parents. We've seen how they live for their kids and we're not going to do that."

He put his arm around Casey and smiled at her. She beamed back and chimed in, "That's right. We're going to live for each other now." She reached for Dad's free hand and squeezed it.

Dad said, "Your lives are your own."

We four exchanged quizzical looks. Roger shrugged. Debbie asked, "Are you going to make dinner? Maybe we could wait in the playroom."

Dad and Casey laughed as if what Debbie had just said was hilarious.

"Yes," Dad said, "we plan to feed, clothe, and put a roof over your heads for a while. And we wish you good luck."

We slid off the bar stools and headed for the playroom.

But the bar was the pulsing place where the action was—where, as Casey said, "we got down to the real nitty-gritty." Dad was breezy and Casey probed, their variation on good cop/bad cop. Casey had radar for sensitivities, blind spots, whatever made anyone wince or dissemble. She leaned into exposed nerves until they surrendered their secrets. There on the barstools we learned to deflect attention from ourselves—to duck the spotlight, the hot seat, and to offer each other up for sacrifice. We waited to see if dinner was served or abandoned as Jack and Casey drank themselves into a range of preferred moods. We read the signs, knew the exact moment we could slip away, hungry, forgotten, free.

Three

Palm Springs

Palm Springs was a natural oasis in the Coachella Valley desert, ringed by the San Jacinto Mountain range. Tall stands of palm trees grew where groundwater hit fault planes and sprang to the surface. Flash floods carved ravines that creased the desert floor and became dry washes. After a downpour, the air was pungent with creosote, acacia, and citrus. Fuzzy rods of cholla cactus, squat and spiky barrels, and stately Joshua trees and yucca shared space and what scant water there was. Funnels of dust whirled in the dry distance. Things that needed little water did well here.

Mother's affair with a Frenchman, who had four names I still remember, was short-lived. Her new boyfriend, Dr. John Henry Scott, a chiropractor, told us how he had awoken one morning in Tahquitz Canyon in his sleeping bag, and had seen a diamondback rattler in his direct line of sight, a spiral sleeping on his chest. Dr. Scott had remained motionless until the snake awoke, flicked the air, and slowly, in the growing warmth of morning, uncoiled and slid from his bag.

Carol and I learned how to tie off, slash, and suck out venom if we were struck by a rattlesnake; we never were. We learned how to cut the top off a barrel cactus for its lifesaving drink; we never had to do that either. We made a fort under the tamarisk trees Mother said were "dirty trees, full of spiders."

We invited the neighborhood kids, a mixed bunch of savvy nature sprites, over to play, and our new tribe showed us stone stairs embedded in the hillside behind our house, ascending partway up the mountain in perfect camouflage. American Indians had built them. They had always lived there, and their descendents still did. Some were made mega-wealthy when the area was checker-boarded, divided equally into public and tribal land. Portions of Palm Canyon Drive, the main drag, and downtown were allotted to some; others received worthless stretches of sand. It was an arbitrary assignment of gifts and deficits, as random as human birth.

We learned about lizards we couldn't tame; a tail came off in my hand when I grabbed it. A boy pulled a plastic magnifying glass out of his pocket, held the lizard in the notch behind its front legs, and tried to burn it with the sun's focused rays. To distract him, I suggested we search for scorpions. We sifted through sand for the translucent warriors armed for the battles he then staged. Tarantulas traveled in pairs, prodded the air with furry forelegs. Quail families hurried by, swathed in capes like 1920s Frenchwomen with feathered cloches on their heads, and herded thumb-sized chicks. Prairie dogs peeped out from tunnels, frozen in place, then dug furiously and dove into their underworld network, popping up again a few yards away. Roadrunners skimmed the sand. Chuckwallas, barely detectable, sat and glared. Fitting in so well that one disappeared was another survival skill in the desert.

Sometimes Dad and Casey drove to Palm Springs with Debbie and Roger and we rented bicycles, or hiked to Tahquitz Canyon. One weekend they painted a friend's condominium and made a party of it. Friends stopped by, had drinks, pitched in. One friend was a retired, Olympic-level ice skater whom Debbie called "an old and tired ice skater," which everyone, including the skater, found funny.

We kids spent the weekend in the pool. On breaks, shriveled skin wrapped in towels, Debbie organized us to sing *"Zip-a-Dee-Doo-Dah"* in rounds. We put our fingers in our ears so we wouldn't get confused, and watched for Debbie's cue, chimed in with the staggered phrases until we all sang something different at the same time. We produced a cheerful cacophony until we were dizzy and blissed out, falling all over each other like puppies on the lounge chairs, then cannon-balling back into the pool still zip-a-dee-doo-dah-ing.

Casey taught Carol, Debbie and me how to walk a catwalk on the diving board, how to forget ourselves and just think about clothes, how to be models.

Portuguese Bend Club

Carol and I flew to LAX on Friday when we visited Portuguese Bend. Then on Sunday evening, after dinner in some lounge, Casey and Dad dropped us off at the airport to rush to our gate. We kissed Dad goodbye at check-in and ran.

One visit included a trip to Porterville State Hospital. We didn't know where we were going or why. They said they wanted to show us something. We entered the sprawling property surrounded by a chain-link fence topped with barbed wire, and cleared the guard gate. We toured the grounds past barracks-style buildings, and exercise enclosures within more chain-link fence. On volleyball courts, pajama-clad people played games while men in green scrubs blew whistles and kept order. We parked and walked through a ward full of odd-looking kids, another ward with children confined to their beds in dormitory rows.

Casey finally located a girl with straight blond hair who sat alone. She looked a few years older than I was, but it was hard to tell. Casey called her Diane, enfolded her in a hug, talked nonstop like you would to calm a skittish animal, smoothed her hair behind her ears, and pulled her over to us, where we stood clumped by the door,

"Diane, this is Jack, your new father," Casey said.

Diane extended her hand to Dad. "Hello, Father," she said, in a deep, serious voice. "Hello dear," said Dad, his kind eyes saddened.

"You remember Roger and Debbie," Casey prompted.

Diane turned to Roger, and after a moment, she grinned.

"Hello, Roger. Remember me? I'm your sister, Diane." Roger looked like someone had hit him upside the head with a two-by-four. His mouth hung open; then a glint animated his blue eyes. "I think I DO remember you," he said. Debbie was quiet.

Casey pushed me and Carol forward, said, "and these are your new sisters, Carol and Terry."

We said hello.

We didn't stay long. We never had to go back. Jack and Casey found another place, a private institution. Diane was Casey's first-born—before the term "Down's syndrome" was used, back when the round-faced, hoarse-voiced children like Diane were called Mongoloid Idiots. I listened to Dad and Casey talk on the way home while the others slept. Casey said it was "good exposure" and I suppose it was. Another good exposure was the summer camp we attended with kids from LA slums while Jack and Casey toured Europe.

Casey lit up a room—charmed, entertained, and intimidated. She told it like it was. I believed she and Dad were the arbiters of taste for the Western world, the world they saw together, careening at their own pace, upscale vagabonds.

Diane came home for visits. She and Dad shared an October birthday, and each year we celebrated both with a party on the beach for the children from Diane's home. The parties were affectionate affairs. Diane also had a dark streak: she loved vampires. Dad's investment advisor did imitations of Dracula for her at Christmas.

Four

Palm Springs

The desert had a soft, distinct palette. In spring, cacti bloomed in fuchsia, lime, and shades of ivory. Yuccas sprouted waxy, buttercream blossoms, and orange plumes waved from tamarisk treetops. The smooth Palo Verde trees bristled with yellow fuzz, and the smoke trees were an airbrushed blur.

The cactus garden next door to our house was open to the public by day; at night their peacocks shrieked, jumped our fence, and shat in our pool. We lived on the wind-free south end of town, in a one-level, wood-frame house with a half-circle of gravel drive that skirted an oval of desert landscaping. A concrete planter stretched across the façade, under plate glass windows on either side of the front door. The house was gray and so was our name. In a neighborhood comprised of nuclear families, we were "Kitty Gray and her girls, Terry and Carol."

A portrait photographer, who worked at home, developed prints around the corner from us. Hoagy Carmichael composed tunes on a white piano up the street. A couple from India lived up the block; the doctor husband went to work each morning, and his wife never left home, where stacked magazines and newspapers made room dividers. Russians lived across the street, and we befriended the daughter they treated like a princess.

Carol and I shared a room until Mother enclosed the carport

to make another bedroom, which I claimed in junior high school. Carol imagined a bond between mother and me that excluded her, but we were each on our own. I thought I should do more to make us a family, and I felt guilty when all I did was prepare to walk out the door.

I entered third grade at Cahuilla School, wore squaw dresses with conch belts and lined up for the bus near our house. Voted bus stop monitor, I kept the neighborhood gang in line. A wide, white plastic, bandolier-style belt with a military hat that came to a point in front and back gave me authority.

In class, we wrote about the desert for a radio play. Everyone jumped around that day, frenetic, but I was the new kid, quiet at my desk. Our teacher said that was why she chose me. Sandi, the most popular girl in school, and I would represent the class. We worked on a script, and on Saturday, Sandi and I went to the radio station KDES, where her stepfather worked as a DJ. We acted it out live as we pretended to walk through the desert.

"Look Sandi," I said, "there's a desert tortoise. See how he lumbers along in slow motion?"

"I wonder if he eats Dune primroses. These floppy yellow petals are pretty," Sandi said.

"I like these cushions of purple verbena," I said, "that grow low to the ground for protection from the wind." I was no longer the friend-less, unknown newcomer.

On May Day, the queen sat on her throne, alone in a yellow dress and golden tiara. We princesses attended, my best friend Sandi and I, glad to be together on the second tier—Sandi in pink to my laven-der, an undivided pair. The class surrounded the tetherball pole, held streamers we wove with our bodies. Ducking around each other, we braided ourselves together. I still didn't like Palm Springs. I missed the ocean and Dad. And Mother had sold my piano, said I no longer practiced. But I made a new place for myself in the ruthless desert.

Sandi and I joined Camp Fire Girls, made Indian names by com-bining first syllables from what we valued. Sandi became DaSoHeMu, for dance, song, health and music, and I, SuBeLoHa, for success, beauty, love and happiness. We won merit badges and camped out, strung beads and walked in parades wearing feathered headdresses with our navy-and-white uniforms. Ours vests were full of badges and beads, our hair in matching ponytails.

For a fundraising drive, I stood alone on a downtown street corner offering cans of Camp Fire Girls peanuts for sale. A silver-mustached gentleman stopped to talk to me and left with a case of peanuts under his arm, guaranteeing I'd win the drive. The owner of the store where I stood said, "Do you know who that was?"

I shook my head.

"Do you watch the Mickey Mouse Club?" he asked.

"Yes, of course," I said—the TV program was a popular hit.

"Well, that was Walt Disney."

Portuguese Bend Club

We four ate breakfast up on the barstools. Dad started us off with juice and cereal and we were busy making a mess on the bar. Roger bombed his bowl with grapes—"Look out below!" A few wet Cheerios landed on Debbie's sleeve and she stared her brother down, eyes a slit, mouth pursed.

"Oops, sorry Deb," Roger said in mock horror, and turned back to his private war.

We heard Dad coming down the hall with Casey, hidden behind the floor-to-ceiling partition. They started each day with a dip in the pool, Dad nude, Casey in a one-piece suit and flower-covered cap. This particular morning Casey wore a loose bathrobe and leaned on Dad for support as they cleared the partition and came into view. We watched them continue out the front door, watched Casey negotiate the few steps to the pool. She looked back over her shoulder and yelled to us, "I'm NOT drunk. I took too many pills last night. I'm not drunk." It seemed important to her that she make the distinction. Was it better to take too many pills than to be drunk in the morning, I wondered?

We went camping in Big Bear and agreed never to do it again. Piled into the Jag roadster, Carol, Debbie and I were wedged into a cubbyhole behind the two seats, Dad was at the wheel and Casey rode shotgun. Roger hunched over in a small trailer we towed with our gear and the cooler. We girls watched beer cans arc overhead when Roger saw Dad's signal, his hand in the air ready to catch. Casey leaned over to help steer, and Roger tossed the can against the wind into the open cockpit.

Dad and Casey had seen *Psycho*, the new Hitchcock hit, and thought we'd like it. We stretched out on the hood of Casey's car at the drive-in theater. Just before the shower scene, Dad blasted the horn. We levitated off the hood, flailed, screamed, and scrambled. Great fun.

Five

Palm Springs

The rest of the country judged California shallow, and California suspected sour grapes. We assumed it was envy, the legacy of harsh winters. Hollywood crafted the hedonistic message, and Palm Springs was the playground where Hollywood's secrets were kept. Celebrities and studio execs brought families one weekend, and mistresses the next.

The town protected the privacy of the privileged, created an environment where stars unwound, Presidents retired, and those with money reinvented themselves. Spring Breakers, or college students on a spree, invaded the party town each Easter. A gay scene thrived, and stars with heterosexual cover stories relaxed there with chosen company. The Desert Inn and Racquet Club housed celebrity visitors who bought homes in golf course communities. Bob and Dolores Hope built a saucer-shaped house halfway up the hillside over Araby. Sinatra brought the Rat Pack there; Liberace, his piano; and snowbirds flew in with pale skin, loud clothes and golf clubs. From the air, the desert resembled a color block painting: shapes of white sand, aqua pools, and green golf courses, within a circle of mauve mountains.

Mother moved there before the first streetlight, when the airport was a one-room operation with short hops to and from LA and longer ones that serviced the East Coast. Seasons were cycles of tourism and heat. Summer reduced the playground to a ghost town until refrigeration replaced swamp coolers for year-round, uninterrupted fun.

Petunias fringed the manicured grass that lined broad boulevards, and palms stood at entrances to gated communities. The stage was set. Country clubs filled. The modern, one-story houses became "Palm Springs Style;" sunbathing and golf, drinking, dining, and dancing, "Palm Springs culture."

A sub-culture of hobos survived the winter without shelter. "Desert rats," a brand of eccentrics who thrived in the dry heat, consisted of rock hounds, health nuts, nature freaks, Bible thumpers, and spiritualists. In the high desert around Joshua Tree National Monument, lavender glass gardens grew: bottles and jars stuck on the ends of branches decorated dry shrubs and trees, and the pre-1915 glass contained manganese, which oxidized in the sun and changed from clear to purple.

Citrus trees flourished in the fertile Coachella Valley, and palms grew laden with dates. Date shakes were produced in a shack under a billboard that advertised *The Sex Life of the Date,* a disappointing film about pollination. Indio, a neighboring town, hosted a festival to honor the promiscuous date palms that featured camel races, a carnival, and an Arabian Nights pageant presided over by Queen Scheherazade, a local teen beauty.

Dr. Scott, mother's boyfriend, said that if he wanted to he could stage the Second Coming at the La Brea Tar Pits; he'd play the starring role. People were gullible, he said. Dr Scott alternated between shots of Jack Daniels and fresh juiced vegetables, swallowed vitamins, and gave daily chiropractic adjustments. I learned to align my spine in a series of pops as the vertebrae slid into place. I cocked my head left and right, "pop pop," to finish.

Dr. Scott tried to persuade Mother to cook health foods. Carol and I tried to persuade Mother to cook anything. She made a festive tuna casserole a few times with Campbell's soup, crushed potato chips, and sliced American cheese. Overworked and overwhelmed, Mother could not be bothered.

She woke me up one night, threw me a sweatshirt with a fuzzy poodle appliqué that I shrugged on over my pajamas. I ran to catch up with her; she was already behind the wheel of her new, midnight-blue Thunderbird. Gravel sprayed as we peeled around the half-circle drive.

"Where are we going? Why so fast?" I spoke into the void of a dark desert night. A jackrabbit cleared the front driver's-side tire, and disappeared in an oleander. We turned at the long, tamarisk-lined driveway that led to the Biltmore Hotel, the home of a nightclub I was too young to enter. Besides, I was wearing pajamas. "I can't go in here," I said.

"Be quiet. We're not going in." Mother parked, sandwiching the car between two trucks on the perimeter of the parking lot, and got out. Her sprayed platinum beehive looked like a helmet. She gripped my arm and pulled me toward a gold caddy with fins that I recognized as Dr. Scott's car. We ran stooped low, and I hid behind the bulbous fender of another car as Mother fiddled with Dr. Scott's rear tire. I heard hissing. Then she joined me, collapsed against the car that hid us, and we waited.

A short time later, I recognized a familiar voice and peeked out, and I saw Mother's boyfriend strut by, guiding a woman by her elbow. Mom and I made ourselves small. I pasted my palm across my mouth in case involuntary sounds crept out; I felt bugs crawling up my pant leg, but I didn't dare move.

"I think we have a problem here. Looks like the work of a jealous girlfriend. Ha, ha, ha." Dr. Scott got a flashlight out of his glove compartment and waved a wand of light around the lot, looking for more than his flattened tire. "Come with me," he said to his date, "and I'll call AAA."

"I could wait with the car," she said.

"No, I don't think so," Dr Scott shook his big head. "That could be a mistake, and there have been enough mistakes made tonight."

They walked in the direction of the showroom, where Joey Bishop and Deano were headlining.

"Mom, it's our chance. Let's go."

Her beehive was lopsided now, and a streak of grime dirtied her cheek like war paint. Mascara pooled beneath her eyes. I felt for her hand and pulled her up to standing. She followed, as docile as our pet guinea pig was the time I carried it out to the patio, climbed the stairs to our pool slide, and let it loose at the top. It plopped into the pool, sank, surfaced, and swam for the steps.

Mom wilted when she reached the car, still camouflaged between two trucks. "You drive," she said.

"I don't even have a learner's permit. Come on."

We passed the AAA pickup truck as it came down the long driveway.

Later that week, Mother had no hair. She went out with Dr. Scott one night, and he shaved her head, dropped her off at home, and told her they would be married in the morning. An hour later, a squad car was sitting in our driveway. It belonged to Mother's friend, a vice officer, who had agreed to stay with her a while to ensure her safety. After that, Dr. Scott was out of mother's life.

Carol and I walked to town, tried different Sunday schools, visited the shoe store to put our feet in the x-ray machine and look at our bones and we went to matinees alone. We were loosely connected sisters in a family that didn't touch—never greeted with kisses or parted with hugs.

Portuguese Bend Club

Dad was affectionate with a twist, a kink, a lascivious undertone. Casey was a toucher after five, when the efficiency of day melted into sensual enjoyment with the first martini. In Portuguese Bend we dressed for cocktail hour, felt the anticipation build, witnessed the transformation each night.

A Beat note sounded at the end of the fifties, a hint of radical change to come. Dad wore a beret, a trim moustache and a goatee. He traded martinis for white wine, cigarettes for an angular pipe anchored between his teeth while he talked. Conversations were now punctuated by the tapping, scraping, tamping of his new prop; the air above his head was a personal storm. Dad looked at life from a plateau he had struggled to reach, felt satisfaction at forty: satisfaction with the beach house he'd cut in two and moved when the land began to slide; satisfaction with its new perch at the top of the cliff;

satisfaction with his new wife. He was making a name for himself, and he intended to enjoy everything.

Life wasn't always settled for Dad. When he was six, his mother died. The rest of his childhood was spent rambling about the country with his peripatetic father, Merrill. His older brother Landon stayed with their maternal grandparents, and received a conventional upbringing and an East Coast education. But Dad was happy to follow the "old man." His only memory of his mother was her insistence that he eat vegetables, and the taste of soap when he refused.

Dad's father had a restless vision. He engaged in a printing operation, a mining scheme, and developed a motel and restaurant—The Spanish Gardens Motel and The Sip 'n' Bite—in Albuquerque, prototypes for a nationwide chain, each identical, each a day's drive away. Ahead of his time, Merrill had good ideas with sketchy follow-through. When his dreams failed, he pulled his son from school, salvaged what he could, and moved on. When they reached the Pacific Ocean, Dad attended Santa Monica High School—until his father needed help again. He slept in a cot in an airplane hangar, tried to cash Merrill's hot checks, learned to fly, and got by. That itinerant childhood bred in Dad a desire to shape his fate.

Dad believed humans were a half-step above the animals, each generation a slight improvement on the one before, and that was enough for him. He called himself an atheist—but he was an atheist in love with life, an atheist moved to tears by the KSAT sign-off at two a.m., with its image of a jet in the sky and the recitation of Pilot Officer John Gillespie Magee's poem, "High Flight":

> Oh, I've slipped the surly bonds of Earth,
> And danced the skies on laughter-silvered wings;
> Sunward I've climbed and joined the tumbling mirth
> Of sun-split clouds.

Yes, breaking with gravity—that's what turned Dad on; when he felt the Godlike feelings. Happiest with a wheel gripped in his hands, steering racecars, quarter midgets, boats, airplanes and gliders in and out of currents, lifted and propelled.

And, while with silent lifting mind I've trod
The high un-trespassed sanctity of space,
Put out my hand and touched the face of God.

Dad sniffed, stood and switched off the buzzing, snowy screen, reached in the pocket of his paisley silk robe for a handkerchief, and honked his nose. He strolled outside onto the deck, pissed a stream that arced and fell toward the surf, and sauntered to bed.

Casey commissioned a collaged door of Dad's life, a birthday surprise she installed on the wall between the bar and the hallway that led to the bedrooms. Wine corks lined the edges, framed the memorabilia-filled door. Inside was the cast Dad wore when he and Roger built a go-cart and Dad took it out for a test drive, caught an edge, flipped, and broke his arm. The autographed plaster shell shared space with a framed photo of Carol and me, angelic in choir robes, open-mouthed mid-hymn; an alarm clock set for 4 a.m., Dad's preferred time for sex, sat in a cluster of souvenirs and trophies for tennis, chess, and golf. An ashtray, stolen from the original "Harry's Bar" in Venice, was next to a picture of a young girl dressed in white lace with a matching bow on one side of her dark hair, and eyes that looked like mine.

"Who's she?" I asked. I felt she lived inside me.

"That's dear old Mom," Dad said, "the grandmother you'll never know."

"You told me she died when you were six, Dad, but you never said of what?"

"Abortions were even a bigger gamble in the twenties. She didn't want more kids. I guess she wanted to quit after me," Dad said.

"I'm sure it wasn't personal, Dad." I brushed his shoulder. "You never told me we looked alike."

Dad grinned. "You think you look like my mother?"

"You DO look alike. You looked just like her at that age," Casey said.

"Better watch out, kid," Dad winked. "But I think you'll age better than she did."

Casey bought everyone's gifts, and Dad was in charge of hers:

sky-written messages visible from the deck, QE II Atlantic crossings, and balloon tours in France. Casey was mistress of the domestic arts, a talented interior designer, gourmet cook, and lively hostess. They created a signature look, and their home was a showcase that prospective clients toured. As Dad's reputation grew, he no longer had to deal with others' tastes and idiosyncrasies. He designed and built the house he wanted. Casey furnished it, and people bought their packaged vision. When a spec house sold, Dad and Casey took off, traveled and played, and returned to do it all again.

Six

Palm Springs

When we moved to Palm Springs, my grandparents, Herb and Marie, gave up their horses and bought a modest house in Morongo Valley, a short drive into the mountains surrounding Palm Springs. An investment with Dad financed their retirement, supplemented by Social Security and grandpa's benefits. Herb had been a talented chef who, in his spare time, had invented a roller for applying face cream. The beauty aid received a patent and nothing else. Herb was gassed in World War I, and his lungs remained weak. The unfiltered Pall Malls he smoked didn't help. He wheezed at his desk, and watched boxing matches on television. My mother and grandmother adored him. Herb called me his "little sweetheart," and Carol his "little dumpling."

Herbert was a French-Irish redhead. His mother, a Salvation Army lieutenant, died in a typhus epidemic when he was a boy. After his father remarried, friction with his stepmother caused him to leave home early. Not yet fully grown, he found work as a jockey, and was well-suited to the job. When he finally returned to the small town in France to visit his beloved father, he found him painting inside the church, high on scaffolding near the vaulted ceiling.

"*Mon père, mon père,*" said Herbert. His father, surprised and excited by the return of his son, lost his balance, was killed by the fall, and lay dead at my grandfather's feet.

Marie was youngest in her German Catholic family, a smoky-eyed girl with a ladder of seven older brothers. She held her own with hell-raisers like my grandfather; she had a strong will and deep faith. She attached a plastic font to the door of her room when she visited Palm Springs, filled it with holy water, and dipped her fingers in it to make the sign of the cross. Her rosaries were worn smooth with fingering. Marie made it her mission to save Carol and me. Mom had always been rebellious. Now that she was an unapologetic divorcée, it was official. Kitty was the ex-communicated black sheep of a devout Catholic family.

Grandma took Carol and me out through the kitchen door and around to the back of the patio for heart-to-hearts, and told us puberty would turn boys into monsters. Carol and I were insufficiently alarmed, already walking a wayward path. We often camped out with the Russian princess across the street, on her broad expanse of lawn surrounded by white adobe walls. Inside our tent, we took turns shining a flashlight on each other's changing bodies.

When I was little I had liked going to church with my grandmother. A lace handkerchief covered my head as I entered the cold, cavernous church, my patent leather Mary Janes tapping the stone floor as Grandma and I paced to our pew, she with a death grip on my arm. We bent one knee in unison, and genuflected, slid down the smooth wooden bench. I found the rituals of the Mass mysterious and appealing—the mumbled Latin, the rosary beads I fondled, brass censers smoking with incense, carried swaying down the aisle. An invisible choir sang above and behind, where an organ pumped out chords. Grandma gave me coins and paper money wrapped inside another lace handkerchief. I dropped them into a basket on a long pole that men fed down each aisle, fishing for funds. Flowers bloomed among pyramids of flickering red votive candles.

Sandi and most of my friends were Jewish. I spent the night, ate lox and bagel breakfasts, and sipped matzo ball soup, thinking everyone did. Our thirteenth year was marked by mitzvahs, trips to temple for the ritual passage into adulthood. My friends were a brainy bunch. In seventh grade we changed schools for junior high, and some of us moved into a program for "more capable learners," a college prep program that continued through high school.

My friendship with Sandi transitioned. We double dated. My friend Mike was Sandi's boyfriend, and his friend Alan was mine. But Mike and I were on fire. Most often our more reserved partners stood watch while we provided mischief and fun. We broke into the Plaza's central marquee and rearranged the letters, snuck into movies, and stole neighborhood mail. Later we'd joyride around golf courses, ripping up greens with our cars. I was the tallest girl in my class until the eighth grade when I stopped growing, but I never lost the sense of being tall, not even long after I had to accept my petite status.

The four of us attended a conference on racial equality, sponsored by the Youth Center. When James Meredith became the first Negro admitted to Ole Miss, it set a precedent and put a movement in motion. I loved the weekend seminars with student representatives from all over California. Small biracial groups talked about problems and solutions. I saw a possibility of real change, and couldn't wait to share it.

Herb and Marie drove down for the day from their high desert home in Morongo Valley. I dove into my description of events and Herb exploded, said, "This is the first instance of Communism in my very own family. I won't have it."

"What do you mean, Grandpa? What does Communism have to do with treating everyone alike no matter what their skin color is?" I asked.

"Don't try to confuse me with your new ideas," he said. "I won't have it. Do you hear me? Next thing you know they'll want—"

"What?" I interrupted. "Better jobs? Equal treatment under the law?"

"I've lived in this world longer than you have and I should know a thing or two. And that's THAT." He coughed in emphasis.

And that's THAT reverberated in my brain as I walked to my room. And *"that"* was what, exactly, except the dumbest thing I'd ever heard anyone say? It seemed important to at least try to get over prejudice. After the thoughtful dialogue at the conference, my grandfather sounded lunatic.

Marie proved tireless while Herb wore thin, watched boxing, and struggled to breathe. She served the braided and buttered sweet roll he loved, coated with sugar crystals that gave it a crunch even after he dipped it in his thick ceramic mug. Marie planted trees, put old glass bottles in her garden to turn purple in the sun, and prayed for us all. I got my period at their house. A fan blew hot air around as I sat in a chair upwind of Grandpa. Grandma motioned me into the tiny bedroom off the living room and whispered that I should move to a different chair. My smell, she said, made Grandpa sick. I'd learned about menstruation in sixth grade from a film for girls, so I understood when I felt a cramp and saw fresh blood in my white cotton underpants. I had the curse.

Mother gave birth to my brother, Wayne, when I was fifteen. Wayne had Grandpa's red hair and former spunk. Mother had to work, so Grandma took care of Wayne until Grandpa told Mother she needed to pick up her son right away. Marie was too attached.

Portuguese Bend Club

The meals that did hit the bar in Portuguese Bend were exotic, made from unfamiliar ingredients, paintings on a plate. Casey sent me to the market with a list to fill: 1) Shallots; 2) Hearts of palm; 3) Couscous; 4) Spam. I bought the Spam she'd included as a joke and the fact I had thought her serious made me the butt of the joke. I tried to get up to speed with these hip people who had all the fun.

My stepsister, Debbie, said not to bother. She didn't. Debbie had a disdain beyond her years, was an unwilling participant in family activities. She was biding her time. I understood her authority, her dark moods, and her waiting game. Unlike most people, she didn't think much of Dad, and however mystified I may have been by that, I didn't need her to feel otherwise. We planned a future with limited role models. We didn't want to teach children or go into nursing. Mary Tyler Moore and Marlo Thomas showed us another possibility: single women with secretarial skills taking on the world. It wasn't ideal but it kept us going. We could never have foreseen the seismic social shift to come.

Dad didn't know what to do with someone he couldn't charm, and Casey was wary around her daughter. Once, when they were riding a chairlift—scooted forward on the wide seat, preparing to ski off at the top—Debbie reached over and unhooked her mother's boots and bindings, laughing when the chair tipped her off and Casey fell in a heap on the packed and icy snow.

Debbie feared her future self would resemble her mother. She didn't use the word "alcoholic"—no one did—but I knew what she meant. *Days of Wine and Roses,* a breakthrough film in 1962, had awakened the public to the disease's democratic nature, broken the myth that it was a lower-class problem. Jack and Casey loved the movie: they identified with the characters, kept drinking, and named several boats *Wine and Roses.*

Debbie ate chocolate after dark, stuffed the lurid wrappers into the crevice between her bed and the wall where they furred with dust, to be discovered later. She listened to Lou Reed's dark, edgy, urban music, and led our filial pack. Roger was the sweet one, a pushover for puppies and babies, happiest on his surfboard. Carol and I, part-timers, were closer in this foursome than at home, where we went our own ways. Carol listened to rhythm and blues, Lou Rawls and Marvin Gaye, and Dad's jazz.

Roger and Carol began to explore new feelings for one another. When the folks found out they made a dramatic declaration against it, though I doubted they actually minded, and later Casey wished they had encouraged them.

"Not under our roof," they said.

Roger and Carol, literal-minded teens, went to the first *Wine and Roses*, a twenty four-foot sailboat tucked in a slip at Terminal Island, for private time.

When Roger saw friends off to Hawaii on the Matsonia, he stowed away. The ship's horn sounded and Roger ducked into a stocked lifeboat. He slept in the lifeboat by night and circulated with passengers by day until a crew member discovered him and threw him in the brig. Dad made him drag his prized surfboard up to the highway with a FOR SALE sign on it as a punishment, but we thought what he'd done was daring and cool, and I sensed Dad was proud of his stepson. Later—after Vietnam, after the evening news described Roger as a troubled veteran, after he pulled a series of criminal stunts and spent years in prison—we thought his stowing away should have raised a big red flag.

Seven

Palm Springs

It was tough to define what I valued in the land of make-believe. The town worshipped money, stored in banks that resembled cathedrals. Inside, an awed hush signaled proximity to THE source. My schizophrenic relationship to money developed as Dad gained affluence and Mother struggled to survive. At school, offspring of the rich and famous invited me into opulent homes. Mother trudged on while Dad did what he loved and thrived.

Guys prepared to make money while girls groomed themselves to become their helpmates—good-looking adjuncts. I yearned for attendance to my heart and brain. Who were the A's for? Dad didn't care. He'd never graduated high school. Mother didn't care. She'd aspired to stardom, not higher education. I was the anomaly. I cared. The A's were for me.

I started a list to record my route to an authentic self:

#1 PRESENTATION TO THE WORLD

#2 LEARNING

#3 JUSTICE AND EQUALITY

A hairdresser bleached my dark hair blond and took me to national style shows, where I competed with hair rinsed with shades of blue and green. A fake ID facilitated the trips out of town. My hairdresser wasn't gay. Maybe Mother had assumed he was. But he didn't insist that anything happen in the hotel rooms we shared on the road.

I tried out for DEBS, a group of girls who were chosen, pageant-style, to do PR for the city. Together we spelled out P-A-L-M-S-P-R-I-N-G-S in letters stretched across our chests on t-shirts. Stretchy short shorts, a cinch belt, and black pumps completed our look. The coveted letters were the two P's and S's, worn by girls sent in pairs to events not requiring the entire group. I wore an S.

I had no idea where I was going but I had to leave soon. Mother reminded me when we argued, "You'd better come up with a plan. I'm not paying for you when you turn eighteen."

Trips with the hairdresser gave me new perspective, though Las Vegas and Los Angeles didn't count: LA was a known world, and Las Vegas was as plastic and twisted as Palm Springs. I vowed to experience the wider world.

In a book I got from the library called *I Married Adventure* by Osa Johnson, Osa described her marriage to an anthropologist and the adventures that ensued. Waking up in a tent in Nairobi with cockroaches chewing your fingernails for nourishment seemed so exotic. I didn't question the notion that to have great adventures I needed a great adventurer. Who I would become was still linked to whom I would attract.

Jack and Casey sent me on a West Coast Teen Tour. A bus full of teenagers drove up the coast. San Francisco was a revelation, even the early morning in the park when an old man opened his pants and pissed a stream near the bench I occupied. I vowed to return. We continued north through cool, green Oregon, and on to Seattle, home of the world's fair, where we saw the landmark space needle built for the occasion. We climbed through the Pacific Northwest and entered Canada, my first new country. Lake Louise in Alberta was a pristine, ice-blue mirror, ringed by snowy peaks, and as I peered into its depths I was, for a while, not myself—or I was myself, and I included the majesty I saw. No boundaries or lines of demarcation divided the world. How long the feeling would last I didn't know, but I wanted more. I called Mother to check in, and I told her how fantastic it was and asked, "Why haven't you traveled?"

She seemed stung by the question and snapped, "Because I'm too busy taking care of this house so you and your sister will have a place to live. What is the matter with Palm Springs?"

"It would take too long. I'm sorry I upset you. I'll see you next week," I said and hung up, discouraged.

I added another item to my list of values.

#4 SEEING THE WORLD

Dazzled by the magic and alchemy of art, and impressed by those who created something from nothing, I hung out in the art studio at school. My friend Drew made the wildest things. He worked into a color wash and, with a few strokes, persuaded imagery to appear. A recent transfer from New York named Edna made ornate figures and faces with pen and ink. Her black-and-white patterns seemed to move on the paper with a will of their own, and she played the oddest music. A guy named Bob Dylan sang in a nasal twang about racial struggles; his music was weird and magnetic. Drew and Edna encouraged me to take an art class, but it seemed sacrilegious to dabble and I didn't try. I didn't try to do anything I didn't already know I could do well.

#5 CREATIVE EXPRESSION

I kept the list inside an unabridged dictionary with transparent parchment pages, along with my reading list, vocabulary, letters, and diary entries: all my important papers were tucked inside the pages, pressed and undisturbed. I pasted pictures of Ayn Rand, Albert Camus, and Albert Einstein in my school notebook, and read Dickens, Maugham, Fitzgerald, Hemingway, Plath, Colette, and Graham Greene, and I felt more connected to the worlds contained between book covers than I did to my own life. They promised so much, validated my private thoughts, and filled my emptiness with a family of kindred spirits.

One book stayed with me: *The Razor's Edge* by Somerset Maugham. His protagonist made his way to the Himalayas, studied with a sage, and, after learning healing abilities, left to return to his prior life. In reading that book, the Catholic beliefs I'd never subscribed to gave way to a mystical view of life. I woke myself up in the night to experience being alone in a sleeping world. I loved the quiet. Mother loved television, but seldom watched. TVs set on different channels made background noise when she was home. Lucky for me she worked a lot.

A succession of bad boyfriends and draining marriages had left Mother apathetic and angry. Her guidance took the form of warnings about men: "It's a war out there. Get them before they get you, and NEVER fall in love," she said. "The worse you are, the more they will love you."

As jaded as I was with the platinum hair and the fake ID no one questioned, Mother's advice on love was too cynical for me. I hoped true love was more than Disney programming; I hoped it was the highest value in human life. Meanwhile I was marooned in Mother's absolutism—her bitter black-and-white world.

#6 LOVE

My teachers assumed I'd attend college, but at home we fought about it. Mother wanted to reduce her financial burden by one, and Dad and Casey wouldn't subsidize four years of college. During our one conversation on the subject, Dad became uncomfortable and suggested a scholarship. But his income disqualified me for scholarships based upon need. I discussed it with my guidance counselor, who swiveled his chair around so his back was to me while we talked. He said he needed to be undistracted by my looks while we discussed my future. I wanted an Ivy League education, but that wasn't going to happen.

Life seemed hopeless in this hedonistic town where people came to get warm, play golf, and die. Awake in the middle of the night, I wrote poetry about creosote after a rain, purple verbena springing up out of white sand, colored stars swirling in mysterious patterns. I pictured life outside the sand trap and listened to my relentless heart beat.

#7 NATURE

Mother served cocktails in a baby-doll nightgown and high heels in a popular restaurant and bar, a block from our house. I was mortified and ashamed of feeling mortified. Mother's concern was maintaining the control she thought she had over Carol and me, so she liked working close by. She smoked outside on her breaks and watched the house. But my boyfriend, Jeff, came and went, and she could do nothing to stop it. We did as we pleased.

#8 FREEDOM

Portuguese Bend Club

I was caught in conflicting tides. I wanted to live with Dad, and at sixteen I moved back to Portuguese Bend Club. Dad partitioned off a third of the playroom to create another bedroom, bordered by the sliding glass door to the pool. But I didn't last long. A combination of the "Gray House Rules" and my own restlessness made me want to bolt as soon as I arrived. The "Gray House Rules" were reasonable boundaries and curfews that applied to Debbie, Roger, and me, and if I had ever known restrictions before I might have accepted them. I might even have been comforted to know my limits. But it was too late. I wasn't happy anywhere. I hoped I was special in some way I had yet to discover, but I feared I was worthless. I was shy, though people never guessed that was the case. They thought me conceited, and I let them.

The gateman's job was to limit the number of teenagers admitted to our playroom. On weekends there were two parties at the house: kids in the playroom, and adults in the living room. Jack and Casey were regulars at the Lighthouse Café, a Hermosa Beach dive of a jazz club that people lined up to enter. They often brought the party home. The Howard Rumsey Lighthouse All-Stars set up in our living room for informal after-hours parties.

Casey came on to my dates when they arrived at the house to pick me up. Late one night, after she'd done it yet again, I said, "Do you have to have everyone?"

"Frig you, Tomato," she said.

Boys I liked lost stature in Dad's proximity, and Casey's seductions ruined the rest. My evenings ended with a swim in the ocean while my dates tracked me in their headlight beams, and rounded up towels from the trunks of their cars. No one swam with me at night.

I loved seeing Debbie and Roger every day, but we all hated my being the academic yardstick they were measured against. My everyday ambivalence was great. Casey called me "Bewitched, Bothered, and Bewildered," mocked my dreamy aimlessness.

After just one semester at Palos Verdes High School I called, and Mother came. I went home to Palm Springs, to the house where no one talked. I said good-bye and we left. But I asked Mother to drive around for hours, still tempted to change my mind and stay. I couldn't decide. She turned onto a ramp, and headed home to Palm Springs.

Eight

Palm Springs, November 22, 1963
President John Fitzgerald Kennedy is Assassinated

My mother's evil eye backed everyone off and intimidated the boys. But most often with them she was coquettish. A natural nudist who stripped the minute she was inside the house, she kept her clothes to minimum coverage. She watered foliage around the house while I sat and talked with boyfriends in webbed chairs by the pool. Our conversations were interrupted when Mother bent to douse something low to the ground, revealing white moons under both cheeks in her very short-shorts, the only part of her body not tanned a golden brown. When she straightened back up, their attention turned back to me, and we both pretended to ignore her again.

At seventeen, I worked as a ward clerk at Desert Hospital. I loved being with the marooned patients who rewarded me for favors with smiles and stories from their lives. We talked about family members—those who visited and those who didn't. They opened up, and I was privy to tears, confessions, and hard-earned truths from people forced by illness or accident to stop in this serious, sterile place.

The hospital was a respite from the routine artifice of Palm Springs, the sand trap I longed to escape for good. My job was essentially to be cheerful. I hand-delivered messages jotted down on slips of paper in the nurse's station. It was an easy way to feel I was making a difference. My conversations with Mother's old boyfriend, Dr. Scott, had made me question traditional medicine, but Desert Hospital felt like a healing environment.

As I walked the halls like Harry Haller in *Steppenwolf*, each door was a portal to possibilities waiting to be realized. Sometimes all I got was a full urinal, pulled from beneath the bedcovers and thrust into my hands.

One day I met a patient animated by delirium tremens, a man too shaky to take the message I was holding out to him. I pretended I wasn't horrified as he gave up trying and said, "Just read it to me."

"Okay," I said, smiling, "Sir, your ex-wife called this morning and, ah, she wants you to know that, um, your medical insurance has been cancelled."

He convulsed in my direction, and moaned until a nurse rescued us both from discomfort with a syringe of sedatives.

Mother had to drop me off and pick me up from work, an unwelcome task in her already burdened schedule. I suppose our relationship was typical: she, harassed and angry; me, sullen and rebellious. We were deep into the friction that makes leaving home both imperative and possible. We'd bonded for a while when she shared her little yellow diet pills—the buffered methedrine, marketed as Desoxyn, had focused my mind for study—but Mother had begun to have heart palpitations and we'd both quit cold turkey.

One day, the Thunderbird was parked at the curb in its usual place when I finished work, but when I got in, I sensed something more wrong than usual. Mother held two Styrofoam cups, and the close space was humid and coffee-scented. I didn't drink coffee. Mother, usually in full control, handed me a cup with a hand that shook, and I took it and waited for her to speak.

"Honey," she began.

I saw she was crying behind her big, rhinestone-trimmed sunglasses. Tears from her were rare. I waited, frozen, for more.

"Honey," she tried again, "I'm so sorry to have to tell you this." She paused.

"Debbie is dead."

"What? How? No!" I demanded insanely, brain shutting down,

functions folding into a tight, protected knot. Perception lockdown: high-threat alert.

"Asphyxiation," she said, as if the unfamiliar word was something to which she could cling. I knew what was coming, and from the roaring tunnel in my head, I saw her lips mouth the words, "She killed herself last night."

If there was a way to make a casual suicide attempt, I had done so a couple of months before. As the eldest, I knew my gesture endorsed Debbie's act. I'd taken some pills, then slashed my wrists horizontally and gone to bed. I hadn't been upset; I'd been numb. Neither having swallowed enough pills nor slashed deeply enough to die, I awakened with the sheets stuck to my wrists. When I pulled them away, there was fresh bleeding, and I had to wake Mother for a trip to the family doctor for stitches. He had seen me through childhood illnesses, and had prescribed the diet pills. Mother and I were quiet as he sewed me up in November.

Debbie had come for Christmas. Unhappy at home, shuttling between friends' houses, she'd asked if she could live with us. Mother said it would be okay, but we all doubted Casey would accept her daughter's choice to live with her husband's ex-wife. One night I came home from a date and found Debbie holding a large kitchen knife. She said, "I thought I would have the courage to do it when I heard you drive up, but I still couldn't."

I said, "Oh Debbie, don't do it that way." I never said *don't do it at all*.

Later Carol explained to Debbie that the best way would be in the garage. She told her if she sealed the openings around the doors with towels, rugs, and rags, she'd drift into a painless sleep.

Parents of Debbie's friends had become concerned about her, so Jack and Casey took her to UCLA's Neuropsychiatry Institute, or NPI, for a battery of diagnostic tests, and she lived with her father while they awaited her test results. If Debbie proved stable, Casey would allow her to live with us in Palm Springs. She returned to Portuguese Bend for the weekend, for the meeting where they would receive recommendations. Her future would be decided Monday morning.

Saturday night, Jack and Casey threw a party, a loud party that went late. Debbie flounced through the playroom with a pillow and a blanket, announced to Roger and his friend that she was going to see if it was quieter in the garage. Roger went cruising in his friend's car, and when they returned to the house, they heard the engine running inside the garage. Roger went to his room. His friend entered the party, found Dad dancing in the living room, tapped him on the shoulder, said, "Mr. Gray, I think you should…"

At first Dad thought he was cutting in. He moved aside in an expansive gesture that drew him into the dance.

"No, Mr. Gray, please sir, you need to check the garage."

Dad's smile died in slow motion as the meaning of his words washed over him in waves. Months before Debbie had cried out, "I'm going to kill myself," and Dad had said, frustrated, "For Christ's sake, Debbie, *do* something."

"You need to check the garage *RIGHT NOW*, sir."

Dad raced past the bedrooms, through the playroom, purple with drink and apprehension.

⌐

A guy I was dating drove me to Portuguese Bend and dropped me off. The somber gateman nodded, raised the bar, and gave a brisk salute as we entered. The house was open and empty. Casey was somewhere, and Dad was with her. Roger was with friends.

I walked down the steps to the circle perched in the middle of the cliff, and listened to the ocean's relentless sounding.

Carol arrived the next day and Dad picked us up to view Debbie's overly made up and definitely dead body at the mortuary. Carol and I saw Casey at Debbie's funeral. Uncle Landon and Casey's ice skater friend guided Carol and me toward the family room. Uncle Landon opened the door and held it for us to enter. Casey saw us at the threshold and screamed, "Get them out of here! They're alive, and Debbie's dead. Get them out of here!" Carol and I backed up, stiff, wondered where to go.

Nine

After Debbie's suicide, I came down with mononucleosis, was prescribed bed rest, and missed most of the spring semester of my senior year. As I recovered—still weak, feeling overwhelmed by the work required to graduate with my class, and knowing my nearly perfect grade point average would suffer—I followed a twisted logic to an unexpected conclusion: I quit.

Becalmed, with lots of time on my hands, I meandered—magnetized here, drifting there—surprised and embarrassed to still be alive.

One night I noticed a boy sitting by himself at a party. I'd never seen him before, and I felt an attraction. I approached him, and realized he was very drunk, and indifferent to me. A challenge, I thought, and I tried to draw him out.

"Where do you go to school?"

"Judson, Palm Valley, but that's over," he said, his voice heavy and flat. I recognized the schools as private alternatives to public high school.

"Oh yeah? What's your name?" I asked.

"George III."

"Are you a royal?"

"Just rich," he said sadly, a wry grimace lifting one corner of his Clara Bow mouth.

His eyelashes were even longer than Carol's, his face stamped with mischief and pain. He was George Cameron III, a name I recognized. His father owned the local newspaper and radio station. George said he was living in a suite of rooms in his father's business offices at Cameron Center. He told a story about living in Hawaii with his father, about a surfboard gone missing. How his father interrogated him for days until George wasn't sure if he'd stolen the board or not and finally confessed to end the harangue. He came to Palm Springs and his father's business manager saw to his needs.

What George needed was love, and I wanted to give it to him. Parked at the end of Rocky Point, overlooking glitter town, we laughed until we cried about the expectations the world had of us.

"Marrying well," I offered and we dissolved in giggles.

"Making one's mark on the world," George said, with a forward thrust of his fist, and we swept over the falls of hilarity.

We wondered what we might create instead. Nina Simone's "Black Swan" was our anthem, and we spiraled down into the wet depression we shared. I moved in with him. We told friends we'd gone to Tijuana and gotten married. We were both drunk the night we first had sex. There was no pain, no blood, nothing unfamiliar. George said he was sorry he couldn't remember what he had wanted so much.

We went to a party in a north end motel room. A man sitting in a chair outside charged us a small fee and let us in. The room was cramped, full of smoke and black people who shifted a little so we could see. Tina Turner shimmied and crooned, closed eyes, thrown-back head, and legs that never stopped, while Ike strummed a guitar in the background. It was an acoustic set but Tina was electrifying. She sang of love like a prisoner with a life sentence, bringing on the rapture mixed with suffering. In that tiny, shabby motel room was a surplus of soul. We two, just a couple of high school kids, were lucky to experience it, and we knew it.

On another night I don't remember clearly, George was upset and roared off in his modified Chevy 409, then brought it back, saying, "I don't want to wreck this one." He stormed away again in his Austin Healy. I waited to see what would happen next. Mike Ellis showed up and held my hand. Mike had been my partner in junior high antics, and in the *More Capable Learner Program* in high school; he was a trusted friend. Then Mother was in the room. She let herself in the unlocked door and found us in back. Michael knew Mother and I weren't getting along and he was protective. He stood between us saying, "Stay away from her. If you don't stay away from her I'll take her away and you'll never see her again."

Mother cried, "George had an accident. He flipped his car in front of my house. I thought you were with him." We rode to Desert Hospital in mother's car, were told George would have no permanent injuries—he was all right. I collapsed outside the emergency room and slid down the pale green wall. Someone lifted me to a bed; I stiffened into catatonia there, and they admitted me. When I regained consciousness, I overheard a nurse telling another that I was the ward clerk who worked there. I heard her intake of breath, her shock. There was confusion around who was responsible for me, not yet eighteen. Had George and I married in Tijuana, as we'd told friends?

The next day the Cameron business manager drove me to UCLA's NPI, where Debbie had gone for her evaluation. My interview began with a questionnaire I couldn't even begin to answer:

Question #1:
WAS YOUR FATHER A GOOD MAN? True or False.

I rambled about the relativity of good and evil and was admitted on the spot for a three-month evaluation. A surreal week of wakefulness followed as the drugs I'd been sedated with cleared my system. They watched me interact with patients from whom I learned new ways to commit suicide. I signed myself out, against medical advice, a week later. Dad and Casey picked me up, and took me to see *One Flew Over the Cuckoo's Nest*, a popular new play adapted from a Ken Kesey novel.

George and I would marry for real. I insisted he reconcile with his mother, Ann. They had been estranged since George burned down the garage of her comfortable San Marino home (hence the time with his Dad in Hawaii). Both of George's parents had remarried, and any communication between them went through the business manager and sometimes surrogate father.

When George and his brothers were young boys, their father powered them to the middle of a lake in a dinghy with an outboard motor, cut off the engine, and said, "There will be no QUEERS in this family or I'll drown you myself. UNDERSTAND?"

Ann was cool, socially adept, and non-maternal for someone who, by the time I met her, was a mother of seven. She welcomed us into her home with a gracious detachment. George's siblings clearly adored him. A young half-brother shared his book on Impressionism with me. Ann herded us through activities for a few days, her rift with George apparently healed. I was startled when, as we were leaving, she said,

"Terry, I'm growing quite fond of you, and I understand you share a birthday with my son, John, whom I really don't care for at all. How interesting."

I thanked my future mother-in-law for I wasn't sure what, leaned into her efficient embrace, and stated what to me was obvious: "You and my parents are going to be very good friends."

We approached George's father next. As a condition for receiving his blessing, he demanded I return to NPI to complete the three-month evaluation. It had become a family proving ground. George's father had done a stint there when his brother, Arthur, tried to have him proven incompetent. There was a measure of "If I could do it, let's see if she can," in his challenge. I accepted. He introduced me to Dr. Brill, the head of the institution, and this time I made an appointment to be admitted in a couple of weeks. I would collect new experiences, and find out about Debbie—and besides, it would make George happy if his father approved of our marriage.

I hadn't appreciated how deeply addicted George Jr.—Mr. Cameron—was to prescription drugs and alcohol, with increasingly volatile results. I'd heard the stories about his incredible constitution. He sought treatment on a regular basis, and then walked out of the hospital a few days later to repeat the cycle.

George Jr. had a chokehold on George III, his favored son, and he expected him to enter the family business. He didn't know if I was a threat or an ally, so his behavior toward me alternated between affection and violent attack. We couldn't anticipate, when we knocked on his door, if he would be friendly or have to be restrained by bodyguards.

George III frayed under the strain of his father's mixed messages—but I took them in stride. George Jr. could be charming and folksy, the kind of dinner guest every hostess loves, right up until he passed out in his plate. I watched how money moved the social wheels. This man was powerful. Much was forgiven. He had an audience for his decline. He also had a new young wife, who ran around town in a white Rolls Royce with red pinstriping, shopping and pulling into Foster's Freeze for ice cream cones, auburn ponytail swinging. She seemed to be having the time of her life.

There were three psychiatrists on Ward B; mine was a resident named Dr. Zaslove, and my case was overseen by Dr. Ungerleider, who chose one case to monitor from each of his three residents. NPI was a diagnostic clearing house—all kinds of patients spent three months there, then went home to continue therapy as outpatients, or were legally committed for a minimum of two years. Dr. Zaslove reminded me of my high school guidance counselor, who had swiveled his desk chair around when we talked. They were just guys. I watched Zaslove from an upstairs window as he walked to his car, observed his cocky gait. He slid into the driver's seat of a candy-apple-red convertible. Like I said, just a guy.

The inmates were fascinating company, however. I met the man who brought Theatre of the Absurd to Los Angeles, a flood victim afraid of water, and a man so obese he rode the freight elevator to recreational therapy, where we did synchronized movements to Julie Andrews' "My Favorite Things." A woman knitted great balls of tangled loops, went for a routine EEG, and came back cured: she knit a lovely sweater she wore home. A teenage boy hung himself in a closet on a home visit. The fragile new mother from Sweden hallucinated deer running around our group therapy session. ("Don't you see them? Really? REALLY? They're right there!")

A sax player I befriended later married Mike Ellis's mother—he would send me a note from the bandstand in 1974 that read, "Where were you the summer of 1964?" A mathematician worked problems all day, head down, marks filling a growing stack of papers. Periodically he berated himself for being "stupid, stupid, stupid."

There was a former child star who had appeared in Westerns in the fifties, who, when her film came on television in the dayroom, identified with the horse, and galloped, whinnied, and bucked around the bulky furniture until she was corralled by three beefy attendants. We all looked back and forth between the pig-tailed girl she used to be, conversing pleasantly with her horse on the screen, to the wild, deranged imitation steed she'd become.

I sat with electroshock therapy patients, repeating their names and describing their families until synapses reconnected: "Yes, they will visit you Tuesday, Joanne and your brother Matt. Yes, you have a brother. You are Andrew. Yes, you have two visitors every Tuesday, your brother Matt and his wife Joanne. Your name is Andrew. Yes, Andrew."

That month's Playboy centerfold arrived after a suicide attempt. She'd lied about her age to Playboy and wasn't much older than I was. Her Hollywood friends brought fruitcake stuffed with marijuana, and I tried some. I liked it better than the vodka I had smuggled onto the ward, which I mixed with 7-Up and sipped undetected. We grew bold, smoking pot in the ugly green bathroom at night. Things didn't seem so serious when I was high. In fact, it was all funny sometimes. Like the night the fire department came and men ran through the ward with their hose toward the back offices, where a paper fire had set off an alarm. Their nervousness was hilarious, scared eyes behind goggles, helmeted heads jerking right and left. We giggled, in hysterics, playing our parts.

"BOO!" someone said, and we laughed harder.

I asked about Debbie, and met with the doctors who had interviewed and evaluated her. They shared their recommendations after the fact of her suicide. They would have urged the three-month residential program I was now in if they'd had the chance.

About two months into my three-month stint, Dr. Ungerleider met with me and insisted I request a new doctor. He claimed Dr. Zaslove had lost his objectivity, and had a personal agenda that would not be helpful to me. He would back me up, but the request had to originate with me. I decided to leave instead, again.

That night I joined a group with privileges on a chaperoned trip to see "Hamlet" at the campus theater, a short walk away. The centerfold and I positioned ourselves at the back of the group and slipped away, then caught a cab to the Beverly Hills Hotel, where she called Frank Sinatra, who guaranteed our bill.

Dad came to visit that evening, and when the hospital told him I was gone, he stopped at a bar in Westwood and met a Brit, a woman fleeing an affair with a married man in London. She began another one with Dad that night. Casey was in Europe with her friend, the ice skater—an experimental period for them, she told me later, that didn't go anywhere. "Travel is my kind of therapy," she'd told Dr. Zaslove when I was first admitted.

When Casey returned and realized Dad was packed to leave her, she removed the clothes from his bag and persuaded Roger to zip her up in his suitcase. Dad tried to pick up the bag and couldn't, unzipped it, found Casey, and stayed another forty years.

"How can you leave a woman with a sense of humor like that!?" he said.

Mom and I returned to NPI a week later to retrieve my things. Dr. Zaslove strong-armed her, told her I'd most certainly kill myself and it would be her fault unless she signed a two-year commitment order now, while she still had some authority. I would soon be eighteen.

He did a good job of scaring her. I took her arm and steered her out of his office, saying, "Okay, you've made your case. We're going to lunch now and when we get back she can make her decision." I had to promise her I would never end my life—that she would never regret her decision to set me free. I had to convince her I was fine.

We returned to the hospital after lunch and I said to Zaslove, "Sorry, we're going now," picked up my things, and got us both out of there.

That fall, Mother saw a photo in the *Los Angeles Times* that she thought, at first glance, was me. She read further: it was Dr. Zaslove's engagement announcement to my lookalike.

Ten

I was eighteen and getting married. I saw Watts burn from the freeway when I went for fittings in town; bought monogrammed silver boxes for the wedding party, antique gold bridesmaid's dresses, and my own ivory charmeuse gown with a handmade lace coat and mantilla. I lost ten pounds I couldn't comfortably lose.

"Stress," I was told. "Even good change is stressful," someone reassured me.

I went through the motions: booked the glass church for the ceremony and lined up the Princess Louise cruise ship for the reception. I felt I was in a movie with a cast I slightly knew, waiting for real life to begin. I longed for something I couldn't name; freedom trumped security.

Dad walked me down the aisle of the handsome church made of glass, the Wayfarer's Chapel in Palos Verdes. He looked distinguished—balding early and not yet wearing hats of hair. He and Mother were cautious around each other, cordial. She, blond now, wore a tiered lace dress the color of money. Casey sat in the front pew in a cut-velvet coat in primary colors, hard to miss.

Dad and I paced the aisle, our dress shoes striking smooth stone in unison. Behind the altar, crossed wooden beams formed abstract shapes, the chapel's central juncture an open circle. No crosses or religious imagery marked the altar. The chapel was dedicated to the Swedish scientist and philosopher, Emanuel Swedenborg, who, informed by dreams and visions, entered Heaven and Hell at will. His writing inspired poets and mystics like Blake, Baudelaire, Balzac, and Carl Jung.

We stood in a glade, encased in glass, lit by moon and stars. Spotlights at the base of each surrounding tree cast a circular glow up into their canopies. The church interior was candlelit by pulsing white pillars that lined the walls, and the altar flickered with strings of tapers. The chapel was both modern and grounded, airy and earthy—filled with the scent of flowers. Bridesmaids promenaded in shades of antique gold. I followed in sleeveless silk, covered by a lace coat with a cascading train, crowned with a lace mantilla. I felt a tug and knew it was Drew—he held my train a moment, and pulled me back into myself, made me gasp and smile. Dad and I continued past his pew. My cousin's daughter scattered flower petals before us in tandem with my brother, who held a satin pillow with our rings tied with ribbon. Dad and I were solemn as we moved through the moonlight that shone through the glass ceiling.

We reached the altar. Bridesmaids to my left, groomsmen on the right, and a smiling George front and center. Dad passed me off to him and took his place beside Casey.

Vows we'd composed, recited; the connecting ritual consummated in the kiss. We rotated to present to guests, now on their feet in a whoosh of reaching out, congratulations, festivity spilling out of the chapel behind us. There was a rush to cars for the drive to the dock in nearby San Pedro, where we would board the Princess Louise for a harbor tour reception.

Our guests were an eclectic mix of George's Hawaiian surfer buddies, my artist and dancer friends, and Palos Verdes and Pasadena's social register. George's brothers had refused their father's demand that they kidnap George before his wedding, and stood up for him instead. Their father, who paid all the bills except for the rehearsal dinner, which was on Jack and Casey, did not attend.

One of George's groomsmen, a blond Indian who didn't drink well, insulted Casey. Someone sprang to her defense and a scuffle ensued. It wasn't Dad—he was never pugnacious, more inclined to finesse a situation than turn it confrontational. But someone Casey was cultivating tried to defend her with his fists. George rushed in while Casey looked on, amused, and subdued his unruly grooms-man. Peace was restored, and the party resumed, but I took it as a sign and plotted my getaway, said a few good-byes, and left George with his friends.

The Princess Louise slid back into her berth and the party con-tinued. I managed to walk the gangway unnoticed, and escaped to collapse in my hotel room. I'd thrown up all day, so much so that Mother had reminded me I didn't need to go through with it. I sup-posed it had been a good wedding, but I was on automatic, following momentum I'd put into motion. I'd coursed through my wedding, a shadow figure, more quicksilver than bedrock, more ethereal than corporeal, more shooting star than firmament. The black-and-white photos were crisp, but in my memory of the evening diffuse shapes slid in and out of focus. There were ghosts in attendance. It was not the happiest day of my life, not the culmination of the promising teens; it was an act of compliance that marked more of an ending than a beginning.

Portuguese Bend Club
Photo credit: Jack Gray

Three

Flower Child

⌒

*If you want to find the secrets of the universe, think in
terms of energy, frequency, and vibration.*

Nicola Tesla

Terry in Golden Gate Park
Photo credit: George Cameron

One

*W*e arrived in Montecito in a white Lincoln convertible with red upholstery that we drove off the showroom floor at a time when we were enjoying George Jr.'s good graces. We settled in a rental on the water. A house full of nuns from the local Carmelite order lived next door. I walked the beach in a black Rudi Gernreich bathing suit: a wide mesh V began at my collarbone and tapered to a point above my pubic bone. My pet ocelot, Glee, played in the surf at the end of his leash. People snapped photos. The oversized hat and sunglasses, the dramatic designer suit, and the exotic animal on a leash convinced them I must be somebody. Nuns watched from their deck.

A short walk up the beach, another of George Jr.'s ex-wives lived with her actor husband, John Ireland, and George's half-brother, Cameron Cameron. We lunched at their club and showed up at their house for cocktail hour. George had disappointed his father with his refusal to enter the family business, a communications conglomerate—an acrimonious split I supported, and thought essential for George's well-being. He enrolled at Brooks Institute of Photography and tapped the educational trust his father couldn't reverse.

George was generous, and he welcomed my artist friends Drew and Edna, my buddy Mike Ellis, and my high school boyfriend Jeff, who came for extended visits. I wanted us to buy an island, someplace where everyone could create not only art but a new way of life. Change began to have its way with us. We molted, smoked pot, skipped cocktail hour, said good-bye to the nuns, and moved to a ramshackle place in the woods by the water. The house had an adjacent three-story tower where we installed Glee, the ocelot, hoping he would feel he occupied the upper branches of a forest. The first floor we filled with dogs rescued from the pound. George photographed me with the animals in various woodland settings for his studies at the Institute.

After a semester, we moved on to Sausalito in the Bay Area's Marin County, where we sold toys to finance a new life, letting go of surfboards, the Chevy 409, and the wedding silver. George and I commuted to jobs in the city: George apprenticed to a fine cabinetmaker in the Marina, and I enrolled in Patricia Stevens Finishing School on O'Farrell to train as a model.

Jeff and Drew made us four. Edna, a New York City girl, lived in San Francisco with George's brother. They had a flat with space for Edna to do her artwork, those complex pen-and-ink drawings of intricate, patterned faces. My dear friend, Mike Ellis, lived in Sausalito with Martha, who had long, straight blond hair like Mary Travers from Peter, Paul and Mary. Mike had told me he had feelings for Martha, and said he'd never loved anyone but me, and wanted to make sure it was alright. It pinched, but I wanted him to be happy.

Martha and Mike lived with Martha's mother, Reba, secretary of the NAACP's California chapter. She had long mentored Drew when we lived in Palm Springs, and Drew and his friends called her "Ma." Mike and Martha looked like a couple, could have been brother and sister, with their same straight blond hair and wire-rimmed glasses, their same wholesome appearance. In high school, Mike and I had stood in his mother's dressing room, looked at our multiple reflections in her infinity mirror, and laughed at the clear mismatch. Mike was a super bright, basic guy, happiest riding Appaloosa ponies. I looked like I had more to prove, wanted more, and I suppose I did.

The animals had new homes. Glee, the ocelot who had only been eight inches long when I fell in love with him at the wild animal store in Manhattan Beach, grew to be three feet long. His favorite place was on top of the refrigerator. He sprang onto the backs of whoever walked by or bent to look inside the fridge for food. We thought it cruel to trim his claws, so we were raked with scratches, scarred by tooth marks, and the baby talk we'd always used to soothe him became an irritant to him instead. He still loved to play in the surf, but he was wild. An architect in Palm Springs who had long coveted him, offered to become his new, more stable owner, and we gave him up with reluctance.

The Sausalito property was a former Victorian mansion, divided into apartments. It was managed by Ralph, an effeminate man in his early thirties. Ralph lived with the octogenarian dowager who owned the place and kept Ralph like a pet. Drew and Jeff became his play-mates, while George and I spent our weekdays in the city.

Sausalito was a small artist colony/fishing village then. Located on the edge of Marin County closest to the Golden Gate Bridge, it had the easiest access to, and best views of, San Francisco. This was before hip restaurants and tourists clogged Sausalito's main street, before the social earthquake cracked open the buttoned-down life. We sat in the park across from the broad steps that climbed the hill to residential neighborhoods, and marveled at our terrific timing and great good fortune in being there. The Bay Area felt ripe and ready to burst—electrically charged—and we were thrilled to be part of the change.

The front gate of our house opened onto a lavish, tiered garden lit with globe lights that looked from our apartment above like float-ing orbs. We had the mansion's main kitchen, pantry, and dining room, with a small room off to the right with three large unscreened windows. With a push at their top, the windows swung open on their center hinges and admitted a blast of damp, salty air and a spectacu-lar view: Angel Island front and center and the city on the right. We slept and awakened in this room, side by side on single mattresses.

Our entry door opened onto the dining room. Walnut walls glowed with hints of green and violet, and floor-to-ceiling cabinets held books behind old glass doors. A stained-glass candelabrum lit the elegant room we'd furnished with low tables and floor pillows; area rugs left expanses of wood exposed. A gray marble-framed fireplace heated the sumptuous room. In the desert, we had become accustomed to spare design stripped of ornamentation—buildings that looked as sterile as the desert itself (without its spring carpet, that is). Nurtured by the space and the moist sea air and free from the sand trap at last, we settled.

On O'Farrell, we models in training practiced our runway walks, and paired off with photographers to build up our portfolios at the Japanese Tea Gardens in Golden Gate Park, the Maritime Museum, and the Legion of Honor Hall. We did photo shoots on location, runway shows, and were occasionally filmed for local TV while we continued our training.

The four of us led an increasingly double life in the pause that linked the beatnik movement to the psychedelic revolution. Pot produced a pleasant buzz, not as big a deal as booze, was more subtle, not so dangerous—ironic, as it was illegal. I was on a quest for something that worked as well for me as alcohol did for my family. I thought maybe I'd found it.

Two

Carol's best friend Gerri, an African-American dancer from Palm Springs, came to visit, and we took her to North Beach to see Nina Simone. We had traded in the convertible for a blue Volkswagen bus with a sunroof, and, as we crossed the Golden Gate Bridge, we swallowed a half dose of something called D-lysergic acid that we'd bought in the park. We were told it had no effect on the body, was undetectable after being absorbed into the system, but was a catalyst for expanded consciousness, whatever that meant.

We parked by a neon-purple sign we made a point of remembering as a landmark, and found the small nightclub where Nina was performing. In a lounge outside the showroom we lined up on an upholstered red leather banquette, and waited for the next show to begin. After a while the door to the showroom swung open and out of the blackness came a roar—half growl, half lament—that pinned me against my seat with its intensity. I caught a glimpse of Nina, the jungle goddess, in a leopard-print bodysuit, and she looked mad. I balked, afraid to go in. The bench beneath me shifted, slid sideways and bucked slightly, so I got to my feet, swaying but upright, and said, "What's going on?" Everything moved. The mirrored wall behind the banquette with its faux marbling looked like a sheet of quivering, fractured mercury, and in it was my warped reflection. My burgundy velvet dress vibrated. The image wobbled and threatened to break apart. Everything I looked at was made of particles in motion, expanding and contracting, generating patterns. The draperies undulated; the jewel-toned, patterned carpet snaked and pulsed, its blues and reds melting into purple pools. Nothing was solid. Drew giggled and Jeff stared at the palms of his hands, muttering about maps, arterial highways. Gerri looked like she might cry. "What time is it?" she asked.

The hands on my watch were spinning so I asked a man in slow motion, "W-h-a-t t-i-m-e i-s i-t? I pointed to my watch to illustrate the foreign language I spoke. My words floated through the air, popped, and dissolved in front of his face. He answered, and I saw the time on a limp, Dali-esque clock face. I passed it on to Gerri, who looked relieved for one full second, then asked again, "What time is it?"

"I have no idea," I said.

George wore a goofy grin, looked like he had something to say. His lips moved but nothing came out. His wavy blond hair was long now, and those dimples. The door opened again, and everyone stood. We became part of a stream moving inside, slipping into seats around rectangular cocktail tables. From my chair, left of the stage, I saw a portly man standing in the wings on the opposite side. He wore knee breeches and a lace cravat. Headphones cupped his ears under a three-cornered hat. He did a sound check and nodded to someone above and behind me. I'd just finished a Ben Franklin biography, and there he was at the edge of the stage, half hidden behind the curtain. Somewhere in the distance sticks stirred a snare drum, and a lone piccolo piped. Ben removed his wire-rimmed spectacles and winked at me, then turned and walked offstage, kicking up puffs of red, white, and blue spangles that erupted around his buckled shoes.

When the house lights went dark there were explosions of color in my field of vision. I'd never liked the Fourth of July's warlike connotation, and I had always stayed home with Dr. Scott, who had shell shock, while Mother and Carol drove to the park to watch fireworks. This was different. The explosions took shape, and a subtly striated, star-encrusted panorama opened up and stretched out before me. Surges of symphonic sound passed in crescendos of color; waves crested and curled in frothy ripples of strings.

Suggestions of ancient civilizations gathered and dispersed. Gorgeous architectures triumphed, eroded, and fell into the void that gave rise to everything.

Nina appeared on the small, spot lit stage, galvanizing all attention. She stood beside a glossy piano and glared at us, dark queen, panther, and conscience—sad little Southern girl holding a notebook and pencil, humming along with crickets and cicadas, skipping down a dusty North Carolina lane. She moaned out octaves of her pain, and it was my pain too, told stories my imagination illustrated. When she sang of the lynchings, sycamore trees grew and filigreed the curtains behind her, bore in silhouette the swollen bodies, pecked by crows, that "strange and bitter fruit."

She launched into "Sinnerman" and the room jittered with agitation. My adrenaline spiked, and I fought an urge to stand and fight, defend or condemn, or just get the hell out of there. She slowed and began our favorite, "Black Swan," and I squeezed George's shoulder. He leaned toward me, brushed his cheek against my hand. *"Black swan, take me down with you."*

Returning my attention to the stage, a whirlpool of tears appeared and invited me to drown in their depths. I held onto my seat like I would on an airplane in turbulence. I held on tight, but the vortex at Nina's feet was too strong to resist. I closed my eyes and let go, swirled down, down, down, drifted into spiraling eddies, was buoyed up and bounced over falls, and when I opened my eyes I was back in the room, back at my seat. The lights were on, and people were filing out of the showroom. We shuffled after them and staggered out into the North Beach night with neon signs flashing purple in every direction.

"How are we going to find the car?" Gerri asked. I laughed, a little hysterically, and Drew joined in, finding everything hilarious. George wasn't laughing. I knew he needed to find the car but what then? We couldn't drive home like this, and no one had any idea how long it would last. North Beach throbbed with a seedy Saturday night verve. Carol Doda flaunted her gifts. Hot jazz spilled into the street. Men stood outside strip clubs and beckoned the milling crowd to enter.

We wanted to find our car. It took all five of us, and it took all five of us to drive home. George took the wheel. I rode shotgun, and Gerri positioned herself in front of the clock on the dashboard. Drew and Jeff crowded around the front seats, offering suggestions. We all focused on staying on the right side of the white line and encouraged George to pick up speed, to flow with the traffic.

Jeff said, "George, if you don't want to drive, I will. It's like we're coursing through the bloodstream of a giant organism. We're the vessels, the atoms, the molecules, and it's all a dance, a grand cosmic dance. Come on, Gerri, relax, it's a dance."

Jeff and Gerri had studied for years at Trixie Jarrette's dance studio in Palm Springs. I had first seen them in recital on an early visit, before Mother moved us there. I was seven, and I'd thought Jeff *was* the prince he danced in *Sleeping Beauty*.

"No, that's alright. I'll get us there," George said. We took Van Ness to the Golden Gate Bridge, the route familiar from our weekday commute. The bridge was a diamond dragon stretched across the Bay. The bus arced over its back and dropped down onto the Sausalito turnoff. We made it home, and paused in silence as the engine settled, then pushed and slid open the doors. George opened and held the gate and we entered the tiered garden, lit with its glowing globes. Jeff and Drew streaked ahead. George walked with Gerri, who moved jerkily and left angular afterimages in her wake like Marcel Duchamp's *Nude Descending the Staircase*. Her body and spirit, so fluid when she danced, were tight with fear. I gave her a small alarm clock that she clutched the rest of the night.

George was cold and shivering, and I suggested a hot shower, which sounded good—but judging the temperature of the water became another group activity. Jeff and I opened the three picture windows and heard a cat crying in the garden. Should we rescue it like we had the dogs at the pound in Carpenteria? Then we would be responsible for it. Jeff said no, we shouldn't—we'd just have to feed it—but I was already headed out the door. It was a tiny tiger stripe, weightless in my hands. I held it against my chest and felt its heart beat against mine through the thin skins that separated us. I carried the kitten inside and put it down on the middle of the floor. It gagged and threw up.

"See, I told you not to bring it in," Jeff said. "I'm not cleaning it up."

"What? You are not your brother's keeper?" I asked.

In truth, I'd lost interest in the cat and didn't want to clean up after it either. George walked in dressed in his bathrobe, drying his hair with a small towel—feeling better, I could tell. "Oh, look who's here." He used the towel to wipe up the mess but didn't pick up our interloper. George was more wounded king than nurturer. He took care of us all in broad strokes, but was nervous dealing with the details we generally spared him.

If George was king, Drew was jester. I knew I'd be the one to take care of the cat. I moved toward it, and said, "Maybe just because I brought her in doesn't mean she's ours now. Dogs and cats are over-domesticated, I think, I'll just put it back outside."

Gerri picked up the cat, wrapped it in her coat, slipped the ticking clock into a pocket, and, curling up on a mattress, said, "Thanks for a very interesting night."

Three

*L*SD produced no demonstrable effect upon the body, but it took a toll. Sunday mornings, I wished for a medieval rack for some light stretching. Instead I rolled out a yoga mat and the guys joined in, and we started a morning practice. Yoga meant "union," the union of everything we experienced in the first phase of our journeys. This union we longed to extend, and sought to reach without drugs. Ancient diagrams showed how energy moved through the body, and gave us language to describe our experience: chi, chakras, kundalini, and auras. Eyes closed, we followed light trails blazed the prior weekend, and as we became sensitized, pot had the power to catapult us further.

We cleaned up our diet to support the yoga, which supported the trips. What I'd learned from Dr. Scott served us now, as we lived on English muffin creations, mounds of random ingredients topped with cheese, melted in the toaster oven. Barbecued spare ribs, artichokes, and champagne was formal fare. I threw out the Uncle Ben's rice and brought home Chico-San's brown. We gave up meat, aspirin, alcohol, coffee, cigarettes, birth control pills, and negativity. The change began here. One day a week we took only water, tea, and juice, and a week's fast began each season. George and I continued our commute to the city on weekdays, and reserved Saturday nights for LSD.

Drew disappeared to eat hamburgers and seduce men. Being our resident artist and freest spirit, he was entitled. I bought paint, brushes and pens and watched him wet the paper, tape it to a board and lay in bold, free color fields in red, blue, and green. A representational Buddha head emerged from the amorphous, saturated wash; a few lines added with a dry brush supplied the closed-eyed, tranquil expression.

Something was happening—something equal in importance to the discovery of fire, or the invention of the wheel. This something required us to pay close attention to ourselves, each other, and the possibilities in each moment. Our actions were imbued with significance, as if on Saturday nights the universe looked through us, searched for a reason to intervene in humanity's path to self-destruction.

San Francisco bookstores combined cutting-edge and classic literature. From San Francisco's City Lights, and The Tides in Sausalito, I brought home ecstatic poetry by William Blake, Aldous Huxley's *The Doors of Perception,* and the *Tibetan Book of the Dead,* an eerie echo of our LSD ego-death and rebirth. Former Harvard psychologist Timothy Leary had based his 1964 book *The Psychedelic Experience* upon it, and we read both Leary's and the original. I picked up the *I Ching* or *Chinese Book of Changes,* and cast hexagrams. My high school favorite, *The Razor's Edge,* where Larry sees a procession of prior selves—past incarnations—was even more relevant now.

Reincarnation made sense of things, in a way. The bomb that Debbie's suicide had exploded had spun my family into separate orbits. I longed for revelation, wanted to understand how life and death worked and what they expected of me. Mother's Catholic lineage relegated Debbie to purgatory. I wanted to believe more comforting stories. I now considered another possibility: the Void, the Clear White Light of undifferentiated being.

The therapeutic potential of LSD was obvious. Patients I'd met at NPI could be rescued from their psychic kink, their mental detours, by practitioners willing to merge doctor with patient. Leary emphasized "set and setting," and our night in North Beach persuaded us he was right. We were open and impressionable, and owed it to ourselves to provide as pleasing, safe, and interesting an environment as possible. A cut from Stan Getz's album *Focus* became our soundtrack for bliss, before boundaries and separation set in. Jeff perfected his timing. My first awareness of external reality when we tripped was the soft scratch of a needle circling grooved vinyl, followed by ineffable release into freedom's song. We basked in the unabashed innocence of stars being born, as Getz's horn pushed higher, caught, tremulous, on precipices, and then soared.

We never wanted to come down. It was always, "Oh, no, here we go again," nostalgic for what we couldn't frame in words. Everything came up for review in the stages of re-entry—the passage through *bardos* en route to re-incarnation. Words and ideas drifted through consciousness, along with self-recriminations and song lyrics. The scope of awareness narrowed until, back in the body, I surrendered the illusion of control, a little at a time, and softened.

Pot wasn't killer weed, so we sifted through lies about drugs and a morality we found repressive. The generation who had thrilled to the Beatles' "I Want to Hold Your Hand" started a sexual revolution. We saw attempts to control sensuality as immoral, and what the culture feared as hedonism, we considered choice. What looked like anarchy was freedom giving birth to natural order, the joyous rebellion of a flower's push through concrete.

I sewed us four velvet capes. People asked if we were a theatrical troupe. Sometimes we wore them to watch the sunset. Jeff's was electric blue, Drew's gold, and mine deep violet. George's rose-colored cape had an embossed floral lining. Ascetic by nature, George was more interested in our new spirituality than he was in me, but I didn't mind. I was not proprietary, or jealous.

Jeff was sensual, and solicitous of George, while mildly covetous of his authority and alliance with me. I delighted in Drew and Jeff; their levity and love balanced George's seriousness for me, the fulcrum of our foursome. George, glad I had playmates, was always hardest on himself. His mood at times grew grave, his devotions disciplined, and we tried to lighten his burden. It was an unspoken and unconventional agreement, a system of dividing roles and affections that lasted a few years.

Four

*W*e wanted to be outside, and thought we could handle the exposure. So we wrapped sleeping bags, pillows, and soft duffels full of clothes in the Spanish bedspread we used for yoga and tied it to the luggage rack. The back compartment of the VW bus held grooming kits, a Coleman stove, and supplies. Floor pillows and an Oriental rug replaced the middle seat. We glued an incense burner to the dashboard and hung crystals from the mirror, and we were ready to go. I gave the modeling agency notice, and George took time off from work; we locked our Sausalito apartment, and went south to Laguna Beach, where Jeff knew the Brotherhood.

"The Brotherhood of Eternal Love" manufactured and distributed psychedelics (from the Greek meaning "mind manifesting") to a broad network that included Millbrook, the New York mansion where Tim Leary and Richard Alpert conducted drug experiments. Funded by heirs to the Mellon fortune, Millbrook operated under the auspices of the "League for Spiritual Discovery," or LSD.

"We saw ourselves," Leary said, "as anthropologists from the twenty-first century inhabiting a time module set somewhere in the dark ages of the 1960s. On this space colony we were attempting to create a new paganism and a new dedication to life as art."

The LSD we took came from Sandoz Pharmaceuticals in Switzerland, where it had been discovered and developed. Members of the Brotherhood were older and followed traditional gender roles, whereas George gravitated to the kitchen and I hung out with the guys, listening to music, and passing joints that looked like cigars.

We set up camp in Laguna Canyon, a fairyland setting of cottages marked off with picket fences on flower-filled lanes. Laguna Beach police wore shorts and rode bicycles. Artists and craftspeople lived in the lush canyon, and sold their work in fairs. One man perforated tin cans that projected patterns when you burned a candle inside them. We bought several, thought them ingenious, and added roach clips fashioned from hemostats and antique spoons. In a more efficient world, we told one another, recycling materials would play an important part.

An artist painted an enormous canvas outside under a canopy. In the center, a single cell divided, and the evolution of life spiraled out, each species depicted in painstaking detail, sketched first upon the canvas, now being painted. One night while on LSD, he told us, he realized what his hands were for, and began.

Joshua Tree National Monument was a short drive over the San Bernadino Mountain range, in the high desert above Palm Springs. The majestic cacti and boulder-studded terrain was another good venue for camping and dropping acid. The air was thin and the vibratory rate was high at Giant Rock, a WWII radio transmission site. After the war, George Van Tassel bought the property and established a Flying Saucer Institute with a landing strip and metaphysical library, hospitable to the curious and host to an Annual Flying Saucer Convention, which drew hundreds. Van Tassel claimed to have built his Integratron, housed inside a geodesic dome, from instructions received from extraterrestrials; its purpose, he said, was antigravity, time travel, and rejuvenation.

One reason to be outside was to distance city lights so we could scan the sky we hoped was full of friends. A sense of being monitored persisted. We channeled information we couldn't explain, were certain a higher intelligence was interested in the human race. It seemed possible that extraterrestrials had dropped the idea of LSD into the mind of Albert Hoffman, the Swiss chemist Sandoz had hired in 1927. He'd first synthesized LSD in 1938, and then set it aside for five years before returning to it, at which point he absorbed a small quantity through his fingertips by accident and discovered its power-ful effects.

"I perceived an uninterrupted stream of fantastic pictures, extraordinary shapes with an intense kaleidoscopic play of colors." Hoffman chose chemistry as a career, though tempted to pursue art, because "mystical experiences in childhood in which nature was altered in magical ways" had provoked questions concerning the external material world, and chemistry was the scientific field which might afford insights into this.

In George Van Tassel's library we reviewed the literature on repeated UFO sightings around nuclear facilities worldwide. Our crude technology and ignorance of waste disposal, combined with our warlike nature, presented a potential threat. Man's technology *was* crude. Planes struggled for lift off, spewed toxic exhaust, shud-dered as they picked up speed. A more sophisticated system of light and sound frequencies would explain the phenomena we witnessed, the silent lights that traversed the sky in a flash, on diagonal trajec-tories. Weather balloons and space stations didn't zigzag across the upper realms, but something did.

The nights were so clear and star-studded I saw the curvature of the earth reflected overhead. Beyond the hill, the dull glow of distant civilization lit the horizon. Someone stood at the hill's apex and held a guitar high in the air. I watched its silhouette from our campsite, and listened to the wind blowing through its strings and thrumming it into an eerie, howling hum. Eyes skyward, we waited.

Carl Jung considered UFO phenomena to be mankind's quest for wholeness, projected onto a neutral cosmos. In a book on Nikola Tesla, I read that his childhood bed had to be placed on stacks of felt—so sensitive was Nikola to vibrations as a boy that footfalls in adjoining rooms disturbed him. I wondered how sensitive it was advisable to become. My hair was a bouquet of sense receivers with a will of its own. I identified minerals around me, and lost conscious-ness when we drove through Los Angeles, curled up in the backseat, defenseless against the smog.

We listened to Ravi Shankar. His centered presence, the complex-ity of his chord structures and rhythms, his relentless progressions and exquisitely rendered instruments, the *sitars* and *tablas,* drew us like magnets: we were riveted by the complicated, meditative music. After one of our seasonal fasts, dressed in our velvet capes, we went to the Hollywood Bowl to see him. The four of us burst into tears as the first note was plucked, bowed, tapped, sounded.

In Palm Springs, Dr. Scott sold us food supplements and brain foods, and gave us tips on how to manage our vegetarian diet. We checked in with our families, and Jeff found a long black velvet coat that belonged to his dancer aunt. It was a perfect fit, and I couldn't resist a visit to I. Magnin with Drew in tow, where I scored a short, white dress covered with butterflies, and matching tights.

When we returned to San Francisco we saw evidence of change in the local culture. A new rag, *The Oracle,* published articles by Leary, Ferlinghetti, and Ginsberg. Bizarre art deco concert flyers were tacked up around town, the imagery reminiscent of being high, and the text more legible when we were.

Stanley Mouse became the premier psychedelic artist, and Bill Graham booked the Fillmore West for a "Family Dog" concert to benefit The San Francisco Mime Troupe. I wore the antique coat and new dress. Under black light, surrounded by a show of pulsing shapes, the white dress glowed fluorescent. I moved and spun, the day-glo butterflies circling the surrounding air.

Five

$\mathcal{M}$a—Martha's mother Reba—wanted to try LSD. She was still secretary of the NAACP's California Chapter, and had moved with her two daughters to Sausalito at the same time we had. Reba was expansive and experimental, full-figured and commanding. I thought of her as Reba, Mother of the Gods, and of her Sausalito Victorian as Olympus. Her eldest daughter, bookish and serious, attended Berkeley; the younger, Martha, was Mike Ellis's playful blonde girlfriend.

Reba was unconventional: a white woman who championed black causes, a widow whose home served as a refuge for artists, writers, and activists. Now she wanted a psychedelic journey, and she sent out an epic summons. We had introduced many friends to LSD by that time, and though the results were never predictable, they followed a pattern that had become familiar.

We gathered in the parlor of the grand Victorian: Mike and Martha, Drew and Jeff, George and I, and Reba and her cat, Richmond, who arced across the room, frozen in midair poses, crackling with static electricity. Richmond's levitation, the language no one spoke that surprised us in conversation, and eerie fingers of light poking through walls, led us to suspect a craft. So, after Reba ascended the stairs to her tower, satisfied with her introduction to psychedelics, Jeff and I ventured out to see what circled the area.

Jeff wore a monk's robe and sandals, carried a candle on a carved wood base, as we proceeded down Sausalito's residential streets. The subtle activity of plant life quieted us, stealthy and hyper-alert, as we passed houses that made an amusing ruckus with humming and gurgling sounds.

Far in the distance, but growing closer and louder, was the sound of a single car, tires screeching around corners. A squad car braked to a stop near us, an apparition of flashing lights in the night. I emptied the rolled joints from my pocket and stashed them under a bush as a nervous cop who resembled Barney Fife of Mayberry disembarked from his squad car. He looked at us and called for back up while we struggled to be serious.

It may have been Jeff's monk's robe and candle that caused him to ask, in a quavering, hoarse soprano, "Are you on a trip?" Barney's voice cracked on the word "trip."

We nodded, smiling, tried to make him comfortable as we waited for the second squad car, and when it arrived, Jeff gathered his robe with the cowl pushed back, and ducked into the backseat. The beefy cop blew out the candle and laid it on the passenger seat. The caged backseat of the first squad car was for me. We left in tandem for the San Rafael Sheriff station.

Jeff told me later that his officer relayed his life story as he drove. He wanted to be a lawyer fighting for people's rights—he was a good man doing a job, demoralized by being called "pig" by a portion of those he served. Mine tried for calm as we crossed the San Rafael Bridge, the car's engine cutting out, restarting, and cutting out again as the squad car continued its pace. The headlights flickered. The radio emitted static mixed with language and electronic sounds. The policeman's head swiveled from windshield to radio to me, laughing in the backseat.

They booked us for "being drunk in public." Psychedelics were so new that no laws against them were yet on the books. Don Knotts wrapped his hand around his coffee mug to hide the nickname written on it in red block print—"Giggles." Tough to consider these young men adversaries, easier for me to agree with Lenny Bruce that anger was misspent on public servants like these.

I shared a cell with two women, one a victim of domestic abuse, one on a suicide watch. Arguably we were there for our own protection. Interrupted by Jeff's occasional screams—"Terry, get me out of here. You have to get me out of here"—we passed a pleasant night. Jeff's cellmates warned him not to slip on semen in the bathroom, and spooked him with lascivious threats because he was an easy target. In the morning we were free to go. Jeff later went to court, expunged the arrest from his record. I never bothered.

I spent the following week fasting and enjoying altered states. I had connected with Debbie, I thought, the night of Reba's acid trip, and now believed she persisted somewhere. I called to reassure Jack and Casey and they sent the Suicide Control Squad. When I heard the sirens and saw the flashing lights, I hoped it was the Beatles pulling up to Reba's house—they were scheduled to play at Candlestick Park. I waited in Reba's tower.

White-uniformed attendants walked me to the ambulance, strapped me to a stretcher, and raced to Marin General Hospital. A nurse gave me a vial of lavender liquid I explained would break my fast. I drank it, gagged, and proved my system empty of food and drugs. They sedated me for a drive to Napa State Mental Hospital.

At the hospital, two women rummaged through a box of donated clothing, trying on and discarding identities with the clothes. They riffed like musicians, playing off each other, as they moved through time, culminating in a scene between Jackie Kennedy and her lady's maid the morning of JFK's assassination.

"Dallas is a tacky town to die in," one said, placing a pink pill box hat on her head, frowning into a hand mirror.

"Wear the pink suit," the second woman said.

"Won't it clash?"

"No, they're wearing pink and red these days. And even if it clashes, you're a trendsetter."

"But what a tragic trend to set."

Old people sat motionless alongside the young and listless, torsos caved in, faces collapsed—all self-appointed failures. A boy shared drawings of heavens and hells inside his body, and a girl encouraged me to eat. I'd be hooked up to an IV if I didn't, she said, and at lunch she gave me a peeled, hard-boiled egg. I carried it outside to a patch of garden and sat on a cement bench. Absorbed in the egg's slick, shiny surface, I carved symbols with my fingernail.

A boy handed me a multi-petaled flower I didn't recognize.

"Is that a lotus?"

"No," he said, "but it may be the flowering of the human spirit." I planted the flower in the egg, and carried it the rest of the day. In the evening, I broke my fast, and threw up pieces of symbol-scored protein.

A psychiatrist asked about the symbols. "You have symbols of your own to decipher," I said, "and they will provide the insight you seek through us, your patients." He balked, as did my first-grade teacher when I suggested I was the authority of my own life, the source of answers to my own questions.

A week later, George showed up with his best friend Bruce to sign me out. I could leave if someone took responsibility. Only half of George's face worked, and his lop-sided smile made me unsure I wanted to go. Bruce waited in the cramped VW bug they had driven up from Los Angeles, where George had stayed with a girl who shared her pharmaceutical drugs—hence the facial paralysis. I slept all the way home.

⌇

The next day at the Tides bookstore, I fixed upon an oversized book on symbolism, opened it at random, and stared at a familiar image: a flower growing out of an egg. Underneath, the caption read, "The Lotus and the Egg: Hindu Symbol for Health and Eternity." The evening with Reba had run full circle, and I closed the book, complete.

Reading Jung had been the catalyst; my guilty grief over Debbie was the ground that generated a play I wrote and starred in as I struggled toward resolution. Jung spoke of a twentieth-century gap—the split between mind and spirit, science and religion, physical and psychic reality, which resulted in an inherent loss of meaning. He said in *The Undiscovered Self* that it was "universally believed that man was merely what his conscious mind knew of itself, and so he regarded himself as harmless, adding stupidity to the rest of his evils."

The cure, then, was direct revelation; the task, to identify our human failings and discover something more. The value of my experience was not in what it revealed of reality, but what it revealed within me, the connection between the actual and the symbolic, the personal and the collective—the bridge across the twentieth-century gap.

Six

Death dragged us back into the family fold. It was surreal to wear tailored black, stockings, and high heels; they were relics from the past. My afro was severely anchored into a chignon, a familiar look that would elicit known responses from my family-through-marriage—it was George's uncle we were burying—but inside there had been radical change.

I had trouble recognizing George with his new haircut. The wavy, shoulder-length locks that made him look like a blue-eyed, Anglo Jesus (in Giant Rock at the flying saucer convention, more than one person had come up and thanked him for "walking amongst us") were gone.

He sat beside me now inside the glossy limo staring at his tight Italian shoes. His face looked thinner without its frame. I squeezed his hand knowing he was shaken from seeing his father at the service, and again at the graveside as Uncle Arthur's body was lowered into the ground. They hadn't spoken. We were unsure if his father would be at Arthur's house, to which we were now being driven for the reception for the family, their handlers, and their attorneys. We moved as a grim caravan through the streets of Beverly Hills.

We tried to keep up our end, replying to each "How are you doing?" with "Fine, fine, and you?"

The "*What* are you doing?"s were tougher to finesse. Did they really want to know we were doing psychedelic drugs, yoga, and

macrobiotics, or camping out and scanning the skies for flying sau-
cers? Probably not.

Arthur's "boys" sat across from us in the limo looking wooden, set
on paths we'd sidestepped. They helped themselves to drinks from
the burnished maple bar between them. The plush backseat smelled
of leather, scotch, and money, and I wished we could open a window,
but the one-way glass provided stale privacy. We were trapped within
the family vault.

We tried to listen and respond appropriately. Ah, yes, they were
finished with college, needed now to take over their father's business: oil futures, communications, and commodities. *War profits*, I
thought. "Hmm, yes, of course," we nodded amiably, as if we could
relate.

Uncle Arthur and his younger brother, George Jr., had worked their
way up in the Oklahoma oilfields. They were second-generation Scottish
Americans, sons of a Baptist minister and a mother who breastfed her
kids for a dozen years. They left home to go "wildcatting," worked in
shifts around the clock for weeks at a time, and shared a bed in the tent
city. They'd known a young Clark Gable who alternated sleeping shifts
with a Chinaman and swore that "if he ever had more than two nickels
to rub together he'd have clean sheets every night!"

The brothers worked hard, purchased land they thought promising, struck it rich, and moved to California, where they invested
in communications and each built a small empire. The relationship
became more competitive than filial, which is why Arthur at one
point tried to have his younger brother George declared incompetent. But George Jr. emerged from three months at NPI certifiably in
control of his faculties and his holdings.

Hatchets now buried along with Arthur, we'd been summoned,
and George had been dreading seeing his father again. The last time
they'd been together was shortly after our wedding, when George
III made it clear he would not be entering the family business. Now,
San Francisco had had its way with us and we lived as typical "flower
children," gypsies with the quintessential bus, liquidating toys left
over from our early marriage when we needed money. This was not
the prodigal son's return.

Our procession moved past one mansion after another. Each groomed, walled expanse was penetrated by a steep drive that curved up and away behind a screen of trees. We turned into one, ascended, and the limos lined up before the fortress-like facade. Several servants helped us disembark, took our coats in the deep foyer, which was lined on its left with a staircase that existed solely for making entrances—there were elevators farther down the broad hall that provided everyday access to the upper floors. The open end of the gallery-style entry led into a ballroom for lavish entertaining (dance was the widow's "thing"). I glimpsed an empty bandstand.

We were ushered into an adjacent sitting room with half a dozen groupings of plush couches, leather club chairs, and spindly, scrolled antiques, arranged around Persian carpets and gleaming coffee tables. We settled into the nearest couch, and there we sat, a clot of family, awaiting our star. Drinks were served and the collective thirst was great. "Another?" Those assembled nodded, eager for a relief that wouldn't come.

How strange it was to be surrounded again by people who drank. We ordered fruit juice, an anomaly there, and even though I looked calm, George's nervousness was contagious. I knew what dangers lurked when these people had had a few. I remembered how quickly a polite exchange could turn nasty with lubrication and I grew tense, as anxious as George was for this to be over. Luckily, his father was not present.

"And where exactly are you living now, George?" *Oh no*, I thought, cringing.

"Well, we're doing some traveling,"

Good—always an acceptable beginning for restless Californians. Maybe he won't describe our volleying up and down the coast of California, staying with friends and guiding their first LSD trips.

We all paused as the widow descended her stairs. She had changed from her weeds into something glittering and long with deep slits that revealed her famous legs. She strutted down the steps, posed on the landing as if standing over paparazzi.

"Ah, there you all are. How good of you to come and comfort me." Her trained voice projected powerfully. "Have you been well cared for? More drinks, Louis, the funeral is over."

With a little kick she sashayed down the last of the stairs, giving us the full benefit of her profile. I noticed Ann wore the same black, lacquered-back chignon I did—evidently it was the *de rigueur* hairstyle for women of the Cameron clan. I had a flash of us draped in tartan plaid, surrounded by Scotsmen with bony knees and bagpipes. She strode across the hall, head up, shoulders back, glitter rippling, arms opened wide.

Ann was larger than life and feral in her intensity. I shrank further into the deep cushions but knew there was no escaping her. Ann Miller, minor star of the silver screen, hoofer extraordinaire! She shared herself with each guest, all flounces and "Darling!"s, leaning in to deliver air kisses near both cheeks, careful to protect her makeup. Full body contact disarmed the men. I had a cartoon vision of us all as chickens in a coop, feathers ruffled as the salivating wolf stepped in and surveyed the crowd. I was afraid of her; I wondered if she'd sense it and attack.

I tried to talk myself down. After all, what could she do to me? I watched as she worked the crowd, knowing she'd get to me eventually. Paralyzed, I tried to look blasé. When she spotted us, she advanced purposefully, big red lips bared in a voracious smile.

"Ah, the Cameron curse—beautiful women!" Briefly she averted her gaze to include her nephew, "Georgie darling, where *do* you keep yourselves these days? Are these rumors I hear about LSD true?"

Turning to me, she gave George no chance to answer. She grabbed both of my hands, hauled me to my feet. I tottered on my high heels, cowering before the supreme confidence of her celebrity. I tried to speak, but she had other plans for me. She pulled me out of the sitting room. The assembly scrambled to follow. They grabbed their drinks and formed a wobbly parade, trailing their hostess. We were headed down the hall.

Reaching the ballroom, she began to whirl me around in a kind of Fred Astaire/Ginger Rogers swooping waltz, singing out in her formidable voice, "What's the matter with the REAL WORLD, darling?"

"Real world?" I croaked, concentrating hard on keeping up with her.

"I hear you're part of that Haight-Ashbury scene now and I must know: what's a girl like you doing in a place like that? Tell me NOW: what IS the matter with the REAL WORLD?"

Her words were our rhythmic accompaniment as we careened around the room, looping by our audience in laps. Again and again, crazily, she sang out her mantra,

"What's the matter with the REAL world?"

I had a vision of Anna and the King of Siam, Deborah Kerr in a floor-length hoop skirt, propelled around a room by a forceful Yul Brynner. This was my first partner dance since high school—except for swing dancing with Dad, of course. It was too hilarious, and mid-dance I finally got the joke that was on me and relaxed, laughed, surrendered to this force of nature in the same way I'd learned to let go when we invited the ego-death that was our ritual transformation each week. I envisioned Ann and me at the Fillmore, twirling under the black lights that made our teeth and eyeballs glow purple-white. The surrounding walls blurred with our movement, and we could have as easily been in the pulsating light shows there as here in this private ballroom, in this Hollywood set of a home, in this excruciatingly public life.

We wound down and I knew I was crimson with exertion and embarrassment. I had literally been carried outside of my self; I gasped and asked, helplessly giggling now,

"Is THIS the REAL world, Ann?"

Seven

*J*eff and Drew announced we'd been evicted. What the guys had done to alienate delicate Ralph was unclear, and didn't matter. We needed to move, so I prepped George for a different adventure. We'd drive south to the desert, leave the bus with Jeff and Drew, and go to Mexico. The land south of the border had always called me in hip-swinging, shamanistic, sun-spiced rhythms. George agreed; he wanted to try the natural psychedelics that grew there, the mescaline cactus and psilocybin mushrooms rumored to produce a more organic high. A woman named Maria conducted trips, put gringos in hammocks while their minds soared. We'd find her if we made it as far as Oaxaca.

I. Magnin offered me the coveted Sunday ad in the *San Francisco Chronicle*, and my agency was unhappy I was making other plans. One photo shoot remained: a formal portrait in profile. I sat before an antique French mirror under a crystal chandelier in a floor-length, strapless gown with vertical stripes in bold black and white. I'd been chosen in part for my classic hairstyle, but I showed up in a short, angular, Vidal Sassoon cut Drew gave me—easier to care for on the road.

In Palm Springs, Dr. Scott told us he wanted to dive for abalone and said he'd take us as far as Guaymas. We rode into Mexico in the tuck-and-rolled backseat of his gold Cadillac convertible: Miss Nicaragua, his current girlfriend, rode shotgun. Mother's former lover had matinee idol looks, a Tarzan physique, and the white teeth for which mother had a weakness. Miss Nicaragua wore white short shorts and a halter top that drew the gawking attention she craved but pretended annoyed her. George and I, fresh refugees from the San Francisco scene, completed our incongruous quartet.

We parked for the night on a bluff over a cove bordered on one side by a rocky finger extending into the water. George and I carried gear from the trunk of the Caddy and gathered stones in a circle for the promised abalone dinner. Scott emerged from behind a boulder in a makeshift loincloth, slit to the waist, into the waistband of which he tucked a knife and miniature crowbar. He padded, waddling in oversized flippers, into the water, his snorkel dangling from his mask. He waved a gloved hand as he entered the waves, a mesh bag floating behind him. Miss Nicaragua ducked behind the boulder, sarong in hand, to dress for dinner.

George and I made a passable pot of brown rice while we waited for the great white hunter from Oklahoma to return with his bag full of shells. When he did, we pried the flesh loose, sliced it into steaks, pounded it tender, then basted it with olive oil and garlic, pan fried it, and served it with lemon wedges. The twentieth-century slipped away, its sole reminder a bottle of Jack Daniels George and I declined and Dr. Scott and Miss Nicaragua relished.

Birdcalls woke us, and we reached Guaymas the next day. We parked in front of a beachfront hotel. The surf was wild, but I assumed I could handle it; I swam out and dove beneath breaking waves. I caught one, and felt the familiar lift of the swell—but as it crested I somersaulted and tumbled between sick green light and darkness until the ocean spit me out onto the hard-packed sand. Mexico had initiated and humbled me.

We slept on the beach, and in the morning Dr. Scott said we could shower in the maid's quarters. The doctor radiated a heartiness and gift for bullshit that opened many doors and slammed others. The Mexican maids loved him, but their *novios* bristled when they found him, freshly showered and chatting up their girlfriends in their rooms. I rinsed off the salt and sand and got dressed *pronto*.

Dr. Scott exchanged hot words I didn't understand with a growing number of angry men, body language aggressive on both sides. George was loading gear into the car where Miss Nicaragua sat, her seat belt buckled, and watched. The *hombres* were half Dr. Scott's size, but compensated for that with their *machismo*, and they had the doctor surrounded. Hot-headed Scott threw a handful of coins at the feet of the now-livid men and yelled "*Vámonos!*" and George and I scrambled into the back seat. Scott took the wheel, gunned the engine, squeezed Miss Nicaragua's knee and winked, as if he had planned this entertainment. We roared off laughing.

But when I looked behind us through a funnel of red dust, a pickup truck full of *muchachos* with shotguns was gaining on us.

"They're coming!" I screamed, and Scott floored it. Dense jungle foliage whipped by as we sped around curves. Scott yelled back, "Get ready!" and slammed on the brakes. We jumped out and leapt behind leaves twice our size waving *adios* to the caddy which was still moving. It disappeared, and moments later the pickup cranked by in pursuit.

Escapees from expectations, we were on our own in a moist, green, unfamiliar land. We stuck out our thumbs and gambled on rides, ran from putrid smells and mariachis, avoided tap water, and followed our instincts.

⤶

We settled in the sleepy coastal town of San Blas and hitchhiked along the winding road to inland Guadalajara's three-tiered market-place. A stall on the second level sold fresh peyote buttons wrapped in newspaper. No honing device, hand signal or password located the vendor amongst pyramids of fruit, caged birds, stuffed iguanas, automotive parts, candy, fly-specked carcasses, and huaraches. An old man spotted us and beckoned with a crooked finger, tipped off to our interest by the woven bags we wore bandolier-style, our beaded Huichol bracelets and belts, and our wide-open, kaleidoscope eyes.

We hitched home to the jungle beach hotel, scraped strychnine from the buds, and peeled and diced the bitter buttons into fruit salads. Then we lay in pools, ignoring crocodiles, and followed the movements of hand-sized, electric blue butterflies as they flashed through the jungle, also home to snowy white egrets, owls, and herons.

The hotel had a second-floor common room with couches in the center that faced a wall of windows overlooking treetops. George sat on a couch and watched the skies explode into lightning and subside into blackness as he came on to mescaline. He was peaking when the glass panel shattered and a tree branch-turned-missile cleared him by only a couple of feet. From our room I heard the crash, and I found him still sitting, eyes closed, covered with splinters and studded with needle-like glass shards.

I spoke near his ear and hoped my voice was reassuring: "It'll be alright. Keep your eyes closed and stand." I took his hand and guided him to ground level, outside into wind and rain. I peeled wet, gauzy layers from his body as rain and tears of shock and despair rinsed glass from his face and sun-blond hair. His vulnerability broke my heart as I led him back inside, naked and shivering, shaken and weeping. Pinpoints of blood marked his skin like a star map. His trips were always a serious matter, fraught with crises, spiritual or otherwise. George was searching for something missing, attracting older men who served as father figures, seeking an elusive God.

I couldn't, nor did I want to, compete. I enjoyed a freedom I recognized when I was in it—to be myself when world and cosmos spun inside my silent core. I was spark and conflagration, ignited in love for the puny and the noble, the base and the divine. It was enough to be alive, to be breathed, to be breath itself. It seemed immodest and ungrateful to want more.

We spotted others of our tribe—travelers, not tourists—by their native dress and laid-back receptivity, and the knowing look in their eyes. Nodding to each other on the street, on the beach, across the open-air, thatch-roofed *palapas*, we gravitated into the ritual circle, got high, and split apart. Deprivation and intimacy, hidden in the States, was here laid bare: raw pleasure, hunger, and hustle. Gravity felt different when we grounded in fertile red earth. Our cozy vantage point at the top of the food chain was gone: we were part of the ceaseless animation that exhilarated and exhausted, making it up as we went. Farmers who had never seen blue eyes laid pot at our feet in a cardboard box. We pressed pesos into gnarled hands, made deals. The verdant world vibrated; the sun torched each day, and we burned.

I had brought the Tolkien *Lord of the Rings* trilogy: *The Fellowship of the Ring*, *The Two Towers*, and *The Return of the King*. It was a perfect match for mystical Mexico, a complex retelling of the battle between good and evil that resonated with our quest, and I spent days identifying with the characters in the convoluted tomes. I spotted a July 15, 1966 *Time* magazine; the cover photo was of a New York subway station where someone had scrawled, "Frodo lives." I was surprised by the trilogy's popularity, and pleased to be part of a wave of young people who were adopting the tale as symbolic of their own journey.

It was time to go home, time to see what had transpired in our absence, these few months that seemed like years. We spent our last week in Guadalajara in a shabby hotel, the entire block without electricity, poverty romanticized in candlelight. To return we rode the train, straddling the bucking couplings between cars to toke.

Culture shock drove home how much we'd changed. Palm Springs appeared even more frivolous than before; American resort life, a study in frenzied distraction. Jeff and Drew were well-fed hobbits, and everyone moved and talked in triple time. The funky bus, with its carpet and tapestries, crystals and precision engine, was a sumptuous, portable palace.

Mother kept saying, "Fix yourself up. At least take that rag off your head and put on lipstick." Friends were attracted and repelled. We had evidently become a skinny, mutant, telepathic couple: Jesus and Sheena, Queen of the Jungle.

Dr. Scott recommended and administered B-12 shots. When we didn't respond to him in our usual way, when we smiled patient smiles and waited out his jocular monologue, he said, "Hey guys, do you realize you're no longer talking?"

I exchanged a look with George that said it all.

Eight

We parked the bus at the trailhead to Tahquitz Canyon, a lush crevasse with a two-mile loop of sandy hiking trail that wound around crystalline pools, boulders, and old-growth palms and led to Tahquitz Falls, a curtain of water crashing into a pool of snow melt. We pretended we were Indians occupying the canyon in an earlier time, sunbathing on rocks in the middle of the stream, gathering firewood, and organizing our diet of oranges, nuts, and seeds. The weekly acid explorations continued at night when we had the canyon to ourselves. Except for an occasional drunk staggering into camp, no one bothered us.

My engagement ring, a dome of small diamonds, looked like crumpled up aluminum foil when I was high. I placed it in a gift box, left it on top of a prominent boulder, and went for a swim; I smiled and felt lighter as I toweled off and noticed it was gone.

In town, we circulated petitions to "Save the Canyon." I have no idea what we meant to save it from, as in fact the greatest threat to the canyon was us. In 1937 Frank Capra had filmed *Lost Horizon* in Tahquitz. Now in the sixties, word of the original Shangri-La spread, and hippies descended in droves. Helicopters and bullhorns herded them to the canyon's mouth, where they were rounded up in nets. After that Tahquitz Canyon was available by appointment only. But that was later.

We'd all grown up hiking to the falls. One time Debbie stepped on glass, invisible in the water, and Dad carried her to the parking lot, her foot wrapped in a piece of his shirt, and drove her to Desert Hospital for stitches. When I was old enough I walked to the canyon from my house, and in high school we parked at the trailhead to make out.

One evening we lay on our sleeping bags around the fire, coming on to Owsley's red liquid LSD. A cracking noise like lightning electrified the night. I remembered the Kundalini energy, coiled like a serpent at the base of the spine, and resolved to stay still, as it released itself. It was vital to remain centered in the early stage of an eight-hour trip, when phenomena appeared real and could pull me out of the dream before I reached the Clear White Light. Just as I made this resolution, Jeff jumped up and ran over to me, pulled down his pants, thrust his ass in my face, and screamed, "I've been bit by a rattlesnake. Help me, Terry, LOOK. Can you see it? I've been bit by a RATTLER."

I made my voice calm and said, "Yes, Jeff. It's Kundalini. Please lie back down and calm your self. I promise it will be alright."

"Oh? Okay, really?"

"Yes, really," I said, lay back down, and closed my eyes.

Jeff accepted my reassurance, returned to his bag, and stretched out. We settled, focused on our breath and got quiet. Then the film rewound and replayed the lightning crack at the base of the spine. Jeff jumped to his feet for a second time.

"I've been bit by a rattlesnake! I KNOW I have. I want my mother!"

No guidance, no mantra, no placating words could stop him. He showed me his ass again, and I assured him there were no fang marks and nothing to be done but to surrender to the rest of the night. George and Drew looked at Jeff's ass too, but they were looking through layers of colors and moving patterns by then, and Jeff knew it. He was panicky, determined to run home to his mother who lived about six miles away. I couldn't stop him. He returned the next morning.

Snow Creek

The day I met John Barrymore Jr. was typical, sunny, the sky a vivid blue. I filled the bus with friends and drove to visit other friends living outside of Palm Springs in Snow Creek, a narrow canyon at the foot of the San Jacinto Mountains. I wondered if the people from Joshua Tree who kept lions would be there.

The house was ultramodern, experimental, circular. When the wind blew, it cycled through the spiral roof and whistled. Inside, cloistered and cozy, was a round room lined with windows, trimmed in stained glass. Around the perimeter were bedrooms, baths, and small sitting rooms, the central space supported by tall beams, a skylight perched at the apex of the ceiling.

We pulled up in front, where the spiral dipped like a saucer. The front door was open. A half-moon of rock formed a shallow entry, and a low rock wall encircled the house. He stood outside in a loincloth, a wisp of fabric wound around the middle of his tall, emaciated body. My friends tumbled out of the bus, walked around the wraith, and went inside. He extended his hand, and spoke.

"How do you do," he said in a snappy British accent with a nod of his head. He continued in French as we raised and lowered our hands in his bony, bird-claw grip, *"Avec plaisir, Mademoiselle. Vous êtes très charmante. Je suis enchanté."*

The whispered French lulled me, and I listed in his direction. He was one-part movie star and one-part Indian ascetic—tan, glamorous, and gaunt. I felt stoned looking into his eyes. We leaned in toward each other, heads cocked to one side, in another birdlike gesture. He became W.C. Fields, doffed a top hat, bent at the waist: "Pleased ta meet ja."

He had an impressive repertoire, and the mellifluous voice of his forebears. John, his splendid father, Uncle Lionel, and Aunt Ethel Barrymore had set the thespian bar high: they were acting's first family, their voices cultured and nuanced, their deliveries impeccable. This was Drew Barrymore's feckless, drug-addled father before he conceived her. He was in his desert period, subsisting on purslane and shepherd's lettuce, yoga and meditation, alcohol and heroin.

I hadn't closed my mouth since I opened it to introduce myself. I pressed my lips into an amused smile and tried to get it together. I knew I'd never be up to speed in this company, in this conversation with this intriguing man. I said, "Yes, lovely to meet you," retrieved the hand he held, and went inside the saucer to see who else might be there that day—maybe those people with the lions from Joshua Tree.

Nine

Arthur's "boy," Artie Jr., was indeed set on a path we'd side-stepped, but it was not the one prescribed by his father as we'd assumed at his father's funeral. Artie invited us to his rented castle in Agoura in the San Fernando Valley. We circled horse farms, searching for an entry road, certain the pseudo-Gothic castle on the only hilltop in sight must be the place. The blue bus traversed the flatland on a frontage road between two plots, and churned up a steep incline, releasing dust clouds in its wake. The stone castle sat squat and incongruous on a level hilltop that overlooked the countryside. Its central tower was a three-story cylinder flanked by one-story wings. We pulled up to the entrance and parked, got out, and stretched, stiff from the morning drive. A few horses stood in a circle in front of stables at the back of the house, next to an open-air arena ringed by bleachers.

"Let's get to that later, come on, come in," Artie said. He stood in the doorway, arms stretched between the frame. An embroidered Chinese robe fell open to the floor, his chest bare above a pair of blue jeans and cowboy boots. His hair was spiked in dark tufts.

George embraced his cousin. "Hey man, how are you? Nice castle."

"Come in. Come in." Artie and George, arms around each other's shoulders, entered first, and Drew and Jeff and I followed. We moved through the massive carved door and the temperature plummeted, a welcome change from the hot, dry day. The house had rudimentary furniture—area rugs and low tables were scattered about, and, as our eyes adjusted to the cool gloom, we saw people lying on bare mattresses that lined the room's circumference. Artie offered drinks and said, "There's catching up to do."

"Oh, no thanks," I said. "Water?"

Bottles and cigarette butts littered the tabletops. Cocaine crystals striped the surfaces of mirrors.

"Or would you like something stronger?" Artie asked.

The dark room resembled a make-shift clinic in a bizarre encampment—so many bodies populated the space in the half light.

"Later," said George. "Let's get our stuff."

"Sure man," Artie said. "Empty rooms upstairs. Take your pick."

We spiraled up the stone staircase and chose rooms. George and I unfolded our thick Spanish bedspread, then unrolled our sleeping bags and zipped them together. Jeff and Drew parked their gear in a room a few doors away.

Downstairs the sedated crowd listened to deafening music that eliminated any possibility of conversation:

"I can't get no satisfaction."

We passed a joint from our stash and a quarter of those present roused themselves to partake. *"Cause I try and I try and I try and I try,"* the Stones droned on in frustration.

"I can't get no, I can't get no."

We had decamped early from Tahquitz Canyon for the three-hour drive and, having reached the day's destination, we relaxed along with the others. There were no other women present.

"Mexico was good for you two. You look *muy* relaxed."

"Yeah man, it was far out. What's up with you? We thought you were going into the family biz," said George.

"No man. Let the lawyers run the show. And let Ann manage them; she's good at that."

Ann was Artie and his brother's stepmother. Their biological mother had been a model, on the covers of *Life*, *Redbook*, and the *Ladies Home Journal*—that's how she had attracted the attention of their oil tycoon father. I'd heard stories of her kindness, of how wounded she'd felt to be replaced by Ann's brassy, public persona.

"How's your mother?" George asked.

"She's fine," Artie said, his face softening into sadness, as it always did when he spoke of her.

The Rolling Stones droned on and Arthur revved, roused his troops for the promised entertainment: "Come on, you lazy-assed degenerates, there's fucking to see."

The magic word stirred the zombies, who followed their host into the sizzling summer light, past the stables and to the arena where we climbed a few rows and took seats. I didn't understand until a groom led a mare by a short rope into the oval, made her stand sideways before us, and held her steady as a rambunctious stud fell in behind, where the crowd bade him to mount her. "Come on boy, make me proud," Artie said. The drugged audience murmured lewd encouragements. The horses joined together in an orchestrated mating dance, and the burnouts cheered. Since Mexico I'd felt more spectator than participant, a neutral witness. It was over in a few colorful minutes, and vicarious pleasures consummated, we ambled back to Castle Cameron to continue the morning's indulgence.

"Doesn't anyone here eat?" I asked no one in particular as I scouted the house. After finding the filthy kitchen, I decided to unload the Coleman stove, and set it up under an oak tree by the bus. I started the brown rice, ground gomashio from toasted sesame seeds and sea salt in a mortar and pestle, and added a few vegetables and soy sauce to the rice. Jeff and Drew found me and circled like excited puppies.

"These guys are smack freaks. Can you believe it?" Drew said.

"I'm afraid so. I knew it when Arthur offered something stronger," I said, stirring the pot. "Sad."

"I thought he meant cocaine," Jeff said.

"No one moved fast enough for it to be coke," I said, "except Artie playing host. We'll crash early and leave first thing in the morning. Tell George food is ready."

Portuguese Bend Club

At Portuguese Bend, the gateman let us in, and we pulled the bus in front of the garage where Debbie committed suicide. The entry opened onto a landing over a pool, where we paused and looked through the glass walls of the house to the Pacific Ocean. We stepped to the decking, crossed the patio and entered the open door. Casey and Dad, who had been sitting on the L-shaped couch, rose for hugs. It upset them that George looked prettier than I did, his wavy brown hair still streaked gold from the Mexican sun. His blue eyes shone, fringed with their impressive lashes; his cheeks were smooth-shaven, his dimples on display. I'd let it go and wore no makeup. A bandana covered my hair. I was the female bird, my plain brownness subordinate to my showy mate.

"You mean we have to look at you like this?" Casey said.

I tried to tell them it didn't matter, that our focus was on exploring inner worlds now, and that superficial looks were unimportant. Deaf ears, so I suggested something experiential to move us past the cognitive stalemate.

"As long as we're talking about it, do you mind if we smoke a joint?" I said.

Casey rose and stood over me with her hands on her hips, "I don't care what you do," she said, nostrils flared, "but never, I mean *never*, call my house a JOINT!"

Communication did not improve in the ensuing hours, and our visit was short.

Ten

*O*n our way up the coast we stopped in Santa Barbara to visit students at the university, and noticed a flyer. Jimi Hendrix was performing that night. We'd stay for the show.

The queue for the concert was six across, and wrapped around the auditorium. When the double glass doors opened and the crowd pushed forward I raised my hands in the air and, pressed between bodies, my feet off the floor, the throng carried me inside.

The students looked stunned by Jimi's unbridled style, and he made little effort to connect with the crowd. He rubbed his electric guitar up and down his crotch, as absorbed in the movement as if he was masturbating on stage. The voice that accompanied his amplified fingering was pure celebration. He pulled out of his personal reverie long enough to say, "You have no idea how much fun I'm having up here," and then launched into chords that accompanied the emotional power of his voice: *"Have you ever been to E-lec-tric Lady-land?"*

George and I couldn't sit still. This was the sound we'd been waiting for without knowing it. We thought we *did* know how much fun he was having. We danced in an open space in front of the stage. No one else danced that night, and we didn't care. George shook off his father, his family, and the heartbreak of his early years. Loose-limbed and rakish, he included me without touch, and we both included Jimi in the ecstatic energy of the night. The students would catch this freedom that could not be contained.

Up the Big Sur coastline, through Monterey and Carmel, we reached San Francisco the next day and found a rental on Haight Street, right in the thick of things. Haight-Ashbury was a residential area that students found affordable and well located, as did we. It was a free zone south of the Panhandle, with wealthy Pacific Heights to the south and black Fillmore to the east.

More odd-looking posters advertised a free concert, a "HUMAN BE-IN" featuring an eastern sadhu, a third eye within a triangle superimposed upon his face, surrounded by Deco design and the lettering you had to be high to read. The Berkeley Barb, sometimes critical of the Haight-Ashbury scene, enthused instead over the coming event: "The spiritual revolution will be manifest and proven. In unity we shall shower the country with waves of ecstasy and purification. Fear will be washed away; ignorance will be exposed to sunlight; profits and empire will lie dying on deserted beaches; violence will be submerged and transmuted in rhythm and dancing."

The Human Be-In, or Gathering of the Tribes, was held on January 14, 1967 at the Polo Fields at Golden Gate Park. The Diggers, a grassroots organization, passed out sandwiches made from seventy-five donated turkeys. Owsley's White Lightning LSD had been added to the bread dough. In addition, Owsley's agents passed out 300,000 hits of free acid to the crowd while the music played. We staked out space near the stage for Moby Grape, Jefferson Airplane, The Freudian Slips, The Chosen Few, The Grateful Dead, and Big Brother and the Holding Company.

Timothy Leary addressed the crowd and spoke his directive—"Tune in, turn on, drop out"—for the first time. Thirty thousand people converged. Many looked like they had time traveled; others as if they had been summoned from solitary caves to take part. Frontier dudes in frock coats and stovepipe hats danced with girls in granny dresses, miniskirts, and Indian textiles. Painted faces and bodies swirled in paisley patterns. Gypsies spread cards on the grass and read fortunes, auras, and palms. Jugglers juggled; mothers nursed babies; children played, and balloons bobbed on air waves. Jeff, George, Drew and I, wrapped in our velvet capes, were part of the cobbled-together crazy quilt.

A white-faced mime handed me a flower, put a finger to his lips to stem my thanks, and disappeared into the gyrating crowd. We walked through a kaleidoscope of characters, all ages represented, as if we gathered in a cosmic symposium. Hair curled around heads in clouds and coursed long, full of flowers and beads. Mustaches and beards were in profusion and, with their addition, the men took on full character.

A procession of saffron-robed men, heads shaved but for a topknot that jounced, hopped along chanting, "Hare Rama, Hare Rama, Hare Krishna, Hare Hare." Dervishes whirled; gurus stood with clumps of devotees amid belly dancers, students, and runaways.

At five in the afternoon, poet Gary Snyder blew his conch, and Allen Ginsberg led the crowd in chanting Om Sri Maitreya, the mantra of the Buddha of the Future. Then they led a team to clean up trash. As the sun sank, thousands of people walked east toward the Pacific Ocean, crossed the highway to watch the sun set from the Ocean Beach strand, built fires and walked the beach. Allen Ginsberg later called that day "the last idealistic hippie event."

The sixties "decade" lasted two years, three at the most. It started slow and undercover, and by the time it exploded into public consciousness it was already sliding into something else, a corrupted after-image of our original pure intention. The "Love Generation," a term coined by San Francisco's Chief of Police, referred to those with specific timing—inner astronauts who discovered psychedelics early, excited to explore uncharted terrain. The media labeled us unwashed hippies and dope addicts, but we were the nation's children, swallowing powerful chemicals to discover ancient roots. We crawled from the sea as single-celled organisms and witnessed the birth of complexity. For located in memories were not only the events of our limited lives, but the history of life on earth—evolution stamped in the cell's DNA code.

We had the glue, the music, the shared disillusionment over the war. We had pageantry, ecstasy, and mind-altering drugs. Poets inspired us and gave eloquent voice to our concerns and demands, our tribal identity, and our war-battered idealism. Our swelling numbers convinced us we had the momentum to make a difference, a freak flag worth flying.

The Human Be-In was the last uncomplicated day of pure potential on the West Coast. That night the police swept Haight Street and arrested fifty people. A concerned group showed up at the Fillmore, where The Doors and The Dead were playing, to collect bail money from the crowd, and Bill Graham denied them entrance. Soft drug dealers were driven off the scene or arrested, and within weeks heroin and amphetamines flooded the area. The mood of innocent abandon on Haight Street was then one of abandon, and destructive drugs went on the rise. In July, huge numbers of disaffected youth arrived for "The Summer of Love."

Eleven

*W*e staked our camp under the arms of a Monterey pine near the county fairgrounds. Our footsteps flattened mounds of pine needles as we walked off our boundaries, happy to be out of the bus after the morning drive from San Francisco Bay to the Monterey Peninsula. Drew, Jeff, George, and I stretched the corners of our gold bedspread across the soft ground, arranged pillows and sleeping bags, and scoped out water sources and waste disposal options. We seated the Coleman stove upon a waist-high tree stump.

We were making our camp as roadies were working on the stage, setting up the cutting-edge sound and recording equipment and erecting scaffolding to light the three-day festival that would go late into each night. The well-known jazz venue was preparing for rock and roll. We intended to be in the audience as much as possible, and we'd hear the rest from our comfortable camp.

Monterey Pop: thirty-two bands performed between June 16th and 18th. Many musicians met each other there for the first time, most played for free, and several broke onto the international scene in a big way that weekend. Sharing the roster were The Mamas & the Papas, Electric Flag, Janis Joplin (with her band, Big Brother and the Holding Company), Jimi Hendrix, The Grateful Dead, The Who, Simon & Garfunkel, The Byrds, Moby Grape, Laura Nyro, Hugh Masekela, the Quicksilver Messenger Service, and the Jefferson Airplane. Ravi Shankar calmed the crowd with Indian ragas between rock and roll sets, and he played for four hours straight on Sunday, mesmerizing and resplendent.

Jimi Hendrix scorched it, burning himself into the consciousness of those present. Ending with a loose rendition of "Wild Thing," he doused his guitar with lighter fluid, lit it on fire, bashed it to the stage seven times, and flung the remains into the astonished audience. Janis Joplin, too, held nothing back; she delivered her gravel vibrato straight from her oversized heart. "Ball and Chain" brought the stunned house down, and her reputation was made. In short, Monterey Pop was successful beyond anyone's expectations. It would serve as a template for Woodstock two years later, but the world's attention was focused on San Francisco that summer.

Bill Graham booked the Fillmore auditorium, and later the Winterland and Avalon Ballrooms, and became rock and roll's biggest concert promoter. Graham, a German Jew who'd escaped Berlin in 1938, had dropped out of a promising business career to manage the San Francisco Mime Troupe, and backed the Grateful Dead's early efforts. Now he provided San Francisco nights with rock and roll concerts.

The Summer of Love touched many with its infectious spirit. Tourists gawked. Cynics came to ridicule, and some were quickened by the simple ecstasy. Others feared anarchy as a hundred thousand runaways flooded into the Haight-Ashbury free zone. San Francisco had grassroots organizations in place, but the numbers stretched thin the Diggers' capacity to feed them, the Free Clinic's capacity to treat them, and the city's capacity to maintain order. Waves of youths were a formidable presence on the streets and in the parks. People milled, protestors marched, and gurus led groups of chanting followers. Everyday life was street theater. Americans watched the volatility from their living rooms, along with images of flag-draped coffins coming home from Vietnam.

The war galvanized our discontent and gave disparate movements a central focus. Proponents of civil rights and women's lib funneled their efforts into tentative coalitions with war protestors and peace activists in an all-out bid for unilateral change. Individuals banded together. Draft dodgers burned their induction cards, women their bras, and Buddhist monks themselves.

Survivors of hellish trips were hospitalized, and Unit 2-South, the ward I'd occupied at UCLA's NPI, became a repository for drug freakouts. Dr. Ungerleider, the doctor who had encouraged me to request that Dr. Zaslove be replaced by another physician, was now an expert on psychedelics. On television he warned the country of their dangers. But it was the speed, heroin, and alcohol that defeated most—they, along with the body count in Vietnam, tallied up an awesome toll, and took a bite out of the bulging baby boomer generation.

We were a narrow band in a multilayered generation: those with specific timing; those psychedelics catapulted through quantum leaps. But we felt we represented a broad movement that could save us all. Some accepted things as they were, and persisted. As Jerry Garcia of The Grateful Dead, a band with incredible longevity, said, "I thought we were experiencing a lucky vacation from the rest of consensual reality to try stuff out. I didn't have anything invested in the idea that the world was going to change. OUR world certainly changed. Our part of it did what it was supposed to do, and it's continuing to do it, continuing to evolve. It's a process."

Hippies migrated out of corrupted cities, and took their idealism back to the land, eschewing chemical pesticides. Earth's bounty had limits, and stewardship was required; an ecology movement was born.

The mold of mechanical obedience was broken, and we entered a time when no teaching was secret, no mystery taboo. If we failed to change the world, we had at least demonstrated a willingness to change ourselves. The neural branches that didn't serve the brain tree had been clipped, false starts and detours culled out. We had intended to open a way to what we could not yet imagine, believing as R. Buckminster Fuller posited, with his Trim Tab Theory, that small acts are pivotal and can produce big results—that looking for what is wanted and needed in any situation is what makes us powerful. Yet failure—falling from grace after glimpsing pure potential—landed us in awkward positions. Trips ended with re-entry—with tours through the blood-soaked jungle battlefields of Vietnam.

Twelve

*Y*ogi Bhajan came to town. We chanted, and did the Breath of Fire, and practiced natural ways to get high. I made enchiladas for the fire-breathing yogis using a recipe from the Desert House of Health in Palm Springs, where skinny, hunched-over Mike and pudgy, pasty Olga ran the lunch counter.

January 1968...Dr. Benjamin Spock goes on trial for inciting American youth to refuse the military draft.

George connected with an older man—an ex-sergeant in the Marines named Rodney—and brought him home. Rodney was loquacious, instructive, and funny. He held court and passed a pipe packed with exquisite smoke. This was Rodney's "thing." He expounded, laughed at our expense, bent our minds, and in return we granted him Guru Status. Rodney was short and slight, with curly black hair shot with silver. His authority, however, was magnetic.

February 1968...Vietnam burns in the Tet Offensive.

We met Sufi Sam Lewis, an unassuming gardener who made himself available for discourse. While Vietnam burned from end to end in the Tet offensive, we sat on his carpet in a San Francisco apartment. On weekends at his house in Novato, he taught us Sufi dances in his spacious patio. The dances mimed planetary orbits and we entered the ecstasy of dervishes, spinning to lose ourselves in the will of God. There were lots of lovely young women. My guys were entranced, ready to convert. George wanted to give himself to the Order. I wanted to get out of the city.

March 1968...My Lai massacre, reported eighteen months later.

I conceived Yohosame mid-day in our rented house on Haight Street. The room was flooded with colored lights, and pulsating shapes shuttled about the room. Street noise clattered in the background.

April 4, 1968...Martin Luther King is assassinated. Rioting nearly engulfs the Capitol.

In June I stood in my mother's kitchen, and looked out the window at George and his fifteen-year old, pregnant lover. They frolicked in the pool while I made a strawberry and avocado sandwich, added mayonnaise and peanut butter, and thought, *you'd think I was the one who was pregnant.* That's when I knew I was.

June 6, 1968...Robert Kennedy is assassinated after delivering his speech for the California Primary.

George enjoyed his affair while I explored an attraction to a sculptor with a shaved head, laser-blue eyes, and a vocal timbre that drew me. I had been drawn, painted, and photographed, and now I would be carved in stone. When my lover began grappling with hallucinations of time-traveling alter egos, however, I got bored, and eventually exhausted by his madness. George's girlfriend was lovely—a Virgo just like George and she smelled of jasmine, their birth flower. (Even after her skin was scrubbed pink with sand at Tahquitz and she was carried to the stream and rinsed off—she smelled of jasmine still.)

August 1968...In Chicago, police brutally beat demonstrators, journalists, and delegates at the Democratic Convention.

George had a dilemma: two pregnant women, one fifteen-year old flower and one his mature twenty-one-year-old wife. We became the alpha couple again, and she moved to Hawaii with her family to continue high school. She miscarried; a sad event closed her chapter with George.

September 1968...The Beatles record "Helter Skelter," giving the volatile time its anthem.

While we proceeded with our personal lives, the events of 1968 dealt body blows to our idealism. We had watched as John Kennedy was cut down, had grieved and renewed our commitment to his ideals. But when Martin Luther King and then Robert Kennedy were killed, our conviction we could combat and cure the nation's ills was shaken. If we couldn't keep true leadership alive, we were forced to see ourselves as powerless. This crippling of our good intentions made us cynical about a future we'd vowed to make exemplary. We drew inward, sick to death of death, and of this new view of ourselves as party to the mindless violence.

October 1968...There is a massacre of students in Mexico City. Victorious athletes give Black Power salutes at the Mexico City Olympics.

George and I applied for assistance at the welfare office. I sat in the hard plastic chair and cried, while we waited for an interview. George sat next to me and held my hand. A guy approached—burnt out, manic, skinny, and unwashed—and gave George a thumbs-up, and leaned in to whisper, "You guys are a shoo-in. She's doing great." This stranger thought I was acting. I cried harder, knowing welfare was never meant to give middle class kids an extended adolescence. I was deeply ashamed it had come to this, and I understood the irony. I was a dropout, and was now dependent upon the state.

October 1968...The Civil Rights movement in Ireland, mod-eled on the American one, begins. For the first and last time in decades, Catholic and Protestant activists march together. The moment evokes a violent response from authorities.

I moved to Clear Lake and hitchhiked back and forth to San Francisco every two weeks to pick up and cash my welfare check. While in the city, I visited obstetricians. One doctor offered a new (and unintended) solution when he said, angry, "I spent years learning how to deliver a baby safely and you kids are giving birth at home like it's the most natural thing in the world."

His statement was an epiphany for me. I warmed to the idea of a home birth, and realized that if my son was kept under the radar, not issued a birth certificate, he would never be inducted into any future war. And I expected a son. I'd held a gold ring on a thread over my stomach and it had swung back and forth, not in the circular motion that would have meant I carried a girl. I also just knew. I returned to Clear Lake convinced I'd have my baby at home, without professional help.

November 1968...Richard M. Nixon is elected after making a secret and illegal agreement with the South Vietnamese gener-als to continue the war.

The last time I hitchhiked the three-hour drive to San Francisco before Yohosame was born it was late December, and I was eight and a half months pregnant. I was visiting friends when two slick-looking men arrived at the door, and the guy next to me on the couch asked, "Who are they?"

"I'm not sure," I said, "but I think the one on the left is George."

George had transformed himself under yet another new friend's influence. His hair was cut short; a buttoned-down, Ivy League shirt had replaced his East Indian tunic. He wore the Italian leather lace-up shoes he'd bought for Uncle Arthur's funeral; no sign of his usual huaraches. He said he'd been in Palm Springs petitioning the busi-ness office to back his friend in a restaurant, and he wanted me to get a doctor right away—to eschew the home birth. I said no, and hitched back to Clear Lake.

December 1968...Apollo 8 orbits the moon for the first time and Captain James Lovell Jr. describes the earth as "a grand oasis in the big vastness of space."

Thirteen

On January 9th, 1969, the contractions began. The muscular gathering and release felt familiar, exactly like coming on to LSD, when the entire universe expanded and contracted. I breathed into and through the searing intensity. George was in Clear Lake that afternoon, so awed by cloud formations he coaxed me at intervals to look at the sky. I staggered outside, a ship at full sail, looked up, said "Wow," and settled back into the progressing labor.

Twelve hours later, purple with panting and pushing, I gave birth to a boy. The umbilical cord encircled my son's neck twice. I slid the rubbery tether loose, and his color warmed.

"It's a baby!" George said, as if he realized only in that moment what I'd been doing for nine months. This was it. From conception in a light-flooded room to the emergence of this old man in brand-new form, life cracked open and revealed its secrets. I was saturated in sanctity—part of a process that stretched backward and forward through time. I noticed now the suppressed child's gaze winking out of adult faces. The world was full of tenderness, and life was simple.

George called his mother, Ann, to tell her we'd had a boy, her first grandchild.

"What's his name?" she asked.

"Yohosame Freeborn Cameron."

"Call me back when you change it," she said, and hung up the phone.

I rejected the name Granville Ewen Cameron IV, unwilling to chain my son to the baggage of lineage. I meditated, instead, to know his true name, and, in the fifth month of pregnancy I heard "Yohosame" and spelled it phonetically. I added "Freeborn" lest either of us forget.

My partnership with George phased out. Neither of us carried forward a sense of failure. Our parents had all had multiple marriages; the message, absorbed long ago, was that nothing lasted forever. Parallel paths split apart. We promised lifelong friendship, and George said that if he ever received any money, he'd share. He continued with the Sufis, and studied with Sam Lewis. When Pir Valayhit Khan, head of the Sufi Order, visited San Francisco, he appointed George secretary and changed his name to Yusuf. They left soon after for France to build an ashram.

I was glad George had found new direction; I'd been more mother than wife for a long time, and now, with an actual baby to care for, moving on as a family looked harder than single parenting. I needed to drop welfare and be self-supporting more than I needed to spin like a dervish.

I passed my first year of motherhood in a state of happy, albeit sleep-deprived, optimism. I looked at Yohosame and wondered what he'd say, whom he'd love, and what exposures I needed to provide. We left a communal house in Marin, and I drove to Palm Springs with a new friend—red-haired Louise, who had also grown up in the desert and was homesick.

A constellation of cousins, aunts and uncles, and grandparents greeted Yohosame upon our arrival. Mother was happy to have me back in her life. In her swimming pool, we took turns holding Yohosame—an outgoing, energetic water baby—counting to three, exaggerating inhalations, puffing out cheeks, mirroring held breath, and dipping. Eyes open wide under water, we surfaced in smiles. I carried him up the steps of the slide and he sluiced down the chute, plunged, and swam to the steps underwater.

In Portuguese Bend, Yohosame discovered the beach, the tide pools, and his other grandparents, Jack and Casey. Disappointed when I became pregnant, they now embraced us both. Dad said I was an exemplary mother, and Casey set out to seduce the family's new male.

In June, I contracted hepatitis A. I called Dr. Scott, delirious, and he sent an ambulance. My skin glowed orange. I pissed Coca Cola, and my shit was white. Yohosame was returned to me, after my crisis passed, now a weaned, bottle-toting toddler with a natural immunity to hepatitis he'd gained from my breast milk. He lived in a playpen in my room: nurses and orderlies stopped to play with him each day, and three weeks later when I was well enough to leave, the entire staff cheered for us and offered hugs goodbye.

ᔥ

I regained strength and returned to Marin County with Louise. A crib stood in the back of the bus, covered with Peter Max sheets—a cobalt firmament salted with white stars and golden-ringed Saturns. At night we climbed a hill in Fairfax to a platform we'd found built into the cliff side. Mirrors, crystals, and colored spheres dangled from branches overhead: it was a natural crib mobile. People in a nearby house where we showered in the mornings called us "Hollywood Beatniks."

Altamont brutalized what was left of the sixties. Jeff, Drew, and I—and Yohosame who was now almost a year old—showed up to see the Rolling Stones. We staked out space on the grassy hill, but the atmosphere was so negative, the danger so palpable, I feared what would happen as daylight drained to darkness. We packed up and left before the Hell's Angels, hired for security, ended up dealing death.

As man walked on the moon in 1969, Earth's concerns were a snarl. Political assassinations dealt a vicious blow, and the ugly war dragged on. Drugs that did not inspire visions of a better world spiked in popularity. The center could not hold. We lowered our light and proceeded with our lives—no longer hoping to change the world, but to live within it. We needed to individuate, and—in time, per-haps—to connect the luminous dots of our experience.

Louise stayed in San Francisco, and I steered the bus south for Palm Springs one more time. In the rearview mirror, I saw

Yohosame's ecstatic face at eye level. He gripped the bars of his bed rails and bounced, standing for the first time. A week later, he spoke his first word, chanting it in two distinct syllables as he rocked back and forth on sturdy, tree-trunk legs: "ALLAH."

Yohosame Freeborn Cameron
Photo credit: Terry Baldwin

Forty Years Later

~

Though we encounter it as suffering, grief is in fact an
affirmation. The indifferent do not grieve, the uncommit-
ted do not grieve, the loveless do not grieve. We mourn
only the loss of what we have loved and what we have
valued, and in this way mourning darkly refreshes our
knowledge of the causes of our loves and the reasons for
our values. Our sorrow restores us to the splendors of
our connectedness to people and to principles.
It is the yes of a broken heart.

Leon Wieseltier

Four

Flyboy

～

I want to stay as close to the edge as I can without going over. On the edge you can see all kinds of things you can't see from the center.

Kurt Vonnegut, Jr.

Jack and Casey Gray
Photo credit: anonymous

Dad's Memorial Cruise

October 2010

"And I could not ask for more," piped into the lounge on the ship's sound system on day thirteen of dad's memorial cruise. We were in Venice at high tide, water slapping the dock, overflowing into flooded streets, sloshing into shops in waves, and standing two feet deep in San Marcos Square. The famous plaza was lined with people waiting for the lake to subside. We bought thigh-high plastic waders to navigate areas not traversable on the raised planks that zigzagged across the city. Our ship floated in yesterday before sunrise, the air a fine mist, fuzzy auras surrounding the lights that draped the boat, the Duomo, and the Doge's Palace. Looking down on the familiar landmarks from the bow of the ship, I knew where the perfect postcard images came from: the middle of the channel, ten floors high.

"These are the moments I know heaven must exist. These are the moments I know all I need is this. I have all I've waited for, and I could not ask for more."

This morning in the sculpture garden at Peggy Guggenheim's museum, on Yoko Ono's wishing tree, I wrote *"no más esperando— solamente ser"*—"No more wishing—only being."

"And I could not ask for more."

Venice, like Paris, is a city of romance, heightened sensation, and baroque opulence. In Paris, one longed to be in love. In Venice, one *was* in love. Part of the magic was that its beauty was seen in

139

reflection. The bridges, domes, and spires—one saw the static image above, and below its watery, marbled abstraction. Venice floated. Thoroughfares were canals that ranged from narrow alleyways of water to the broad promenade that was the Grand Canal, lined with residential palaces. Arched footbridges with ornamental iron railings connected the canals.

To walk through the narrow curving streets was to experience a visual feast. Designers had stores there, and shops sold the distinctive glass produced on the island of Murano. On another nearby isle, women made lace, and thick stacks of tablecloths were displayed, draped like tapestries against the walls of shops that resembled jewel boxes. Exquisite papers, calligraphy pens, and books bound in colorful leather beckoned. Even the kiosks selling carnival souvenirs were evocative. *Carnevale* was for tourists now, but the sight of the brocade masks bound in feathers, the costumed dolls with lace at their wrists and throats, carried one back to a time when Venice was a wealthy, independent port city known for its sumptuous style.

The cruise, planned to be one more trip with Dad, had become instead his memorial, shared with my sister Carol, my son Yohosame, and a friend from Mexico. Mexico, where Dad spent his last chapter in my home, Mexico which we toured as three generations, first to Copper Canyon in October for Dad's ninetieth birthday, then to Oaxaca for Christmas—we escaped to the beach in January—then to Chiapas in March, weeks before my spinal surgery brought a pause to our wanderings. The surgery and ensuing recuperation were hard on all of us. Dad felt helpless. Watching his daughter fall apart was an uncomfortable reminder of how every body broke down; every form died. Dad played tennis, danced at Arthur Murray's, drank a bottle of white wine every day, and wanted to live forever. For me, though, the first month post-op was more about pain management than pleasure seeking—then, the incremental amnesia set in, and I surprised myself with an intense desire to see the Mediterranean. A synchronistic e-mailed itinerary for October arrived: Monte Carlo, Cannes, Cinque Terra, Florence, Rome, Capri, Taormina, Corfu, Montenegro, Croatia, Slovenia, Venice... OR, Venice, Croatia, Corfu, Messina, Naples,

Rome, Cinque Terra, Florence, Monte Carlo, Provence, Palma de Mallorca, Valencia, Barcelona... HMMM! A late October cruise to celebrate Dad's ninety-first.

"Here's our next trip, dad. Which one would you like to do?"

"Let's do them both," was his characteristic response. "Why not?"

Why not, indeed? We'd been going to Italy and Greece with Carol for a few years, and she was finally enjoying the relationship with Dad she had always wanted. I included Yohosame in appreciation for his care, and because we were a portable family seeing the world. Staterooms reserved and flights booked, we turned our attention to finding a fix for Dad's worsening acid reflux. His appetite wasn't good but he wanted to enjoy the food onboard the ship. Lately, our meals had often ended with Dad ignoring symptoms obvious to everyone else until it was too late. We'd left several restaurants tipping well and apologizing for the mess.

We visited a doctor who suggested an endoscopy to rule out tumors. Dad was familiar with the procedure which he called roto-rootering, and he agreed. Early in the morning, suited up in shower cap, gown, and booties, Dad said, "Wouldn't it be funny if I died from this routine procedure?"

"No, Dad, it wouldn't be funny," I said.

"Oh, I think it would be," he said, as technicians wheeled him out of pre-op.

When he returned to the recovery room, he shook his head and said, "*No bueno.*" His color was cadaverous, and he was uncontrollably shitting in the bed.

"He'll be fine after the anesthesia wears off," they said when I expressed concern.

When I was back at Dad's bedside, he rose up, eyes wide, and leaned his full weight against me. I was only able to support five pounds at this stage in my recovery, and Yohosame was fresh from rotator cuff repair, so although we did our best to support him, we couldn't prevent Dad's slide to the floor. That got everyone's attention.

Dad answered their questions by saying he wanted to go to sleep. Even the x-rating-worthy nurse, who looked like she had just got off work at a strip club, failed to arouse more than a glance into her impressive cleavage as she leaned in to check his vitals. His temperature and blood pressure spiked as his kidney function sputtered.

They sent us home for the night, and I returned to ICU the next morning to find Dad in a party mood.

"Look, honey, they're planning my meals," he said, pointing to a row of IV bottles. Cheerful, he gave the finger to the other patients in the room who looked embalmed and ready for burial. The sensor clipped to his middle digit provided dramatic emphasis.

They moved him into a private room; Dad was too irreverent and irrepressible for the ICU. I was relieved, but it was temporary. He did not improve, and they told me I must let him go. I called Carol, and she said she would come right away. They started Dad on morphine, amazed at his determination to survive.

One night before he stopped speaking, I climbed in bed with him and he asked, "What will you do with me now? Just put me someplace out of the way."

"I'm not going to put you anywhere, Dad. You've always been the center of life. I am not going to put you someplace out of the way," I said.

"Then I'll be with you?" he asked.

"You *are* with me, Dad. You can come home or you can leave now. Just relax and concentrate on your breathing," I said, prepared to draw upon my experience with yoga and guiding people through LSD trips in the sixties.

He said, "Okay," closed his eyes, and was quiet for a time.

Was I doing this? Guiding my father to a final surrender? To that which fueled his flight, his risk-taking, his dismissive approach to the body for any use but pleasure? He shrugged off the cuts and bruises on his builder's, sportsman's, sculptor's hands, folded across his chest, rising and settling with the breath upon which I'd suggested he concentrate.

His blue eyes flew open and looked at me where I now sat, perched on the edge of his bed, "Well, when are we going?" he asked.

"You're in a hospital, dad, and we're not going anywhere tonight," I said. I decided to suggest sleep's temporary surrender. "Just rest and I'll be here on the couch."

"Oh, you'll be there on the couch," he said, resigned.

The next day he spoke of colors swirling around him: reds, blues, and yellows, absorbed in a personal vision, both cosmic and immediate. He spoke of birds flying. When I asked if he was flying with them, he replied, rapturous, "Oh, yes." He was always a creature of the air himself—"I'm flying with them," he said.

Dad developed a passion for flight early, for the sensation of speed which shaped his life. As a teenager he raced sports cars and quarter midgets. Success brought planes of his own, and a travel-filled life. A world map covered an entire wall in his den, and it was studded with different-colored pins representing the many places he and Casey had flown to, both commercially and in their own plane.

Casey had an attraction to flyboys and Dad was the third she'd married, but still she was nervous in their four-seated Mooney. To soothe her anxiety, Dad gave her a gold medallion, an airplane on its front and "good sport" engraved on the back, which she wore on a charm bracelet. Dad loved soaring too—loved the sensation of free-falling through the sky without an engine—then steering into thermals to catch a lift, in the same way he turned his body in and out of waves to ride the surf. One night I remember the seas shone phosphorescent with plankton—the red tide gave everything a blue glow as he water-skied behind our boat, and declared his own magnificence, cutting a swath through the luminous waves. He and the night were starlit and exultant, awash in light.

"These are the moments I thank God that I'm alive. These are the moments I'll remember all my life. I've got all I've waited for and I could not ask for more."

The next day Dad was mute, working on something in the air before him with his hands. It looked like he was sewing, and he was annoyed by the nurse's interruptions. There were no more words until the next morning when Carol arrived and he said, "Hi, baby." He knew she was there.

It was a last great gift. The Fourth of July came and went with Carol sleeping on the couch by his bed. Finally, we brought him home, where he died two days later with Carol, Yohosame, and me at his bedside.

Carol and Yohosame assumed we'd cancel the cruise, but I knew Dad, who never missed a chance to have a good time, would have considered that a sacrilege. So we'd remember him in the places we had visited with him these past few years: a bittersweet tribute, a fitting memorial.

A few months had passed since we had brought him home to die—blurred and busy months spent forgetting he was gone, falling into the habitual groove of our lives together and then remembering. The numbness of shock gave way to painful clarity again and again. I realized life was the same as it had always been for family who saw him once a year. He was still the colorful patriarch cherished from afar, even farther now. But for me, accustomed to his daily presence—his comings and goings matched to my own in the rhythm of our days—his absence felt like amputation, and there was much phantom pain.

⤸

We departed the floating city in the afternoon. The next morning we approached, through a scattering of forested islands, today's destination, Dubrovnik. The air and sea were clear, the early sun highlighting the furred shapes of land. We slowed our pace, glided past island villages, and arrived at the medieval wall that surrounded the old city. Claimed by various empires at various times, long accustomed to invasion and occupation, Dubrovnik was proud in the morning sun, and today within the ancient walls we found a mosque, the third oldest pharmacy in Europe, and a custom hat shop.

On the other side of the island, we wandered the curve of the yacht harbor. It was Sunday, a day of leisure. We were charmed by Dubrovnik as our memory of the jewel Venice receded, creating a fine scrim beneath these new impressions. Experiences blended at this pace; a new port and often a new country greeted our floating global community each day.

And I was still awash like Venice, in sensory memories of Dad and me at various ages: as a child when he defined my world; as a teenager, when I took his arm and we walked the aisle of the Wayfarer's

Chapel so he could give me away; as an adult when he marveled at my capacity for motherhood, and was a little jealous of his grandson. We socialized and traveled together as adults and shared grief in November of 2003, when both my first husband and Casey died on the same day. All of our closeness, all of our mutual regard, all of the years—and yet when he came to live with me we became acquainted anew, and made adjustments that startled and challenged us both.

And now he was gone, his story final and finished, and though *"I could not ask for more,"* within myself continued this review, and I was far from simply being.

One

Dear Friends and Relatives,
After sustaining a large financial loss and having been offered
by my daughter Terry Baldwin to live with her in Mexico, I will
drive my Subaru Outback with a utility trailer there around
early March. Being in reasonable shape for an 89-year-old, I am
looking forward to this new adventure.
Jack Gray 2009

Dad drove from Carmel to San Miguel de Allende in three days. I
sent my friend Alan to Laredo to guide him in, assuming they would
overnight en route and arrive in the morning. But Dad refused to
stop, and the two-car caravan pulled up after dark.

Our plan had been that he would park in a secure lot until we
unpacked and unhooked the car and trailer he pulled, and then he
would park in my garage. Now, exhausted, he said it was fine to leave
the whole affair in front of my house, but I had to insist that we follow
through with the plan as cars had been vandalized on my street. The
parking lot was close by, and Alan would lead the way and bring him
back.

When they returned, Alan took me aside to say dad had annoyed
the owner by directing the placement of car and trailer with an
authoritative attitude. Then he reminded Dad that Mexicans have

their own way and wouldn't appreciate being told what to do. "I'm mentioning this," said Alan, "because I suspect it won't be the last time it will be a problem. Good luck."

⤸

I've never been good with money, but I saw the real estate bubble and financial meltdown coming like a train, blasting its shrill whistle in warning. I sold real estate in the States and acquired a home in Mexico that would accommodate an eighteen-wheeler's worth of stuff—and family members should the need arise—and left my car behind. I walked everywhere my first three years in San Miguel de Allende, no small adjustment for a southern Californian.

Appalled to learn that Carol wanted to buy an overpriced house she planned to live in for a while before turning it for a profit, I cautioned her that property values would soon fall. "Oh Terry, real estate always appreciates," she said, rolling her eyes. Dad, meanwhile, invested in second mortgages on construction loans—he wasn't listening either. I suggested he redeem his principal, and I sent investment information he put in a file but never read. My warnings of a recession ignored, I contented myself with telling him there was room for him in Mexico.

⤸

Dad and I hugged amid the evening street scene. Earlier I had told everyone on my block, *"Mi papá viene habitar conmigo"*—my father is coming to live with me. Expatriates who could afford to settled into all-gringo gated communities, but I loved being part of a neighborhood, and tried to be a harmonious presence. Having family living with me would make me seem less an oddity to my neighbors. Pueblito, my housekeeper, and her family of nine lived across the street in a house the size of my living room.

Dad looked pale in the light over the gate, so we waved to the neighbors and I brought him inside, sat him at the head of my table, and served him a chilled glass of white wine and a light meal of borscht and bread. He dug in, said Casey never liked beets but he loved them, and declared the meal perfect. That's what I liked to hear. I felt deep, cellular satisfaction at his words.

Dad remembered the guestroom from visits and, as I walked him down the hall, he told me—half asleep and fading fast—that tomorrow we had to move the bed to the other side of the room. Then we'd unhook and unpack the car. The trailer could wait a day. I smiled, recognizing a trait I had inherited. No one had ever accused me of procrastination, and when involved in a project, I, like my dad, was compulsive and absorbed.

I'd had the closet rebuilt to accommodate his shoes: two-toned spectators he wore for everything from dancing to hiking, and tennis shoes he wore to the courts three mornings a week. We retrieved his car and unpacked his clothes and the smaller items it held. One was an unexpected shock: a loaded gun stashed under the driver's seat. *Wait until I tell Alan.*

I had asked Dad to bring a pre-Colombian figurine given to him during a fundraising tour of haciendas in Mexico City's suburbs that he and Casey had gone on after the earthquake, when they were flush. We put it in his rearranged room. I was eager to unload the trailer and see what else he'd brought.

An auction house had picked up what remained, from furnishings to the sculptures he'd produced for ten years, and he hoped to receive full value. I doubted it. But I'd stressed that he should bring all the artwork and, of course, his clothes. If his paintings hung on the walls of his room, I reasoned, it would feel like home.

⤴

We'd gone through Dad's wardrobe after Casey died, when he moved to a smaller condo within the same genteel gated community in Carmel. At eighty-three, he still wanted another season on the slopes. I suggested he try one ski outfit on for size, and we cleared two yards of his closet. "Oh well, if we ski again we have to buy new equipment anyway," I said. "We'll buy clothes, too."

The fresh powder-covered runs, the handsome lodges, people mistaking me for his girlfriend—Dad loved it all. When I moved to Lake

Tahoe in 1978, Jack and Casey had too, their first move after twenty-five years in Portuguese Bend, but not their last. Dad and I skied two seasons before they began their search for Casey's Southern roots.

Casey was the black-haired, black-eyed product of a Georgia belle and a Spaniard who lived as a professional houseguest in Europe. Her given name was Isabel Maria De Cuyas, but Casey Gray suited her. A modern woman, an atypical fifties housewife, she had made a smooth transition into the sixties. Head back, Pucci print palazzo pants flowing to the floor, she walked through the world with pride of ownership. Casey's style was exaggeration within the bounds of very good taste. She had inherited her mother's southern wiles and her father's Latin fire, and became fun, or a little scary, or both, after martinis. Casey said what everyone thought, but never dared say.

Beneath her bold and gregarious exterior, Casey suffered intense insecurities, loved white daisies, possessed true generosity, and had awful nightmares. As a child, I found her emotional nature a shock—my mother was a drier, more ladylike type. But Dad loved her sensitivity, and Casey's kids called him Daddy, and I needed to adapt. So we struck our agreement early: she became the communication link between Dad and me, and the role made her essential, less dangerous. If Casey had wanted to manipulate my father into leaving his past behind, she could have. But she was inclusive, a force of nature, a wicked, acidic wit. I emulated her style.

Dad was vain, but in a nice way. He balded early and wore a toupée because, without hair, he didn't feel fully dressed in a tux. He wore several rugs with increasing coverage over the years as his own hair receded to a fringe. Now, at eighty-nine, he had a puffy island of grizzled fluff, surrounded by skin no amount of combing over covered. What was left of his own hair frizzed around the edges. I talked to him about buying a new hairpiece, but he didn't see himself from the back, so he didn't see the need. People gushed over his appearance, surprised to learn his age, and Dad was confident he looked good.

I liked that he always had on a pressed shirt—with a real collar and usually buttoned at the cuff—that he tucked into slacks belted at the waist. I appreciated that I'd never seen him in a tank top, baseball cap, or blue jeans. Dad's leisurewear was the one-piece belted coveralls that airplane mechanics wear in the hanger. He slept nude year-round and had always begun his days in Portuguese Bend with a dip in the swimming pool—a cure for hangovers he never admitted to having. Every morning we heard him coming down the hall and saw him streak by and fling himself into the water. But that was long ago.

Two

We unpacked the trailer, unloaded cases of "Two Buck Chuck"—the awful wine Trader Joe's bought in bulk and sold for $1.99 a bottle—rusted tools, and *no* artwork. The auction house sent checks and itemized sales. I begged Dad not to read the list out loud, but it was too fun for him to watch my reaction.

"One French armoire $150, lead crystal decanters $10 each, an embossed Alvar—"

"Stop, I can't stand it," I said, fingers in my ears.

He chuckled and said, "Alabaster statue $49, art deco humidor—"

I was glad Casey wasn't alive to see this, and although I thought I was being petty, I was upset. Dad mentioned that three of his sculptures were in a show at the club, and if they didn't sell, they would go to auction also. Hundreds of dollars later, the sculptures arrived in Mexico, and I was glad we'd at least salvaged his best work.

⌒

When Dad and Casey moved to Carmel in 1994, they sent out announcements that read *Final Resting Place*, penned on a tombstone drawn by Dad, irreverent as always. Casey loved Carmel, had honeymooned there twice, and she and Dad had good years there until she began to pall.

In 1999 they visited me in Santa Fe and we celebrated Dad's eightieth birthday with a party. Casey and I spent the day of the party arranging flowers and chatting up the caterers, and around noon Dad buzzed the house in his rented airplane. They knew few of my friends, but Casey insisted we must have a party, so I had rounded up a compatible group. My list began with an Austrian friend older than Dad, a concert pianist who had fled to Argentina during the war—she had a daughter my age who had married a southern gentleman—and a couple of others. But three became twenty guests, and over cocktails and hors d'oeuvres, they all met Dad and Casey.

Guests gravitated into preferred groups for a buffet-style dinner, and were herded into another part of the house for dessert. On a spotlit, black lacquered table sat a white sheet cake piled with silver and gold toys: miniature airplanes, cars, surfboards, chess pieces, tennis racquets, golf clubs, slide rules, hammers, ladders, wine glasses, pipes, and tiny houses. Dad made it easy with his many interests. Over coffee, I presented him with a book I'd made, filled with photos, collaged images, and hand-lettered prose—a celebration of his life.

The chemistry between strangers makes magic sometimes, and did that night. But after they returned to Carmel, Casey had stomach pains, and an x-ray showed a toothpick moving through her colon. Then, while recovering from her surgery, in the hospital, she fell and broke her arm. None of the canapés at Dad's party had been served with toothpicks, thank god, but Casey had certainly enjoyed herself that week. One night at the Compound she had fallen down, drunk, and the maitre d' and I had perp-walked her to the car while Dad paid the check. Really, well, it could've happened anywhere.

Casey always said Dad was a brand-new soul. "He likes Tom and Jerry cartoons, for Christ's sake. Look at him. He's a kid, believe me, it's his first time here."

Dad may have been a new soul but Casey had been around the block—or the wheel—a few times. She matched Dad in enthusiasm, but sometimes she was acting. At twenty-one, she gave birth to a daughter with Down's syndrome. Her second daughter committed suicide. Then the evening news described her son as a "troubled

Vietnam vet." After all this happened, Casey got sad, and dark—finished. She had regrets—wished she had developed something just for herself.

Dad was a quick study who did everything well. At twelve, he learned to drive when an explosion at his father's mine forced him to transport the wounded to a hospital miles away. Hired by North American Aviation to design aircraft in his teens, he mastered the slide rule on his lunch hour. He excelled at sports and games, and never threw one to boost a child's self-confidence. Without education, training or a degree, he declared himself an architect and built a successful career doing what he loved—and making it seem easy. In the shadow of our role model's accomplishments, the rest of us family members were unsure how to begin. Dad's advice, always: "Just *do* it."

I formed a belief about nature trumping nurture, about people born prodigies or losers. In her way, Casey confirmed the prodigy/loser theory, taking a number of single classes and dropping out discouraged. Her judgment upon herself was that she just didn't have what it took. I learned that talents can be developed by watching my son progress from playing an air guitar on a tennis racquet to becoming an accomplished musician. But Casey never learned skills beyond gourmet cooking, home décor, and fashion—things that made her a dedicated and decorative partner. As she began to age and travel became more difficult, she lost interest in life.

For fifty years, Dad had opened his eyes at sunrise and dressed in the dark—quiet, puppy-like, eager for the day—excited by a design he worked on, the golf or tennis game he'd play, or his latest alabaster statue. He opened the bedroom door, willed it to be silent, but was unable to prevent the narrow shaft of light from hitting the bed—Casey, awake now, in the unbearably bright and indecently early day.

By the time Casey took her last trip to Mexico—and she loved Mexico—she had shrunk. The brimmed hat, turban, and bias-cut clothing, her trademark look at the beach, wore her. Always a petite woman, she was now tiny and brittle, and I had to lean down when we hugged, as she once had for me. We reminisced about the ways we'd enjoyed Puerto Vallarta over the years, where she and Dad once owned a fabulous house in Conchas Chinas, then a time-share on the beach, then a friend's borrowed condo.

Dad remained busy, and carried a pager so Casey could reach him. She grew passive, stopped spraying silver into her raven hair, and tried to check out. Calls to 911 foiled suicide attempts in the final three years: each time Dad and the paramedics dragged her back. The last time Dad didn't make the call, but she survived anyway. I visited soon after, and Casey, complaining, said, "God damn it, I couldn't keep the pills down."

"You need a Dramamine patch or Darvon to settle your stomach before the barbiturates," I said.

Dad and I walked the dog to the top of the hill. He looked at his shoes as he put one foot in front of the other. "I just don't see how Casey made it," he said, "I decided to let her go, and I know she took a lethal dose."

"She threw them up," I said.

"Oh, I didn't know. It makes sense now."

Casey was bored with Dad. That was so unthinkable—to Dad and everyone else, except my mother—that Casey lost credibility with all of us. The last time I saw her she tried to warn me. "Everyone loves me, and tolerates your father—who is quite the bore, let me tell you," she said.

I laughed. "Isn't that the boring man you've been with for fifty years, who happens to be your sole caretaker now?"

She insisted, "He's got you all fooled."

"Remember me?" I said, "Daddy's girl? You're barking up the wrong tree."

Casey gave up in disgust.

⌒

Dad, in good health at eighty-nine, underwent injections in his eyes for macular degeneration, which slowed his departure a couple of months. The phone rang from creditors he thought he could abandon when he left the country. Why hadn't he dealt with his affairs? Why hadn't he told them he was leaving, and made arrangements to pay his condo fees? Now he thought I should pick up his slack; he didn't want to bother with trifles like an abandoned mortgage. It took us six months to resolve the lingering issues.

Three

$\mathcal{M}$y father had a new habit of speaking over me in a louder voice that dared me to complete my thoughts. Was it a new habit or had it always been this way? It *was* easier to defer to him—to talk about golf, sailing, flying, design, chess, and sculpting—than it would have been to demand equal time. I assumed my life interested him in an abstract way, and that, if I needed him to, he would listen. And, in truth, I preferred his style of benign neglect to that of the authoritarian fathers whom friends complained of, even into adulthood.

I did know I charmed and dazzled my father. Our dance was a sublimated sexual, cool jazz riff, free of traditional roles. I, a DNA reflection that pleased him; he, the standard against which I measured every man, before finding them lacking. We had never quarreled.

We hadn't lived together in more than fifty years, however, and now we faced difficult adjustments. He clung to what he knew: how to be in charge. I tried to be sensitive, but I too was accustomed to autonomy. I'd lived alone since I was widowed in 1989. After a triple bypass left dad with a pig's valve in his chest, his chauvinism had become fodder for humor, and I'd never felt diminished by his worldview. Now, though, I felt I held second-class citizen status, and I resented his sense of male entitlement. He thought I'd be a pushover; I began to disabuse him of the notion.

Dad's insistence upon driving became *the* source of anxiety for me, and I voiced it, though I was aware that driving was a huge part of his identity. He had raced cars, sailed boats, and flown planes—even made cross country trips to Oshkosh for the Wisconsin Air Show in recent years. So I aimed for a neutral tone as we wheeled around a four-way intersection, swerving across lanes. When we cleared a truck by inches, forcing it to fall behind, I screamed, "Dad, look out!"

"What's the matter?" he said, head tilted back, peering through glasses that rode low on the bridge of his nose.

"Why did you cut off that truck?" I said, my hands tensed into fists.

"Because I thought I could," he said, and grinned.

"And why was that important?" I said, my voice raised an octave.

"It wasn't important," he said. "It was fun."

I took my eyes off the road to check out his mischievous grin and returned to back seat driving. "Dad, look out," I said again, as we missed a young girl who walked alongside the highway by a narrow margin.

"Well, if she'd move her fat ass out of the way, it would make it easier to get by," he said.

"Dad, she's no more than twelve years old. Aren't we supposed to watch out for the children?" I said, hoping it was rhetorical, and added, "Maybe it's time for you to give up the wheel."

"None of my wives or girlfriends ever criticized my driving. What is *your* problem?" he asked.

"Dad, you've never been eighty-nine before, so this happy task has befallen me," I said, horrified to be speaking in this way. And then I noticed what had escaped my attention until now. "Dad, are you wearing your reading glasses?"

⌐

If I hadn't always been trying so hard for Dad's love and approval, I might have admitted feeling unsafe long before this point. Dad and I skimmed the sea on a catamaran—a canvas bed stretched across two runners with a sail. We caught an edge, flipped, and surfaced on either side of the capsized cat, laughing to see we still had on our sunglasses and soggy hats. We treaded water until surfers showed up and one paddled me to shore.

When I soared the first time without an engine and threw up into a white bag, I was trying to be Dad's good-time girl, and was ashamed of my body's reaction. Later, we spun toward the looming earth, the glider vertical. I was in front. I saw the ground workers jump into a truck and rush to where they expected us to crash. Dad was frantic behind me, trying to correct, trying to resume control—and then he did, and we pulled out just in time.

When Portuguese Bend Club shifted and slid, Dad treated it as an amusement—when in fact it was splitting our lives open and causing what we knew to disappear. During the Cold War with Russia, while two superpowers pushed each other toward nuclear disaster, Dad bought a bomb shelter, and we spent novel weekends in the concrete bunker: a different party venue, stocked with booze and snacks.

I'd never be a party girl, but I did identify with Dad's love of speed. When I slipped off his lap at that race as a little girl—just as the cars went into a turn—the crowd's noise and the engine's scream blended with gasoline smells and burnt rubber to form an imprint upon me, as I lay there without breath in the sawdust. I came to love motorcycle rallies and car races. What scared me also attracted me—fear and excitement felt the same. Most of my life had passed before I legitimized cautioning impulses and realized that the voice of fear is not always best ignored or overcome. I'd tuned out that voice until I no longer heard it, and I needed silence in which to find it again.

At the end of an El Nino winter, when rivers swelled, I organized a rafting trip in Utah. Dad flew to Albuquerque, where I picked him up for the drive to Arches National Park. We boarded rafts, identical river hats tied under our chins. The Rio Grande float through swollen Cataract Canyon in class V rapids was a thrill ride. We rocketed along, looking up as twenty-five to thirty-foot waves turned river into raging sea. I held on to two ropes, and pried my bloodless hands open when the water calmed. We shared a tent, hiked, and swam, and enjoyed white-liveried service at mealtimes. At Lake Powell, we traded rafts for small planes and retraced our route in turbulent air.

A bumpy, white-knuckled flight for me, but Dad's fear—he confessed later, at home—had been getting DTs in the wilderness.

∽

At sixty, I dreaded telling Dad I'd no longer ride with him. I'd have to kill off the artificial me—the people pleaser, the livelier self that kept up and asked few questions. My intolerance for alcohol made me different from everyone in my family except my mother. As the sun went down, I wound down, just as everyone else was getting started. When they were drunk and happiest, I withdrew into a poisoned boredom. They interrupted each other in surges of animated chatter, exploding in bouts of hilarity, while I suppressed yawns and pretended, fooling no one. Casey said, late one night as we walked home in Puerto Vallarta, "Jack, you'd better get your daughter to the hospital. It's after midnight."

With Dad in his eighty-ninth year, I kept up at last, and we found time for him to answer all my questions.

Four

One morning the neighbor across the street told my housekeeper, Pueblito, that Dad backed his car into her house each time he pulled out of the garage. "Please ask the señora to make him stop," she said.

I hoped for the right moment to relay this to dad.

"Have you seen her house?" he said, amused. "Does it matter?" He *was* more accustomed to gated golf communities than transitional neighborhoods.

"Dad, I know the house doesn't look like much, but she lives on the other side of the wall you hit."

When Dad came home, he zipped into the garage, overshot the awning, and hit the ceramic pots that kept him from driving into the living room every time. When the cracked pots crumbled, I replaced them. Mechanics pounded his dented fenders smooth, and we painted the neighbors' house to match ours. "*Ni modo,*" my favorite Mexican phrase for "*Oh well,*" became a mantra. "Oh Hell" was Dad's response to most everything.

Dad was now a ghost image of his former, vibrant self. He'd had dizzy spells for years that he and Vivien, his girlfriend in Carmel, thought were strokes. Complaints elicited shrugs from his medical team in California.

"Oh boy," he said, each time the world began to spin, "Here we go."

↜

Mexico had drawn me back in a variety of ways since I'd hitchhiked the coast with George in the sixties. With a pre-Columbian art dealer, I rode its length, visiting private collectors. I studied Mayan culture and, with fellow students, climbed pyramids in the Yucatán before they were roped off, before turnstiles, and before vendors crowded the parks. One year Kirk Kerkorian, a friend who owned MGM studios, flew me and another George to Puerto Vallarta, and we sailed his yacht to Las Hades. And, of course, many times I enjoyed Mexico with Casey and Jack. I had somehow missed San Miguel de Allende, and now it was home.

↜

I wondered how the high altitude was affecting Dad, who panted, his brilliant blue eyes opened wide in confusion. He simply refused to drink water, which could have helped. Everything I said I repeated three times, and he guessed at the prompts in his new environment. Dad had taken Spanish classes for years in California, and never spoke a word in Mexico. I hovered, and the role reversal embarrassed us both.

We broke out of the comfortable roles we'd practiced for a lifetime: Dad floating on past momentum, and I—his no-longer-liberated handmaiden—trying to balance his needs with my own. Each morning I talked myself into an improved attitude I couldn't sustain, and I developed a new appreciation for my mother and Casey. Once I had seen them as strident and controlling—and now I understood. When Dad came home from the tennis court covered with tissues dotted red, he was an inspiration to his younger partners, and an annoyance to me.

I needed to return to Al-Anon, but I didn't. I soldiered on, worried, and judged. Whether it was age or alcoholism, the lines had blurred for me, and fifteen years' attendance in a program for those who love alcoholics had not replaced disdain with compassion. I lived in an awkward ambivalence, admiring Dad's good nature, humor, and aesthetics, while at the same time wondering how anyone could be so selfish and cavalier.

Dad went limp and leaned while I struggled with a loss of independence that reminded me of my single parenthood after the sixties. Immersion in the counterculture scene had been an experiment in personal freedom, but that had transformed into devotion to another's care overnight. During that time, I learned to honor details, to be present in small acts, rhythms, and routine. Now I tried to come from the sweet spot of my love and admiration for my father.

He brought a TV that had been in his kitchen, hooked it up, and invited me into his room to check out the reception. When he turned it on I saw a confusing image for a couple of seconds—it was as if someone plunged an arm into someone else's body up to the elbow. I remembered Tony from the Philippines, who claimed to be a psychic surgeon in the seventies. Patients flocked to him, and session tapes looked convincing.

"Oops," Dad said, ejecting his favorite porn tape. "That's not what we want."

The screen turned to noisy snow, then to something innocuous on cable. I agreed the picture was sharp and made my exit, unsure what to think of a man pushing ninety who ingested Viagra to masturbate to porn.

We made a routine doctor's appointment for him, and stopped for lunch at Harry's Bar. Two-for-one—Dad drank a couple of margaritas, and ordered two more. When it was time for us to leave, the waiter poured the unfinished margarita in a to-go cup for Dad to sip as he staggered the block to his appointment. The doctor's visit went well, and no one minded Dad being drunk except me. I offered to drive home, reminding him I had his genes and loved to drive too, but no. Dad slowed at intersections where cross traffic might hit his side of the car. He sailed past the rest. On the passenger side, the side-view mirror hung by a cord, and it banged against the door as we bumped over cobblestones. We'd get it fixed again.

Five

*W*hen Carol visited for my birthday in June, Dad and I were glad to expand our dynamic to include her. He was happy to have a drinking partner, and I hoped to receive a little support and laugh about Dad's new foibles. We spent *El Dia de los Locos* watching the parade and walking around the central plaza. The *Parroquia*, the town's French-inspired cathedral, shimmered pink in the heat. Policemen as handsome as Zorro patrolled on horseback in periwinkle-blue uniforms, black sombreros, and boots with silver spurs. Giant *papier-maché* puppets, and children dressed as flowers and insects, moved through the maze of cobblestone streets.

⤶

Carol and her daughter, Indra, had visited Mexico the year I moved there. Carol announced she would never have the relationship with either of our parents that she needed. I told her that, if it were true, the fault was in part hers, as they were still alive and there was time to do something about it. She listened with less resistance than usual.

For Christmas I gave Dad a book on Italian architects, and after the first of the year he called me in Mexico and said, "You have to go to Italy. Let's do it."

"Sounds great. Everyone has always told me that," I said.

"I'll make the arrangements and call you back with the cost," he said. "No later than May is the time to go."

"May is our hot month, the perfect time to leave," I said. "Wonderful, Dad—I'll talk to you soon."

Dad had been to Italy and the rest of Europe many times with Casey, but this would be his first trip without her. When I mentioned the plan to Indra, Carol called.

"I hear you're going to Italy. I want to go too," she said.

"Hi, Carol. Dad found a two-week tour in May, and we didn't think you would be able to take time off from work," I said.

"It's true I can't afford it now," Carol said, her voice deflated, "but I want to go."

Carol's disappointment was so elaborate we knew we couldn't go without her. Dad and I agreed to split the cost of her tour. Rather than crowding into triple rooms, I suggested that red-haired Louise, my friend from the sixties, join us. If she came we'd be more comfortable in two rooms: one for dad and Carol, and one for Louise and me. Louise agreed.

Carol had broken her ankle rear-ending another car, and the ankle wasn't healing well. We offered to postpone the trip until autumn, but Carol refused to wait—she threw an orthopedic walking boot into her luggage at the last instead. In the San Francisco airport she refused a wheelchair—embarrassed to have it considered—and I reassured the airport employee that he'd done nothing wrong as he pushed the empty wheelchair alongside a limping Carol.

We arrived in Rome to find our group had left for the welcome dinner without us. The next morning Dad introduced himself to Frederica, our guide, saying, "We're sorry you missed us last night." "No," she barked at Dad, "I'm sorry *YOU* missed *ME*."

Frederica was operatic, full of sweeping gestures, threats, and demands. Dad liked her. She had a snaggle-toothed smile, scarier than the scowl she wore for most of the trip. If I raised my hand to ask a question on the bus, she'd leave her seat at the front, sashay down the aisle, and throw the full force of her generous hip into my shoulder as she answered. Frederica proved unsympathetic to Carol and Dad's mobility issues, forging ahead in crowds and leaving us to track the bobbing plastic flower at the top of the wand she wielded like a whip. Even with the walking boot, Carol had difficulty keeping up, so she and Dad found sidewalk cafés to wait inside while the walking tours circled them.

Even Frederica, the devil's ambassador, couldn't spoil Italy. We gawked at Michelangelo's David, and the Amalfi Coast reminded us of Portuguese Bend and the craggy Big Sur coastline. Frederica threatened to abandon us at every stop, and she warned us of her countrymen—sordid opportunists, heirs to debauched appetites and self-destructive excess. In Pompeii, at the Vatican, and in fabulous Venice, we were as independent as we dared, then followed bitchy Frederica's bobbing flower back to our group reality.

The sun shone on silver olive orchards in Tuscany and Umbria, and strands of cypress marched across the landscape. Fields of bright red poppies vibrated under a cerulean and wispy sky. Umbrella pines lined remnants of the Appian Way, which wove in and out of the modern roads we traveled.

On the dock at Capri, cats dozed in a furred knot. We caught the cable car to Capri town, perched high on a ridge. Louise and I walked tree-lined lanes and found the perfect vantage point to view the famous arch rising out of cobalt water streaked with turquoise. Carol and Dad joined us at the spot, and we hired a boat and motored through the arch, around cliffs, in and out of grottos dappled with blue-green light.

Carol grew comfortable with Dad and confident of his love in Italy, so we planned another trip together—this time to Greece, Carol's dream destination. In October 2008, with another friend of mine making us four, we flew to Athens, where Carol and Dad drank ouzo and danced while my friend and I saw *La Bohème* at the opera house.

We climbed the Acropolis, left Dad's camera at the Parthenon, and took a windy ferry ride to the white island of Mykonos. Bleached buildings, trimmed in traditional blue, and a row of windmills protected the island from evil spirits and the elements. We lounged by a saltwater pool, lunched on the beach, and made forays into Little Venice to wander.

An afternoon passage took us to Santorini, land of steep, striated cliffs, gorgeous sunrise and sunset vistas, and homes perched on small footprints. The land had turned up Cycladic figurines, now on display at the Prehistoric Museum. We sat in bistros that hugged the cliffs, an active volcano in view. On the ferry back to Athens, Carol said, "I always thought it would be Greece, but it's Italy, isn't it? I have to go to Italy again."

"Yes, we'll go again," I said.

⌒

For my birthday I had invited friends for a dinner party that filled the dining room table and overflowed into the garden. Carol and Dad sat inside, and I was outside, but I noticed, through the window, Carol's long absence from the table. I found her lying on the tile floor at the top of the stairs, where the acoustics were good. She said, in a hollow voice, "I'm not here—just listening now."

I tried to persuade her to let me help her to her room, but she feared being seen by our guests downstairs. She insisted I leave her where she lay, and I knew better than to argue with her when she'd made up her mind.

The next day a friend filled me in on the gaps in the evening. Carol was drunk, and Dad said, laughing, "And this is my lush daughter." Soon she rose from the table and disappeared.

Dad considered the remark—made many times over the course of our lives—a mild joke, a statement of the obvious. Carol had realized she was alcoholic at fifteen and never sought treatment.

A day or two later, I made the mistake of confiding in my sister how difficult I found life with Dad. The landscape of my communication with her had unexploded charges, but I needed to share with the only one who had been there all along.

Carol minded my new appreciation of our mothers. "What would Mother know about Dad?" she said. "Why listen to her? And what do you mean Casey died of boredom?"

She was disappointed in my response to Dad, and the last night of her visit, in a black-out, she used my own words against me and they found their mark.

"You didn't invite him here to make him miserable, did you?" she said.

I regretted opening up to her and vowed never to again. I felt I'd spent most of our lives atoning for something, and I had had enough. Carol was a talented hairstylist, who owned her own shop for a while and worked hard her entire life. Yet Dad was prouder of me for marrying well—and his favoritism went undisguised. I knew our trips to Italy and Greece had given Carol the relationship she wanted with Dad, and I stopped waiting for the breakthrough to ease our tricky sorority.

I no longer focused on preserving the remains of Dad's estate, either. He and Casey had told us to expect no inheritance—that they would spend and enjoy every cent. Now Dad and I planned travel. On the road, our daily needs attended to by others, we'd do what we did best: escape. Travel was our family's coping mechanism. Typical products of those who went west until they could go no farther and were forced to stop at land's edge, the ocean's churning a mirror for their own.

Six

*W*e began to travel in-country—first with the Audubon Society to Pátzcuaro, its lake cupped by artisan villages. Dad sported brown-and-white spectators for bird watching, day trips, and dining, and charmed everyone. Travel was our answer; maybe we'd return for Day of the Dead, when boats full of flowers and lit candles would glide through the dark waters.

We visited mask makers, copper craftsmen and, my favorite, Tzin Tzun Tzan, where Mexican women wove straw into Christmas ornaments, crèche figures, and mobiles of birds, fish, and skeletons. In the Folk Art Museum, a soft-spoken docent manned each room full of native ceramics and textiles. Strips of bovine vertebrae filled the spaces between stone tiles worn smooth with time.

In October, Dad would be ninety. Two places had already been reserved for Copper Canyon. We returned home in a contented anticipation. We had always been a family of travelers. Dad's favorite aspect of our life together was my wanderlust, and I loved having a ready partner.

While we waited for our departure date, Dad read every book I owned. I no longer built collections but I had kept favorites, and it was sweet to share them with him. Open and emotional, the new genres took him deeper than the pop novels and technical writing he usually enjoyed. When he finished a stack, we donated them to a used book store, where he then had credit to buy more. When he brought books home to read a second time, he insisted they were unfamiliar until he spotted my name inside the cover. So he joined the library and began at "A" in the biography section, absorbing a life story a day.

The *New York Times* arrived at our door each Sunday, and I bought a television, though I hadn't owned one in years, and installed a satellite dish so Dad could have his sports. He was happy when I joined him, but watching golf put me in a stupor, a carryover from Palm Springs, where I'd said more than once, "If I'm ever interested in golf, please shoot me in the head." There, pale East Coast snowbirds had flocked to the desert each winter to knock a ball around with a stick, the sand patched with greens for tourists who wore absurd plaid pants.

Friday nights we watched Bill Maher, an easy audience eager to share in a few irreverent laughs. When the driving Real Time theme music began, we took up our positions. Dad swiveled a wing chair away from the fireplace to face the flat screen, and I flopped back on the love seat tucking pillows under my head and feet.

We emerged from our cocoon to attend concerts—flamenco, jazz, and even chamber music with violins Dad thought he hated until Timothy Fain's solo fiddle and violin concert made him cry and he bought the CD to play during dinner.

Dad was thinner. Casey had been gourmet, but Dad's taste ran to meat and potatoes—nothing green. More than once I'd seen him finish a plate of something incomprehensible as food to me—like Wiener-schnitzel—and leave a lone broccoli flower on his plate. I tried to interest him in healthier foods but he ate a lot of enchiladas and chiles rellenos trying to keep up his weight. Dad's stomach was Méxican.

Pueblito was happy to prepare and serve Dad's lunches, coaxing him with a smile, "Un poco vino, Señor?"

"*Si,*" he responded, expansive. "Why not?" He drained the cases of Two-Buck Chuck.

One day, Dad put on his Captain Jack nametag and joined our local flight instructor on the dusty landing strip off the road to Dr. Mora. Their mission: to get the kids in San Miguel de Allende into the air for the first time. Dad kept the children off the runway when the flight instructor brought his four-seated plane in for a landing. No one lost their life, and dozens of children experienced the thrill of breaking with gravity, and flying over familiar territory, an arrangement of patterns from the sky. Dad came home with a sunburn that took over where his rosacea left off and a contented grin.

People from our tours said hello when we ran into them around town. Dad admitted he recognized no one, but it helped make him feel part of his new community.

In August I left for a week of silent retreat at the Monastery in Atotonilco, a twenty minute drive outside of San Miguel. Dad was unhappy about being abandoned, though Pueblito would be there to meet his needs. I had expected him to have a couple of friends by then, but he didn't. Faithful to Arthur Murray, he showed up for private lessons, but missed the parties where he could meet partners unless I agreed to go with him. I, however, had swung, fox trotted, and faked the salsa until my back said *no más*.

I was nervous leaving for a week, and Dad said it would be "weird" without me, but I needed to go.

On retreat I began to write, and in a counseling session I talked about the inappropriate bonding that takes place sometimes between a parent and child when the parent's marriage is bad. The counselor stressed the importance of changing the agreement in the proper way, without blame or resentment. I resolved to handle things better.

Back in San Miguel, Dad and I screened *The Philadelphia Story*. In the film, Hepburn is angry with her father for his fling with a showgirl. In the climactic scene, father tells daughter that her unconditional affection could have prevented him from pursuing the reassurance of youth elsewhere. Dad smiled through tears, squeezed my hand, and said, "That's right," as he did each time.

A couple of friends and I met with a talented astrologer weekly for work that was deep and dismantling. I'd idealized Dad as a child, when it was natural to do so, and then—absent daily interactions with him after my parents divorced—I had romanticized the loss and formed a pattern of longing for what was not present. Fixated on a missing, essential piece, I had undervalued what was before me, a recipe for misery.

Might chapters of my life read better than they were lived? I decided to see if it was true. I revisited the early years in a writing workshop and explored the past with Dad as well. As a family, we had dealt with Debbie's suicide by pretending it never happened. Dad and Casey had redoubled their pursuit of pleasure as an antidote to grief, and years had passed before we even mentioned her name.

We broke the seal of silence, and mentioned her now. Carol, Roger, and I had known what Debbie planned, and had done nothing to stop it. Dad wondered why. Wasn't the real question, "Why did all four children think suicide was a good idea?" I'd always wondered and I asked it now.

Dad struggled to answer, surrendered and said, "Oh God, honey, I don't know. We were just very selfish people."

⌒

In 1971, I took Dad and Casey to see *Harold & Maude*, a film with Ruth Gordon, one of their favorite actresses. I knew nothing of the film—didn't know it was a dark comedy about teen suicide. Horrified, I sat frozen through scenes where Harold's melodramatic mother finds her son hanging from a rope looped around his neck, or preparing to commit ritual seppuku, a Japanese sword poised to pierce his abdomen. I waited for Casey's sobs, but heard snickers instead. We didn't find a way to talk about Debbie, but we found a way to laugh about suicide.

Then in 1980, at Le Petit Pier, a French restaurant on the North Shore of Lake Tahoe, at dinner with Dad and Casey and a couple of their friends I hadn't met before, Casey became harsh as the evening progressed. The other couple, whom I liked very much, buffered her remarks. When Casey mentioned my hospitalization at NPI—inappropriate dinner chat—the wife said, "To be fair to Terry, wasn't that after Debbie's death, a very upsetting time for everyone?"

Casey said, "To be fair to Debbie, hers was a copycat suicide. She followed Terry's lead."

My world broke up into its component parts, split at the weak, patched-up places, and threatened to fly apart. Casey had voiced her belief that I bore responsibility for Debbie's death. The buzzing in my head made it difficult to concentrate on the rest of the evening.

After a week in emotional chaos, I knew I blamed myself too, and I discovered that it was a gift—a deep, uncomfortable gift—to see what I'd hidden from myself. In meditation I saw a system of gears, levers and pulleys—my psychic governor—rerouting my energy.

I'd created ways to siphon off my aliveness, a hidden, emotional apparatus designed to derail my right to be.

‿

Dad had always insisted he was never depressed; he wore it as a badge of honor, like never having a hangover. Now, as we delved into our past, he said, "I've never been depressed a day in my life—but I'm working on it."

Seven

*Y*ohosame arrived in Mexico, and we gave him the daybed in the living room and invited him to Copper Canyon. He and his grandfather were on good, if superficial, terms. Dad preferred girls, and showed only a perfunctory interest in his three grandsons. My gorgeous niece elicited far more. Dad ogled Indra, who quickly learned to take unwanted male attention in stride. I arranged for Dad and Yohosame to room together for the first part of our trip, and the three of us would share a room once we reached Creel.

⌒

Yohosame had become a musician and songwriter, impressionable and unfettered. He fell in love and married twice—brief and disappointing marriages—and then moved on. For three years he'd studied Arabic with an American Muslim, his father's friend and mentor, who ran a study center in Charlottesville, Virginia. Students from Afghanistan, Somalia, and the Middle East came there, dividing their time between public school and the Islamic center, where Yohosame volunteered.

His father, George, became Yusuf when he adopted Sufism at the end of the sixties. Yohosame and his father enjoyed an easy alliance, free of the problems imposing authority brings, as that was my purview. As a teenager, Yohosame refused to be guilt-tripped when Yusuf said, "If I had been a better father, you'd become Muslim now."

Yusuf moved to Morocco in 1998, and settled in a coastal town that attracted artists and musicians for a summer festival. He died there in 2003. When Yohosame, his father's only son, spent a month there tying up his affairs, he softened to his brand of adopted spirituality, and embraced Islam. I treated it as a phase.

෴

We spent the night in Mexico City, and caught a morning plane north with fifty other "Vagabundos" and dimpled David, our leader. David reminded us that we were responsible for our meals and our happiness, and contributed to both with trips down the aisles of buses, planes and trains, passing out candy. Yohosame declared David the rock star of tour guides. Dad entertained seatmates with family stories, and people warmed to him as the tour unfolded and he proved to be a real trooper. Dad sometimes wobbled, however, so I was vigilant, grabbing him by the collar from behind when he paused at the top of stairs, tipped in slow motion, and threatened to topple.

After a night spent in El Fuerte, we boarded the train to Bahuichivo; from there we drove into Cerocahui where we settled into Hotel Mission, surrounded by spacious gardens. The bushes were in bloom and alive with butterflies and hummingbirds Yohosame captured with his camera as they hovered over petals. We walked to the central plaza and discovered that a festival had ignited the village with music and traditional dancing. Señoritas in yards of skirts, gathered in tiers, rotated around caballeros in short, embroidered jackets, keeping the beat as they clicked their spurred boots and turned in tight circles, twirling their partners.

I wandered into the church across the street in the morning and heard a tenor rehearsing for an evening concert. His name was Oscar, and his voice was sublime. I dragged Dad back in the evening, but he grew bored and hungry in the crowded church, sitting on a hard pew, and left before an electrical storm knocked out the power. Cell phones provided ambient lighting so the musicians could read their music. A sea of children from the orphanage sang in the background while Oscar's voice careened among the upper reaches of the arched ceiling in swells. I floated out of the church under a sky filled with fireworks. Early the next morning, as we waited by the train track, Oscar arrived to another ovation.

On the dramatic train ride to Creel, we skirted the steep canyon in a series of switchbacks: the tracks hugged the mountain on one side, gave way to a sheer drop to the depths on the other. We hurtled over thirty-six bridges, roared through eighty-seven tunnels, and climbed eight thousand feet to Divisadero, on the Continental Divide. We peered at the awesome complex of mountain chains corrugated with fissures, carved by the movement of tectonic plates, and continued on to Creel. I had wanted to do this ever since I read about the thrill ride where the Tarahumara Indians live. The Chihuahua Pacific Railway, or "El Chepe," was nearly one hundred years in the making, some of them spent idle, until technology caught up with the ambitious plan to span 400 miles. Now they hoped to replace it with a tram. We were glad to be there before progress ruined *La Barranca Del Cobre*.

Yohosame fell in love with Mexico, photographed the canyons, the rock formations, and the Tarahumara, or Raramuri, as they call themselves. In their smoky cave dwellings, pine needle baskets held firewood, grains, colorful yarns and stacks of brilliant fabric. Vegetable dyes produced subtle designs in the tight weave of baskets they wove in miniature, the originals too unwieldy to carry home.

Thick pine forest funneled into a narrow side canyon, bordered by steep granite walls. As we followed the flow of a turquoise river, we walked on sand around boulders streaked with yellow and rust, flashing mica in the sunlight. People in bright native garments gathered wood and water, at home in these surroundings.

We heard the broad band of cascading water before we saw it, before we stood in its roar, covered in mist. Cusarare Falls stretched out, exploding 100 feet below, racing to rejoin the larger canyon system. Cusarare means "Land of the Eagles," and refers to a time when golden eagles flourished there.

We backtracked to rejoin the group, but further on were hot

springs with curative powers and shallow, empty caves—shelter for the night.

Dad's ninetieth birthday party was the last night of our tour. He wanted to go horseback riding earlier in the day but his grandson and I weren't up to it. That night, fifty Vagabundos gathered in the hotel bar under a ceiling of streamers and balloons and raised their glasses to my father. There was music, cocktails, and cake, and there was Dad, wearing an oversized sombrero and a big grin. He kissed all the girls and saved the last dance for me.

Eight

We returned to San Miguel de Allende happy and renewed, with Yohosame onboard for Oaxaca at Christmas and the beach trip in January. Carol called me and we made a plan. I just had to convince Dad.

One night as he, Yohosame and I were in the kitchen fixing dinner, I said, "Dad, Carol wants you to visit her over Thanksgiving. What do you think?"

"I'll stay here," he said as he opened the refrigerator and peeled back the foil on his stash of chiles rellenos.

"Dad, I need to visit Mother, and Yohosame needs to fly to the East Coast. We could travel to Lake Havasu together, and Carol could pick you up there. Yohosame can swing back by Palm Desert after he takes care of business so you two can fly back here together before we leave for Oaxaca."

"I don't want to go," he said, his mouth set in a pout.

I poured him a glass of Two Buck Chuck and encouraged him— "The weather is wonderful in the desert this time of year. You can play golf and tennis."

"I don't want to," he said.

I exchanged a look with Yohosame. Mine said *Help* and his said *You're on your own.* I continued to cheerlead. "You're the patriarch. You can see your grandchildren and your great-grandchildren." I'd run out of perks. Neither of my parents liked anyone else's children but their own, and that included grandchildren and great-grandchildren. Dad and Mother had little else in common, except preferring pets to people.

"Carol has those dogs," I added.

"No."

More direct now, I said, "Dad, I could use a break."

"A break from what? Go ahead and take a break. I'm fine right here," he said.

"Carol wants time with you, and I can't leave you here alone while I visit mother. You have to come. We'll all leave together," I said.

He began to cry, escalating into little choked sobs as he headed for his place at the dining room table and crumpled into his chair.

"I want a partner. I haven't had a real partner since Casey died." He was going for a full tantrum, wailing with his head in his hands.

I watched myself hold firm, and said, "I'm glad to hear you say that, Dad. It's true. Casey was your true partner. I'm your daughter, not your partner. But perhaps you'll meet someone and have another partner."

He raised his head, scanned the house, opened his arms in a gesture of innocent inquiry and asked, "Where would we put her?"

There was no more room at the inn. I had bought a proper house, but Yohosame already slept in the living room. I was amazed he would consider moving his next partner in rather than teaming up elsewhere. "Dad, it's possible she'll have her own house."

I tried not to laugh while my father cried. It wasn't funny—but laughter was my response to the outrageous or inappropriate. Dad gave up on the chiles rellenos, picked up the bottle of Two Buck Chuck and his stemmed glass, and went to his room. My sister told me months later that he considered leaving for good that day, but realized it was too late.

After another few days of Dad's insistence that he'd *drive* to the States, we flew to Las Vegas and shuttled to Lake Havasu where Mother lived, and where Carol met us for the night.

Dad cried at movies and books, but I'd only seen him break down twice. The first time was at the mortuary when we went to see Debbie's body. We stared at the open coffin— the lurid, orange pancake makeup on her young face—and Dad cried, "Oh God, if this had been you," and he trailed off in sobs.

The second time was in Lake Tahoe years later. Casey served dinner and the three of us sat at the walnut table by the fireplace. Dad told the story of his father's final days. Dad adored his father, and had continued to give M.R. and his wife, Lucille, money while he worked to build a career in architecture. Dad married Mother, and his brother, Landon, arrived with a wife named Sally and also settled in California. The brothers eventually lost touch with M.R. and Lucille, but when M.R. contracted lung cancer, he ran an ad in the LA Times seeking the whereabouts of his sons, Jack and Landon. Tired of subsidizing the "old man," they said, "We need to raise our own families now."

Dad sobbed in regret at the abandonment of his father years before, saying, "I didn't know I was still so hung up about that."

Casey and I reassured him it was okay, and Dad absolved himself of guilt mostly by blaming my mother.

⌒

I hadn't abandoned Dad but I still felt guilty. I hadn't planned on transforming our old dynamic, and I hadn't anticipated what felt like a fight for my life. I'd had no intention of mothering him, mastering tough love, or making him face what life had carved out of him and what little was left. But that's what happened. I called Mother on Sunday.

"Hi honey, how's it going?" she said.

"It's not so easy."

"I predicted that," she said.

"I remember, but we've always gotten along so well. How did you know it would be a challenge?"

"Because you two are very much alike, and those things he's doing that bother you are the traits you share. You inherited both of your parents' worst qualities."

"Could you be more specific?"

"No."

The guys returned to San Miguel in early December. Dad said he'd had a good time with Carol in Palm Desert. We packed for Oaxaca, and Dad and I spent the two-day bus ride squashed into the last row.

Nine

Christmas in Oaxaca City was all about radishes and riot police. The handcrafted life found its modern voice there in the summer of 2006, when people marched in the streets, shouted their demands, and were beaten back. What had begun as another teacher's strike escalated into a bloody confrontation that lasted several months and left hundreds jailed or hospitalized, and at least twenty dead.

American journalist Brad Will's camera recorded his own slaughter in October of 2006, prompting then-president Vicente Fox to send federal police into Oaxaca. Yohosame and I remembered the jerky footage—the shots and screams; the young man lying limp as his blood fanned out in a flood. The standoff grew further inflamed before an uneasy peace was restored. Three years later, clots of helmeted, shielded, armed soldiers still stood on street corners.

Delicate, carved radish tableaux filled the plaza. We dined on the second floor and took in the scene. Christmas lights winked around the tiered red poinsettias, spiraled up and down the Zócalo's trees, and glittered along rooflines. It had been thirty-five years since I'd last visited Oaxaca, and my memories were closer to the vintage photos that lined the hotel lobby.

I was changed also. In my twenties, I was a typically disenfranchised product of American culture, estranged by choice and reveling in autonomy. In Mexico, I celebrated freedom from the bonds of blood and marveled at the simplicity, the sincerity, the pure, slow enjoyment. Now I traveled bracketed by family, boarding buses to retrace routes I had formerly hitchhiked. Where once I carried what I owned slung over my shoulder, a driver now unloaded my luggage for me. I no longer scored peyote in the marketplace—no longer saw hallucinations in jungle pools. I had exposed nerves no amount of meditation could soothe, and I was far more likely to throw my back out doing yoga than I was to reach nirvana. Mexico, however, was still the mystical, operatic land it always had been, and I still responded—emptied of myself, grateful for its magic.

We ventured out of town to see the rug weavers, and were told of customs and languages preserved—rivers robbed of gold and run dry, primitive clay figurines housed within Catholic saints. We circled the world's second-largest tree on a hot winter day and were thankful for its shade. The thick, variegated trunk spoke of adaptation, detour, and reconnection.

I turned around in my seat on the bus ride back to Oaxaca City and as I did I felt something shift in my spine. Christmas Day I spent in bed, and I wasn't up to the long bus ride home. Yohosame offered to fly with me, and Dad chose to stay with the group.

I had never believed it would come to this. It was surreal to imagine I'd be unconscious for the kind of hammer and crowbar surgery I feared was needed. When I had first arrived in Mexico, a specialist said he would have recommended emergency surgery from my MRI results alone, but when he watched me walk into his office, he recommended I do whatever it was I was doing, because after surgery I would still be in pain. Since then I had continued my regimen of warm-water exercise and walking everywhere.

Each day at home brought greater mobility. We picked Dad up at the bus station and regrouped, unpacked, and repacked for the beach trip nine days later.

Ten

The beach at Rincon de Guayabitos was a hubbub of Mexican families and birds. Black-and-white cormorants made patterns overhead, rotating angles against a cerulean sky. Sandpipers and toddlers waded in the surf. Clumsy, big-billed pelicans, webbed feet wide as snowshoes, waddled over the sand. Seafood vendors shooed them from painted carts mounded with fresh catch. Fishing boats rocked on swells offshore as more pelicans swooped by and arranged themselves on rooftops. Occasionally they lifted off, heavy-bodied, and skimmed the sea. Prey-sighted, their vertical dives made an abrupt stop at their shoulders, at which point they flipped over and floated as the bulky fish made their way down their gullets.

I was indolent and did not board the tour bus all week. I staked out a lounge on the grassy edge of the beach in front of our motel, a pyramid of books on a ceramic-tile table beside me. My father did everything offered: swilled margaritas and swapped stories down the coast in Puerto Vallarta; saw crocodile families on the San Blas river cruise, an hour's drive north; watched whales from a viewing boat offshore and strolled neighboring Sayulita.

Yohosame was a blur of movement, checking in and racing off, just as he had as a child. He turned forty-one while we were there—without fanfare, complete, and in his element.

⤻

Yohosame was a water baby. He stroked deep underwater before he walked. As a child in Venice, California, he marched along the canal's edge, singing, with a string of dogs in tow. When it was time to call him, I visualized a cord of light connecting us—heart to heart—and he appeared within minutes. It worked until he hit his teens, and suddenly nothing worked anymore.

Yohosame was all about the music the world made. He sang instead of talked, danced instead of walked, played air guitar on a tennis racquet, and beat out rhythms on everything. As he played scales on a toy xylophone, striking the keys with a wooden mallet from treble to bass and back again, he sang "This is the way we disappear and reappear."

He frowned and corrected himself, playing this time from bass to treble and back to bass, certain now, "No, *this* is the way we disappear and reappear."

⌐

In Guayabitos I roomed alone and the guys shared one upstairs. When I awoke in the night I lit candles and disturbed no one. The world was quiet. Only the movement of the sea remained, all lesser sound absorbed in the predictable pulling back and cycling forward. I offered my mind's nervous chatter to the blank page before me, surrendered my fate to the sea, and dropped beneath waves into silence. There I put out feelers and found scraps of courage to face the surgery that would fix my spine.

Dad said it wasn't major surgery, as no organs were involved. I'd practiced yoga for forty years, however, so for me it was major. I had never broken a bone or been in an accident, had always been steeped in good health and whole until now. To me, the spine was the stem, the trunk, the central support—a double conduit for energy coursing up and down the body. That energy was now detouring around twists and bends.

⌐

George was a WASP when we married at eighteen, but he emerged from the sixties a Sufi named Yusuf who traveled to France to build an ashram while I tried to master single parenthood. Despite our differences, we remained friends throughout the years.

George/Yusuf married several more times, and fathered two daughters—Sadaf and Shireen, half-sisters Yohosame adored. For a few summers, when the girls were young, Yusuf drove them from Santa Fe to our house in Lake Tahoe, where we spent days on a beach where purple lupine grew and migrating geese gathered. The girls dipped in frigid water and the three of us made art projects in my studio. Their moon-and-star drawings became cards on my simple Japanese printer. I asked Sadaf what her favorite color was, and she tried to decide between silver and gold.

In the evenings, the girls and their big brother raided my closet and sang and danced in feather boas, beaded scarves, and velvet capes. Jeweled belts cinched tunics and togas. Chandelier earrings swung to their shoulders under cocktail hats and turbans. Cabaret scenes turned Arabian nights. The sultan and his harem morphed into the ringmaster and his acrobats, and then the magician and his glamorous assistants brought the makeshift curtain down each night.

ᔐ

At ninety, Dad was still a bon vivant. We caught each other up at the end of each day in a restaurant a short walk up the beach. Yohosame and I always arrived first and settled into a table for four waiting to see which lady friend turned up on Dad's arm.

The restaurant had no walls. Scattered posts supported a thick palm-frond mat in the oversized *palapa*. Tables lined the long narrow room in staggered rows, just a few steps off the beach. Frosted margaritas arrived before dinners of broiled seafood stuffed with avocado, rich and addictive. After dinner we walked the stretch of beach back to our motel. Dad's brown and white spectators shushed through the sand.

ᔐ

Dad's mother died when he was six, at which point he became his restless father's sidekick. Merrill Roberts, or M.R., was a dreamer with a music degree, a head full of ideas, and a gift for persuading backers to bankroll him. What he lacked was follow-through—and conscience. When he failed to make payrolls, produce for clients, or reimburse investors, he sometimes simply vanished overnight.

After my grandmother's death, father and son first moved to New York, where M.R. produced programs for the Zeigfeld Follies. Jack was dazzled by his charismatic father, the Big Apple, and the backstage visits to the Follies, where showgirls bent low to kiss him, feathers tickling his skin as he inhaled their perfumed cleavage. Memories of his mother couldn't compete with the freewheeling life he now enjoyed. M.R. took up with a showgirl named Lucille and left the press with his partner, and the threesome went west.

A decade of failed land development projects, mining ventures, and construction schemes ensued as M.R., Lucille, and Jack crossed the country. They stopped moving only when they reached the Pacific Ocean. That hardscrabble, itinerant childhood nurtured in Dad a strong sense of self-preservation. California was a good fit: a place to settle and test himself, to design and build, and to know pleasure, all linked to the rugged beauty of the natural world. My father's religion was self-reliance and self-gratification.

↫

Each day at the beach, the sun penetrated me more deeply. Knotted muscles stretched, and tortured thoughts loosened their grip. Children played in the broad band of wet, brown, pounded sand, hopping in place on their own eroding footprints. Suds swirled around their feet and were sucked out to sea. Excited, they waited for the next wave's slap down, giggling. The children staggered in to shore, their clothes tucked tight to their gooseflesh, with their wobbly "I'm new at this but very determined" gait.

↫

Yusuf was devout, and so was embraced by the locals in the five years he lived in Morocco. He eventually flew back to the States to keep family bonds intact. In 2001, he buried both his brothers—the youngest first in spring, and then the eldest at summer's end.

For the first memorial, Yusuf and I drove together from New Mexico to La Jolla. We loaded the CD player in my old Mercedes sedan with Stones, Cream, Clapton, vintage Beatles, Jimi and Janis, and the incomparable Dylan. Thirty-five years before, we had awaited each album's release like revelations from the Oracle, and had danced to the music live at Avalon, Winterland, Candlestick, and Golden Gate Park. We were fearless, on the edge of revelation, buoyed up, and alive. Now we sped through the open expanse of desert, with me at the wheel, singing over the engine's hum, shouting over the wind to the sixties road music we loved so well.

Short months later, we memorialized Yusuf's older brother in the Bay Area. Yusuf recited from the Qu'ran, graveside, by heart. The Twin Towers fell the next morning. What was left of the family watched the hypnotic images on television together. Yusuf, his worlds colliding, said, "That isn't Islam: Islam means Peace."

Yusuf died in 2003, the third brother in two years to suffer a fatal heart attack. Yohosame, Sadaf, and Shireen went to Asilah, where their father's body was bathed in rosewater, covered with petals, and carried through the streets accompanied by two hundred chanting Muslim men. They brought him to the cemetery on the hill where they placed him in his grave, wrapped in fabric, on his side, facing east.

～

I softened to the idea of surgery there at the beach, and began to hope I was not beyond repair. I loved this time away to face my fears. I loved the pause at dawn and dusk, the surf as soundtrack for my dreams. Each morning I felt cleansed of concerns as day opened in the crescendo of sunrise. I loved the wheeling birds, the comical pelicans, the shimmering sea. I loved the seaweed chains, the salt crust, and the warm, sugary sand. I reconnected with touchstones for a fearless life—remembered childbirth at home with George, who monitored the sky, who was awed by clouds as his son arrived—and I trusted the universe to deliver.

~

Palm Springs: Yohosame slept in his crib beside my bed. I awoke to a crash, a break-in— the locked, wooden door being kicked in followed by footsteps at the end of the hall. No time to dress, to scoop up the sleeping baby, and run; I locked the door and jumped back in bed. When forced from the other side, the door gave way and slammed against the wall.

They lined up at the foot of my bed: three construction workers I recognized. I had never looked directly at them before, but I had noticed them watching me come and go, alone with my baby, while they worked on the roof next door. Now, their job finished, they had come back in the night. Now they stood at the foot of my bed.

I showed no fear. I made steady eye contact, and concentrated on summoning my power. I stared them down until one of them finally spoke the only words said that night: "Hey man, don't you feel the vibes?" He elbowed the one next to him. "Let's get out of here."

They scrambled over each other to be first through the broken door, the first to run down the hallway, the first to crash back through the broken outer door, the first to get away.

I sat in bed naked, covers up to my neck. I could hear Yohosame's breathing as he slept. And I vowed to remember the night that three burly guys were so dispatched—the night I was absolutely clear that there was nothing to fear.

~

Memories flowed here at the beach. My earliest were of the ocean with Dad. But we were three generations of fully formed adults now, a colorful skein of vagabonds. We went our own ways and accommodated each other's pace and idiosyncrasies, and in the easy way being at the sea makes possible, knew these days were precious.

Eleven

I'd heard rave reviews about Dr. Schmidt for years. The German orthopedic surgeon had a reputation for skill, a high success rate with challenging cases, and a no-nonsense style. Other words used to describe him were "quirky" and "eccentric," which, in combination with the praise for his medical prowess, I found intriguing. He had turned away friends of mine saying they weren't candidates for surgery, recommending instead the warm-water exercise I did several mornings a week. Now that I knew he wasn't an indiscriminate cutter, I was ready to hear what he'd say.

I made an appointment, had an MRI, and showed up at Dr. Schmidt's clinic—it was an hour away from San Miguel—with an over-sized envelope containing my results. I crossed the waiting room to the barrier that was the reception desk, handed over the envelope, and settled into one of the scooped plastic chairs bolted in rows to the cement floor. Chairs filled the room but there were no tables with magazines or potted plants. No attempt was made to lull us into comfort.

We were a curious mix of casualties. Mexican families rallied around each other in animated clumps, alongside solo or paired gringos. We all looked up when the elevator door opened and patients from the upper residential floors emerged—bandaged, dazed, shuffling across the scuffed floor, loaded into cars pulled up to the front door that would take them home. I decided to stay at the nearby hospital if I needed surgery.

Summoned by a nurse, I entered a claustrophobic cubicle with just enough room for a cluttered desk and a vertical light panel where my MRI results were clipped. Dr. Schmidt sat at the desk framed by the tiers of teddy bears that filled the shelves behind him. He swiveled sideways to study the film while I studied him. Haphazardly dressed, short, and slight, the doctor had a small island of scalp ringed by thin, ragged brown hair. He had an unassuming, monkish appearance. He could have been a house painter, or a starving artist working as a house painter, a plumber, or a carpenter—a body carpenter, anyway.

"Well, it doesn't take a doctor to see the problem here," he said.

I looked at the film for the first time. I'd assumed it would be difficult to read, but it was obvious. I had a problem. A dark band obscured the spine at my lower back and the column was 50 percent off-center as it continued down to my coccyx. I emitted an involuntary squeak. Dr. Schmidt turned and looked at me for the first time, and said, "I can fix this. I can have you doing what you used to do."

"I've been putting this off for years," I said. "Did my postponement cause me further damage?"

"Absolutely not," was his confident reply.

He reached out his hand and we shook. His grip was formidable; his eyes clear and steady. I considered putting my life in those strong hands. Equally relieved and terrified, I said, "Okay, I'm ready. Put me on your calendar. The next time we meet I'll be unconscious and you'll be brilliant."

Surgery was scheduled for the last day of March, soon after our return from another "Vagabundos" trip, this time to Chiapas. Now that I had a plan and a timeframe, I decided we needed more room at home whether Dad found a new bride or not. I mentioned to Dad that I wanted to enclose the small terrace on the second floor for Yohosame, and he said, "Good, I'm tired of hearing him jerk off in the living room."

I'd always wanted to add a third-floor studio, so after the simple conversion of the terrace, I designed a third floor to be built before, during, and after my surgery. As a retired architect and builder, Dad was used to being the final authority in this area. He'd retired early but continued to generate ideas. I loved his design sense and respected his expertise, but I knew what I wanted. I loved remodeling, and had completed several projects without his help at this point—and it was crucial to get the builder to share my vision, as I wouldn't be able to supervise most of the project nor any of the finishing work. I'd recuperate in the living room on the ground floor until I could climb stairs.

I paced off the future third floor, talking about light and fan placements, window designs, and where I wanted the glass block bathroom. I marked the interior walls with bricks, and allowed space for a sink, toilet, and tub. The contractor followed, handing me bricks and taking notes. Dad followed him, moving the bricks to where he thought they should be, rearranging them into new configurations.

The contractor said later, "I put the bricks back where you wanted them," and then asked, "What was that all about?" I couldn't explain. I was using what was left of my energy to ensure the house and project would function without me.

The exterior scaffolding was placed right outside Dad's large window, open onto the entry. The workers were prompt and agile, arriving each weekday morning at eight o'clock, carrying their tools and materials up the simple planks that leaned against the sides of the house on two levels.

We resumed our routine in the weeks before Chiapas. Dad's job was to squeeze orange juice for the three of us each morning. One night I heard the juicer's whine and garbage disposal's racket as I was falling asleep. Dad had taken a late-afternoon nap, slept through dinner, and awoken in the dark; he thought it was early morning. I pulled on a bathrobe and rushed downstairs, but he was gone before I could stop him. He waited at the tennis courts until he realized the sky was darkening, not lightening, and no one was showing up for tennis. He returned home embarrassed.

It began to happen more often, the kitchen noise at odd hours, and initially it sent both Yohosame and me into hysterics. Then I got my hilarity under control, and went directly downstairs to tell Dad it wasn't morning yet.

He said, "I'm getting to be a funny guy, aren't I?"

When I just smiled, he said, "Well, I think I am."

Dad was beginning to feel he was in the way, irrelevant. He took my stress personally and felt ignored. After a year of unsuccessful wrangling, he often approached me now with both hands in the air, as if surrendering to the cavalry. When his old girlfriend, Vivien, called from Carmel, I hated hearing him tell her, "I think she's sick of this."

I could tell by Dad's half of the ensuing conversation that Vivien was reminding him that I was in pain and worried about surgery— but both Dad and I knew I was falling down on my true job, which was him.

Twelve

*I*n March we left for Chiapas. Pro-Zapatista graffiti marked fences and buildings as we climbed the Sierra Madre de Chiapas to the high plateau of San Cristóbal de las Casas. Women wore white *huipiles* embroidered with flowers, and thick, shaggy black wool skirts cinched with red belts. They draped sky-blue *rebozos* around their shoulders in which they often carried infants. Men sported Western-style pants and shirts, machine-made hats, long woolen tunics, and high leather boots. Women and girls went barefoot, believing they drew fertility from the ground.

Chiapas had a fiercely independent streak that, when pressed, sparked a revolution. Once controlled by bordering Guatemala, then annexed to Mexico with its distant capital Mexico City, Chiapas was largely ignored for a long time, which suited the indigenous people. But when too much of their land was expropriated, they fought back. An agrarian revolt took place when the Zapatistas stormed seven cities calling for reforms on the day in 1994 that NAFTA took effect. NAFTA would destroy the prospects for indigenous and non-indigenous peasant farmers by flooding the market with US-grown crops. Vast numbers of people, known as *Los Expulsados*, had been driven from their land and communities for joining the Protestant church. Now over 36 percent of the population belonged to a non-Catholic church that co-existed alongside pre-Hispanic beliefs, shamans, and Mayan healing ceremonies. Yohosame even found a fledgling

Muslim community online and planned to taxi to the outskirts of San Cristóbal to connect with them. The Zapatista movement, underground and aggressively suppressed, continued to energize Chiapas, and even though its leader, Commander Marcos, had since come out of hiding, married, written a book, and traveled throughout Mexico, his cause still resonated.

San Cristóbal de las Casas, one of Mexico's finest colonial towns, was built of colorful roof-tiled buildings with wrought iron details. Dad and I did a lot of happy wandering, actually walking two across on sidewalks instead of single file, as we did in San Miguel de Allende's narrow, cobblestone streets. We looked around at the city's landmarks, confident we wouldn't trip, drop into holes, or end up with dog shit on our shoes. Templo Santo Domingo, with carved columns that looked like lace, dominated the plaza, and in the afternoons we sat under trees in front of La Catedral de San Cristóbal, its mustard-colored façade aglow at sunset. Yohosame was thrilled with the Muslim community and all three of us felt we could happily move to this colonial town.

Dad and I visited nearby San Juan Chamula, the largest indigenous community. We parked above the town and walked down past a cemetery with Mayan crosses atop mounded graves covered with wooden doors through which to communicate with the dead on All Saints' Day. We entered the central plaza where the *iglesia* stood, its chalk-white façade decorated with painted blue flowers. The interior was dark except for a forest of lit candles on a floor covered with pine boughs and fresh flowers. This church was left to practice the Mayan ways, visited by a priest only for baptisms. There were statues of Catholic saints covered in bright floral fabrics, mirrors hanging around their necks, housed in glass boxes so the faithful could no longer take out the disappointment of unanswered prayers by breaking off a finger, turning the statue to face the back wall, or even taking it outside to stick its head in the ground.

Revisiting Palenque was sublime. It had changed little in the thirty years since I was there; only a turnstile and museum had been added to the pristine site. Dad decided to skip Palenque, discouraged by the wide stone stairs leading up to the entrance—he preferred to visit the small museum and sit at the edge of the jungle listening to the haunting, raucous cries of howler monkeys—so I spent my time there alone.

In the past, I had climbed the pyramids, descended to inner chambers, and learned of Palenque's Mayan history. On my return, the peace of this place was palpable, and I settled into its pure presence and communed with the trees. The surrounding jungle was relentless, ready to absorb the ruins. Single leaves towered over me, and birdcalls sprinkled the air.

At nearby *Agua Azul*, a swift river plunged through a series of cascades, smoothing limestone pools before rushing on. Last time I was there I had crossed the falls in a bikini, holding onto a cable, and swum in the pools with currents so strong they pushed me right to the edge. Today Dad and I sat in one of the open *palapas* where food was served, and we watched the river flow.

Toward the end of our trip we boarded wooden boats called *lanchas* and cruised downriver through Sumidero Canyon to the Yaxchilan Archaeological site, with Guatemala on one side of the river and Mexico on the other. We pulled in to shore to see gnarly, grinning crocodiles and jeweled iguanas sunning themselves.

Thirteen

*H*ome from our favorite trip so far, I checked on the workers' progress and prepared for surgery. Alan, the friend who had met Dad in Laredo, drove to my mother's house in Lake Havasu and picked up a mechanical bed I'd left. I had climbed onto it on a showroom floor and felt I rested in the palm of God—a concept I doubted, but an experience I couldn't pass up. Perfect for recuperation, it enabled me to raise and lower my head, knees, and feet with the push of a button. The bed even gave a vibrating massage in a wave pattern. It sat in the open living room with arched doorways connecting it to the entry hall and dining room. I would spend the first month there until I was cleared to climb the stairs.

Next to the bed I placed a high, narrow table that held everything I anticipated I'd need: tissues, washcloths, facial cleanser, a water carafe and glass, reading glasses, the TV remote, the bed remote, my sleep mask and earplugs, an ounce of manicured pot, a package of zigzags, a digital clock, pen and paper, a month's supply of vitamins in daily compartments, a thick stack of pesos to keep the house and project going, nightgowns, loose clothing I could pull on over my head, a heating pad, a walker ready for the twenty foot journey to the bathroom and, in case I couldn't make it, a vase I hated.

Pueblito and Antonio, my housekeeper and gardener, moved in with Dad to take care of him while I was gone. I kissed Dad goodbye, assured him we'd be home in five days and that everything would be alright now, and Yohosame and I left.

I was ready at 6 a.m. the next morning for my scheduled surgery, but an emergency moved me to noon, and at one thirty the door banged open and they parked a gurney next to my bed. My attitude had been good in the morning, but as I'd waited, fear had begun to gnaw at my resolve. They lifted me onto the gurney, and we whizzed out of the room and down the hall, late now, in a hurry. I shook and cried without control. A disembodied voice behind my head said, "Are you scared? It's all in God's hands now." If it was meant to reassure me, it didn't.

Several masked and gowned figures were cleaning up from the emergency surgery and preparing for mine. The room was chaos and I was grateful when the anesthesiologist put me out.

I awoke five hours later in recovery with an intense urge to pee, groping for a catheter I didn't find. I gestured to the nurse that I had to go and she brought the cold, hard bedpan. I balked. Should I be arching my back so soon after surgery? The nurse rushed my return to my room so someone else could deal with me. Awake back in bed, I hoisted myself up and over the bedpan, thinking some clever baby boomer must invent a flexible alternative.

The next morning Dr. Schmidt said it was time to get up, and he showed me how to roll on my side, swing my legs around and, using my upper body strength, lift myself to a sitting position on the edge of the bed. He encouraged me to stand straight up with no slumping. Straight up I went, at least seven feet tall, saying, "OH MY GOD" over and over as if I'd left the rest of my vocabulary in the OR. I was a boneless, willowy alien learning to walk on some planet with less gravitational pull. Dr. Schmidt and I executed an awkward shuffle around the room, disengaging at the door to the bathroom I was cleared to use on my own.

When I did, I glimpsed a stranger in the mirror—someone whiter than white, with a blue bruise on one cheekbone. When I asked if it was alright to be so white, Dr. Schmidt said my blood loss had been average, but at 107 pounds, average amounted to a larger share of my total supply, and I might be anemic for a while. He began to adjust my meds.

At first I moved through cycles of escalating pain until I complained. Then an injection boosted me out of my body and around a few galaxies. Finding the right balance was experimental. Over the next several days I improved, and Yohosame and I enjoyed Dr. Schmidt. We learned he never complained, loved classical music, climbed the rock faces of mountains for relaxation, gave pro bono care to the multitudes, and ran himself ragged—a man on a mission.

Five days later, with a bagful of drugs, Yohosame and I climbed into an ambulance with two medics who boasted they could make the drive from the hospital to my door (an hour away) in thirty minutes. I'll never know if it was true, as halfway there I told Yohosame to make them stop. I needed a bedpan, and there wasn't one. We were parked in a lot next to a restaurant, and I was desperate now. I said, "That's okay. I'll go in the restaurant," and I started down the short stairs.

Yohosame yelled, "Stop, Mother, you can't do stairs for a month."

"Oh yes, that's right. I forgot. What's in here that I can use?"

The guys shrugged. I found and emptied a plastic bag of tongue depressors and asked for privacy. Yohosame stayed to help me. Relief was all I knew for a minute before a rivulet ran down my leg and I laughed. Yohosame was tense without hospital support, and was relieved to hear me laugh. I was strapped in again for the wild ride home, until the attendants unloaded me in front of my house. I waved at the neighbors as they wheeled my gurney through the front gate. I was home—and then the fun began.

Consumed by pain, dependency, and my oh-so-slow recovery, I centered in my own experience. Nights were the worst—interminable. Most mornings I wept as I waited for Yohosame to bring food, so I could begin the complicated regimen of meds that failed to dent the pain. Dad, who'd always made himself a good breakfast, woke early and carried orange juice, coffee, and something sugared to the dining room table to the sound of my moaning in the next room. Dad felt helpless and uncomfortable in the face of my pain. He dumped his dirty dishes in the kitchen, and waved at me with a wistful expression as he sauntered back to his room. He didn't know what else to do, and neither did I.

Pueblito was too nervous to help me shower. I needed Yohosame to tape the eight-inch incision, put the plastic chair in the stall, turn on the water, and adjust the temperature. I lurched in my walker to Dad's room while he played tennis. I couldn't sit long. Yohosame gave me a quick shampoo and I made a pass at the rest—clean agony, gratitude leavened with outrage, the humiliation of the helpless.

Pain honed my cynicism, and punctured the illusion that I ever see with clarity—an imaginative creature, set on survival. A fork crashed to the tile floor and my nerves shrieked: it was a cacophony of metal on hard-fired clay. Explosions streaked my vision.

Antonio and Pueblito waved from the doorway. I ducked, burrowed, and growled. A random universe undulated. Brutality wrapped in shock unwound, layers peeled, risked exposure, and recoiled around enfolded sparks. Amnesia rolled in—a cool, cushioning fog. The central bone chain accepted the metal patch and four screws. I imagined myself awake and began to buffer, embroider, and allow. I peeked through a keyhole beneath awareness as the puzzle pieces that comprise my reality reassembled. Forgetfulness reinvented me, and I was here again, and I wanted to see the sea.

After five weeks, Dr. Schmidt examined a new x-ray of the apparatus reminding my spine to align. I had healed well and was cleared to climb stairs and start warm-water exercise again. We returned to the pools outside of town, and I increased my range of movement and strength while Yohosame swam underwater laps just as he did in his first year of life. Dad lounged under the old-growth palms in the hot pool, with a Panama hat, sunglasses, and a book. He was up to the Ms in the biography section at the library.

I'd read that Sophia Loren attributed her well-preserved beauty to good posture, and a refusal to make old people's noises. As I challenged myself to do more, accompanied by sounds of which she would not approve, I said aloud, "Sorry, Sophia."

I had discovered a surprising archetype inside me: a crone who lived to make people miserable. It was humbling to admit that she waited just beneath the surface. I could be pleasant after a good night's sleep, food I liked, and even when dealing with a few problems—but under duress I was not pleasant. And I suspected that I held other self-serving notions as well. During my recuperation I had watched a lot of television, identifying with the most attractive characters and speculating on how I would behave under the circumstances suggested on screen. I gave myself the benefit of any doubt, imagining myself more heroic, altruistic, and loving than I was. This knowledge slipped under the screen of forgetfulness—the screen I used for filtering anything too dense to carry forward, like an actual memory of a traumatic event.

Why was Mexico so awful at pain management? Was it a third-world country lagging behind, or my German surgeon's stoicism? Or was suffering purposeful in a Catholic country? I found that pot, a panacea I'd discovered long ago when I searched for a substitute for alcohol—my family's drug of choice—was far more helpful than the pharmaceuticals I'd been sent home with.

In a documentary called *The Botany of Desire*, Michael Pollan looks at food from the point of view of plants—those best at propagating themselves, specifically. One undisputed champion was marijuana. From Pollan I learned that the areas of the brain affected by marijuana govern movement, thinking, and memory. In memory, the molecule fits the receptor and opens the lock on forgetfulness. Victims of trauma self-medicate—and that was something I'd been doing from time to time since the sixties. As Roger, my Vietnam War veteran stepbrother, once said to Carol and me, "I'm not the only one who has post-traumatic stress disorder—we all have it."

I climbed the stairs to my room, turned on my computer, and scanned the backlog of e-mails. One jumped out at me and I opened it: a Mediterranean cruise itinerary that resonated with my lust for the sea. I showed it to Dad, and he agreed. We booked it. Having turned a corner, we could once again look forward to travel and enjoyment. I would make him feel special again.

Fifteen

*Y*ohosame and I returned to Hospital Angeles to have his rotator cuff repaired, an old injury that caused his shoulder to pop painfully out of place twice a year. Dr. Schmidt performed the laparoscopic surgery and handed Yohosame a DVD we later watched at home. An undersea world waved while a probe sucked up stray algae, the torn tissues removed and repaired. Yohosame was glad something unpleasant he'd postponed was finally over. I was grateful not to have a souvenir DVD of my surgery.

The third-floor studio was finished and close to what I had envisioned, a room with two walls of windows, a view of the Parroquia, a glass-block bathroom, and a terrace built on top of Yohosame's new room. It was a light aerie, perfect for a communal studio. I'd paint and do calligraphy there; Yohosame would use it to play music in, and maybe Dad would sculpt again.

In late May, Dad and I went to Office Depot to buy a desk for his room. We'd agreed earlier that morning to split the cost but as we walked to the check out line, I heard his thoughts and offered, "It's almost Father's Day. This will be my gift, Dad." And he said, "Well, it *will* be yours."

The next month, Dad said, "I've never bought you a birthday present. How about furniture for the living room? We need some." The living room *was* bare without the furniture we'd moved upstairs into the new space. And it was sweet of him to link it to my birthday—presents had always been Casey's job. We began to look together; then, one day, Dad drove alone to the department store on the hill, and when he returned he announced he'd found them. He'd picked out three white couches and three black-and-white tables, saying, "Let's make the living room contemporary; the rest of the house can be old Mexico with an Asian top note, or whatever the hell it is."

I was prepared to love them without argument, and I did. Everything had been delivered except the two love seats, which arrived in the narrow window between the hospice bed and Dad the following month.

The day before Dad's endoscopy, Yohosame accompanied him to Hospital de la Fe for preliminary blood work, and when they were through—for the first time ever—Dad tossed the keys to his grandson and said, "Why don't you drive us home."

Six days later, Yohosame was home with a hospice worker—waiting for Carol and me to bring Dad home from the hospital—when the last pieces arrived from the furniture store. Yohosame lined up the love seats in front of the fireplace, and that's where we sat with Dad in his final two days. He was unconscious by then, slack-jawed, and laboring to breathe, his eyes closed, and we took our time with him, together and alone, speaking quietly, simply sitting. Yohosame recited from the Qu'ran. The hospice workers ministered. I picked a gardenia and placed it over his rising and falling chest. His will to survive was palpable and concentrated there. He struggled peacefully under the assault of the meds that were loosening his hold on life.

A slow, strong intake of breath collapsed into a lengthening pause. I didn't know if he realized he was home, but we were relieved to have him there—grateful also when it was over two days later. The night my father died, an intense thunder and lightning storm blew in, all cracks and booms. We three were present for Dad's last gasp. Carol washed his face with a soft cloth. I felt the warmth recede from the marvelous, scarred, and calloused hand I held, and I watched it whiten knuckle by knuckle. I felt his head, very cool now. I found lingering warmth in the crook of an elbow and went there to be with what was left.

I called the mortuary when I remembered and realized it was time. Two men arrived and bagged him up in black vinyl. With the final zip the gardenia flew into the air and landed on the empty bed. Out into the stormy night went the two men with what was formerly my father. I followed in shock—bone-deep, visceral. This was the origin of love, cast off. Heavy rain washed down the slick streets, the scene electrified by lightning bursts.

The next morning Carol and I pushed the hospice bed out of the living room, the bag of urine leaking and Dad's last fluids running cold down my leg into my slipper. My housekeeper, Pueblito, for whom Dad was a combination of Jesus and Santa Claus, saw two white butterflies in the garden that circled over her head and was convinced that the *muy bueno hombre* was now with God. Dad had called himself an atheist. The only times he'd entered a church was one Christmas when I dragged him to midnight mass, decades earlier, and the previous year in the lavish Cathedral in Puebla where he'd had a dizzy spell. We'd sat on the long pew while he described the chandeliered ceiling's spin.

The hospital handed me a paper envelope with Casey's *good sport* medallion inside. Dad had worn it on a chain around his neck after she died seven years before. A large safety pin served as the clasp I'd meant to replace. The gold was soft, worn smooth and slippery, a talisman made precious by absence. Carol asked for it, and wore it home.

Sixteen

$\mathcal{Y}$ohosame and I shuffled around the house in a haze, unstrung by loss, communicating in a shorthand of simple gestures and looks. The day before he left for the States to take care of some things, I voiced the thought that tortured me: "I feel like I killed my father because it was so difficult to live with him."

It was too raw, too soon—more than Yohosame was ready to absorb. "Oh God, Mother, that's the sickest thing ever. I hope you'll talk to someone."

Someone *else*, he meant. I regretted my unedited remark, and patted his hand to smooth it over. "Sorry, honey. It's alright. It's just a thought. Don't worry."

I was alone now, and I didn't want to be. I tried to tempt out-of-town friends with my air miles and my now-four-bedroom house, but I received no reprieve. I believed Dad had let the procedure kill him because life with me wasn't what he'd expected either. It was time to meet the full complement of my complicated feelings—time for grief and debilitating guilt, and time to get things done.

I climbed the stairs to the studio and wrote a thank-you note to San Miguel in calligraphy, attached a picture Carol had taken of Dad and me on Santorini, and dropped it off at our weekly bilingual paper. The following Friday, I opened it to the familiar photo: "*Thank You San Miguel de Allende, Audubon, Arthur Murray, and Vagabundos for making the last chapter of my father's life one of Adventure, Beauty, and Celebration*," it read. And under the photo: "*Jack Gray, Architect, Pilot, Sculptor died at home with his family on July 6, 2010, at the age of ninety.*"

I wrote a formal obituary for the *LA Times*, whose home section had featured Dad's designs, and one for *The Monterey Herald*, so his friends in Carmel would learn of his death. I cancelled things, wrote letters, called people, made bank transfers, and closed accounts—sent photo albums and alabaster sculptures to Carol and Roger, and to Roger's children, and ordered a plaque to be added to Casey's memorial bench at the Circle Theater in Carmel. The family had sat there often before a play, tracing the quote and touching her name. It read: "*The Sea which calls all things unto her, calls me, and I must embark.*"

I shipped Dad's ashes to California amid friends' concerns that Mexico would screw it up, and I later learned the box sat for a month in the Sacramento post office. When it was finally delivered to the Neptune Society, the ashes were scattered from the sky off the coast of Marin County, near the Golden Gate Bridge.

It was the worst irony that Dad had died in a cobalt-blue hospital in Mexico after the good care he had received in Carmel at CHOMPS, a hospital so pleasant that we went there for lunch to enjoy the food, the live chamber quartet, and the real art on the walls. I agonized over my suggestion that he visit the doctor, for allowing the endoscopy, for refusing him one more dog. Why hadn't I let him take over my life and be the true center of everything? What did I need to prove that I was so unyielding? Had I really needed to learn tough love with my father?

Deep into this cycle of self-recrimination, one night I heard the words: *The work is done.* I saw the thread that stretched from Carol's first visit in Mexico, through our travels to Italy and Greece, and finally to the month Dad spent with her in her home. A new balance had been found after that, a much-needed new balance that had required Dad and me to dismantle our game. I'd become more real with Dad for myself, but a by-product of that change was that Carol had gotten what she needed. Her identification as one who got the short end of every stick Dad held had changed by the time we lost him. At his deathbed, she'd said, "I'm complete in my relationship with my father," and we'd let him go.

This resolution buoyed me for a time. I clung to the shred of redemption and moved forward. It took more time to confirm myself—to own that I was healed by my willingness to meet my own needs. It would take more time still to conclude it had been worthwhile. I said to friends, "If I'd known it would only be for a year and a half, I would've continued to be the perfect daughter. I would have drunk with him every night."

Telling the truth and having boundaries made me feel like a traitor, a code breaker, and a knee-jerk guilt kicked in when I put myself first. I'd joked for years that if my family began to call me selfish, I'd know I'd made progress. It was normal for me to question my own motivations, while others got a pass. Original imprints operated beneath my awareness, and I'd spent years digging, bringing patterns to light, in the ongoing emotional work that offered no place to land.

One day in my twenties, I rode in an elevator with a bunch of businessmen and had the thought, *One of these men is wearing my favorite men's cologne.* Then I knew it was the three-martini lunch wafting from their pores, strong on their boozy breath, that I was inhaling—a smell that repelled me but drew me in, reminiscent of early kisses goodnight.

I lived with mixed feelings and drained each to essence, strained them through a mesh of forgiveness, until I became ready to nourish myself. Killing off the people-pleaser was a catalyst for tapping the wellspring of my broader birthright. I remembered how to wear myself more loosely—to accept and to risk. And it was then that I celebrated the man my father had made of himself, and felt his enthusiasms within my own passions, and experienced gratitude for it all.

Mother was unaware that Dad had written an outline of his life leading up to their divorce, in which he described the infidelity she had suspected. Now that she knew about it, she asked me to send her a copy. I did, and I called her a week later. We talked as Carol styled her hair. Mom had never openly criticized Dad, though her bitterness was blatant, but now she let loose.

"I feel liberated," she said. "I've always felt guilty for breaking up the marriage and making you girls live apart from your father. I thought maybe I'd failed to appreciate this great guy everyone loved so much. Now I know I should have left the son of a bitch sooner."

"The truth shall set you free," I said.

Thank You
San Miguel de Allende,
Audubon, Arthur Murray,
and Vagabundos ~
for making the last chapter
of my father's life one of
adventure, beauty, and
~ celebration ~

Jack Gray
Architect · pilot · Sculptor
died at home with
his family July 6, 2010

Thank You San Miguel de Allende
Photo credit: Carol Gray

Dad's Memorial Cruise

*B*osco, our butler from Bombay, came with the penthouse state-room. He was regal—more royal than servant, so dignified was his bearing, so focused and still was his gaze. He fixed me with his dark eyes and I imagined a third, completing the hypnotic triangle. Yohosame and I were on our best behavior—and were doubly smitten when we learned Bosco had a twin who worked on another cruise line. The twins had awakened one day earlier to see each other's ship docked close—their paths crisscrossing before they finally connected.

The lounge on the top deck at the ship's prow had something for everyone. There was High Tea at four each afternoon, with a string quartet set up on the dance floor to play. At five, waiters stripped the tables and stepped up the music for cocktail hour. Late in the evening I was represented by my son, who filled me in on the disco action over cappuccino and breakfast. He took to the dance floor like his grandfather, whose black-and-white spectators he wore, but with a style all his own. I was so proud of the way he interacted with the international travelers and the staff.

Cruising wasn't at all what I anticipated. The décor was tasteful, not glitzy, with beautifully appointed common rooms and a casual atmosphere. The passengers were not cliquish as I expected, but rather receptive to exchanges that made us feel connected. Everyone was charged with the excitement of travel.

At forty-two, Yohosame may have been our youngest passenger, but he didn't mind. He shared his stunning photography at the end of each day, and we gave him the job of recording the trip for us all. He even had a discreet flirtation with a Danish blonde at the reception desk.

We met Robert from the UK, whose job it was to train and polish the staff's hospitality. He was charming and charismatic—just the man for the job. Robert confided, to Yohosame's delight, that he was on a first-name basis with rock stars and royalty. They formed a bond, and spent hours discussing world religion and current events. Yohosame shared the story of his conversion to Islam with him.

Robert was grooming Bosco for a brilliant career at the highest levels of service. But one day Bosco didn't bring breakfast. His replacement introduced himself and explained: both twins had emergency leave, as their father was dying—waiting for an organ transplant and running out of time. The loss of the father echoed throughout our memorial voyage, and memories of Dad flowed.

Livorno (Port City for Florence and Tuscany)

We docked in Livorno on a Monday when Florence's museums were closed and boarded a bus for the rain-washed Tuscan countryside. Slender cypress trees marched across a landscape of red poppy fields, lemon groves, and silver olive orchards, to the medieval fortress city, Lucca. Inside massive red brick walls was an open square with a Romanesque cathedral at its center. Eyes scanned upward past five tiers of ornately carved columns to a delicate rose window topped by a gabled roof. Carol and our friend settled there, while Yohosame and I circled the square and moved beyond.

It was dark in the heart of Lucca, a spiraling labyrinth of narrow, glistening lanes. The streetlamps were filigreed ironwork: winged dragons held lanterns in their claws. Buildings stood two and three stories high with arched brick doorways. Wheels of sun-dried tomatoes, wreaths of peppers, and baskets of pasta were displayed in ground-floor shop windows. It was timeless within the ancient protective walls. Yohosame and I walked the curved lanes in silence, cloistered within our thoughts, still-tender feelings emerging from their sheath of shock. It had been four months since Dad had died. It was a solace to wander in the gray light together, separate from the others for a while.

Our lane opened onto another square, and we merged with a current of young men and women dressed in black, wearing scribbled wigs in crayon colors—blue, yellow, and red fright wigs made of thick yarn. The women wore rainbow-striped leggings, and the young men carried open umbrellas that matched their hair.

We were surrounded by costumed youth. A sword-carrying swashbuckler strode by, topped by a skull-and-crossbones hat with plumes and an open shirt with voluminous sleeves. A British Parliamentarian in a velvet waistcoat, powdered wig, knickers, and buckled shoes strolled among samurais, Dutch girls in clogs, and corseted wenches strutting in ruffled lace miniskirts, over-the-knee stockings and high heels. Eighteenth- century ladies waltzed by in floor-length gowns, lace collars and gloves. It was an Italian comic book convention—spontaneous street theatre. I picked a bench and watched Yohosame photograph the characters, frozen in grand gestures.

The tableau took place in front of a multistoried white hotel, its green window shutters and flowerboxes planted red, completing the colors of the Italian flag—and Mexico's. The two countries share the three vertical stripes of green, white, and red, though Italy's is absent the central Mexican emblem, the eagle atop a cactus, a serpent gripped in its bloody beak.

Capri

The return to Capri was bittersweet for Carol and me after the idyllic time we spent there with Dad. Cats lazed on the sunny dock. The cable car took us to Capri town, where stores were packed up for winter. It was a first-time delight for Yohosame, that island of blue grottoes. We rode the lift to the top of the island, passing over white marble plots. Raised and planted flower beds covered graves, the grass studded with scalloped crosses. Statuary kept vigil. The circular view from the top quieted all conversation.

Back on the ship, we befriended another pair of sisters traveling with their parents. The father was ailing and walked with difficulty, unable to do much that was offered. But the cruise was his idea, his way of making time memorable. He wore a cowboy hat, walking canes, and a grave expression. His daughters adored him—but bore more complicated feelings toward each other. Each day I imagined how different the trip would have been with Dad, how we would have visited wineries that required little walking, how I would have been watchful, and how, in rough seas after a few glasses of wine, although we would've laughed more, I would have worried.

The tugboats coaxed us out of our berth and bobbed like toys alongside the ship's great length. A pod of porpoises swam parallel—fins cresting among the ferries, fishing trawlers, and cruise ships in the busy harbor.

Under a slim crescent that cupped the full shadow of the moon, we maneuvered onto open waters and hit our churning stride. Away from land, rocked by wind and waves, the sky was pocked with stars so chunky they could have been Chinese lanterns. The harbor soon became a memory—a string of lights that receded in the distance. We were a wedge cleaving the surface of the sea. Frothy arcs of spray marbled indigo water. I stared into the swirling patterns from my eighth-floor veranda and thought of the blue planet as photographed from space. In our wake, a carpet of stars floated upon the inky sea, and made a funnel of nightlight.

In the predawn dim we passed another cruise ship, this one draped with lights like a Christmas tree. The low morning clouds made hills on the horizon. A brilliant sun rose and sank, and blue sky again became black. Waxing and waning, we moved through our time, as our cells cycled through growth and decline. Another sun set fire to the smoke gray clouds—another day.

I loved the cracked-open sense that travel brought—this identification with all I saw. I was an integral part of a rapidly changing world, at ease with myself and memories of my father. Life might eclipse the peace I felt at sea, but I could choose to be porous, let the radiance stream through me, rest in myself, and simply be.

Five

Matriarch

⌇

The truth shall set you free, but not until it's done with you.

David Foster Wallace

From right: Kitty Gray, Wayne Chilton, Carol Gray, Jim Chilton, Terry Gray

photo credit: Marie Burke

One

The last thing Mother said to me before I left her house in Lake Havasu City, Arizona—after a visit spent avoiding eye contact, intensity, and intimacy—was, "If I don't see you again, I want you to know you have been the most exciting thing in my life."

We shared a one-armed hug, our bodies angled away from each other, as if we stood before an invisible audience. I saw her profile out of the corner of my eye as she spoke.

"I haven't always liked it," she said. "Sometimes I haven't liked it at all, but I have to admit, in ninety years of living, you've been the most exciting thing."

"Thank you, Mother, that's, well I'm not sure what that is, but thank you. I love you."

I found them bizarre, these maternal parting words—bizarre, but honest—and, as I learned to do in adulthood, I appreciated her as she was, and took what I could get.

A few months later a cardiologist told Mother she'd had a recent heart attack, a big one. She was certain it was the week Carol rounded up her family and we all converged on Lake Havasu. It had been hectic but Mother had held up, and on the last day she'd suggested we take the boat to the casino on the California shore. When we returned we told her to wait while we went for the car. Instead we found her pale and panting at the top of the steep hill.

In December she couldn't breathe, was rushed to the hospital with congestive heart failure, her lungs filled with fluid. An angioplasty was ruled out as her kidneys wouldn't accommodate surgery. She would go home to hospice care—nothing more to do. I called her hospital room, and she answered on the second ring, her voice strong. She sounded excited, like a teenage girl about to leave on a trip. It was I who was leaving for the beach the next day.

"If I die, you'll find out when you get home," she said.

"No, Mom, Carol can reach me."

"Why should she bother you? You'd shed a few tears and feel a little guilty."

"Why should I feel guilty?" I asked.

"Because I programmed you that way, and I'm good at it."

We laughed as we did on the phone. In person we didn't see the humor, the stern mirror of our faces an uncomfortable reflection. But on the phone, with only our disembodied, identical voice, it was easy to make light of life. I phoned on Sundays to make her laugh.

"I'm a different person with everyone," she said.

"I understand. I'm a double Gemini. Just so you keep it straight within yourself," I said.

"I can always be myself with you."

"That's good, Mom. Most people hide their dark thoughts—they're always on their best behavior. But it's just the mind churning, and I say, 'Let it roll.'"

"And that's a relief," she said, sounding winded, like she needed to catch her breath in silence. As if she wanted to shift her attention to the solitary journey ahead.

"We'd better stop now, Mother. I'll be talking to you soon."

"Not too soon. You're not going to die soon," she said.

"Oh Mom, you'll be back way before I go."

Mother's belief in reincarnation was unshakeable. When I was a young girl she had introduced me to astrology, numerology, and the idea of past and future lives. When the smoke-detector alarm sounded on the one-year anniversary of her fifth husband's death, she considered it proof. Before he died, she had instructed Don to find a way to contact her: "You're smart. You'll figure out how to let me know." Each morning of their twenty-six year marriage, she gave Don a to-do list: his last task was to communicate from the dead.

Now she promised to haunt her children in a rotating cycle. "Look out then," was how she put it.

"But if I'm coming right back, who will I want as parents?" she said.

We exhausted the possibilities in our usual spirit of irreverence. Mother's father had been a proud racist, and most of her progeny of child-bearing age were black. She considered her great-granddaughter, the tattoo artist, who looked like Heidi of the Alps with a body covered in ink, and my son, the bachelor musician.

"Remember when that psychic told me Debbie would come back as Yohosame's child?" I asked.

"A long time ago, but be serious. Who would I choose?" She cycled the conversation back to herself.

"I have no idea. Perhaps it's time to swim in another gene pool."

"Okay, darling, that's enough," she said, tired again now, with even more to contemplate.

"All right, Mother. I'll be seeing you. Fare thee well."

I returned from the beach and packed a suitcase for Guatemala, my next planned trip, but I got the flu and went to bed. I called Lake Havasu for daily reports from my sister, Carol, and my half-brother, Wayne, mother's late-in-life child, born as I plotted my escape. Any minute, they said. There was no time left for me to come.

I said I didn't need to see her again, and I shared her final words last fall and our light-hearted closure by telephone when she was in the hospital. Wayne said whatever I did was okay, no judgment. Yohosame told me everyone was exhausted. Carol commuted on weekends from Palm Springs, where she worked as a hairdresser, and Wayne and his wife, Jane, were using up their vacation time and not sleeping. He encouraged me to come, but with an improved attitude—because I missed her already, not to avoid future guilt. Wayne said Mother was afraid and fighting it. Carol then insisted I come, even if just for an hour, and gave me flight information for the following day. Mother was angry I wasn't there, she said, and refused the phone when I asked to speak with her. Finally I got her answering machine, and talked to it instead.

"Don't be afraid, Mom. Everything will be all right. I can't stand to think of you frightened."

She picked up. "Hello?"

"There you are. How are you, Mom?"

"Pretty good," her voice floated, detached.

"I have the flu, but I'll be there soon."

"Oh, that's convenient. Better hurry," she said.

"I hope you're not angry. Do you remember our telephone conversation when you were in the hospital?"

"Somewhat."

"I'll be there soon."

I got out of bed, grabbed the suitcase for Guatemala, and flew to Las Vegas. Yohosame met me and we drove to Lake Havasu City, Arizona, the unlikely home of the London Bridge. Bob McCulloch, a tool company magnate Dad and I used to ski with, had a vision to transform arid desert into a recreational destination. England advertised the London Bridge for sale as it was sinking into the Thames. McCulloch bought it, carved a channel in the isthmus, leaving an arched land bridge across it, on top of which he reassembled the London Bridge, stone by numbered stone. He scooped it out, dammed up the Colorado River to create a 19,000 acre lake, and called his publicist. Worthless parcels became desirable, and plots sold like crazy. Mother and Don bought one. Mother thought Havasu was heaven, like Palm Springs before overdevelopment.

A town with an identity crisis developed, home to antique stores, gun dealers, retirees, motorcycle and vintage car rallies, and girls gone wild. Tourists drove over, walked across, and sailed under the London Bridge, pointing out howitzer scars from World War II as they cruised around the island in boxy cocktail barges or sleek, garish, racing boats.

Yohosame and I checked into the Heat Hotel in the middle of the night, and stood on the terrace, the bridge draped in lights. Flags flapped against their tethers in a light breeze, and punctured the silence with a metallic whipping sound.

Two

I waited on the L-shaped couch in Mother's living room as hospice caregivers guided her back to bed. She looked rumpled and weak pushing an aluminum walker with chartreuse tennis balls for feet. She took miniscule, halting steps, with an oxygen tank in tow. When she was resettled in bed, I approached and dropped to one knee. I laid my arms on top of the cotton bedspread, stopping short of touching her, and tried for a serene smile.

"Hello Mother."

Glasses lowered, she looked down her patrician nose at me. Carol and I inherited Dad's nose with the knobs on the end, but mother's was especially fine. Her cool, hazel eyes squinted and glared at me "You've aged as much as I have," she said.

Accused, I went for self-defense, and caved in to obsequiousness. "Well, you know, Mother, it's been a stressful time for everyone, and I had the flu, but now I'm here. I'm so glad to be here. Are you glad I'm here?"

"You should have come sooner," she said, and turned her head away. I reached out and ran my hand over one of her tightly folded arms.

"Your hands are cold," she said, "don't touch me. And stop hovering."

↩

After September 11, 2001, I decided to live near my mother for half the year. I found a place on the island, on the water, centered in a cove that faced undeveloped California shoreline. A path off the deck disappeared into tamarisk trees that reminded me of the fort Carol and I had when we were children. I remembered it each time I walked to the shore to paddle my kayak across the lake.

In November, when the weather cooled in New Mexico, I packed the car and headed west on Highway 40, dividing my time between Santa Fe and Lake Havasu. The day's drive ended in a jog south through desert scrub, the road lined with a low screen of lavender mountains that fanned out behind Lake Havasu. The sun set as I crossed the London Bridge to open my place for winter.

My mother and I shared a love of rocks and seashells, and had gasp fests when we displayed new jewelry to one another. We signed up for beading classes, and when she had the energy we went to lunches, plays, and movies. I cooked and invited Mother, my brother Wayne, and his wife Jane for meals on my deck. In May, the desert heat spiked and hinted at an inferno to come. I said good-bye and returned to a Santa Fe monsoon summer and fall. I followed the sun, and avoided its more scorching rays, and spent half the year close to my mother.

One night Mom called to say she was stuck in the bath tub; luckily, her princess phone was at hand. I rushed over and rocked and rolled her until she got her legs under her, and then maneuvered her up and over the rim of the sunken pink Jacuzzi tub. Slumped on its edge, side by side, we giggled and got our breath back. The hot baths Mom lived for, along with sunbathing, were finished. It was time to speak of future needs.

She had forgiven Don for dying ahead of schedule. Her fifth husband was ten years her junior and she had assumed he'd be there for her at the end. But Don was diagnosed with lung cancer instead, and was checked into the VA hospital in Tucson with months to live. After Don died, she wanted husband number six. Instead she broke her ankle, and was forced to stop—forced to feel.

Mother, like others of her generation, had a horror of institutionalized care. She wanted to stay home and die in her own bed. When

I hired a contractor to remodel my place, Mother liked his work and decided to add an apartment for herself onto her home. She then offered Wayne and Jane the adjoining house. They made an arrangement—our mother would die at home.

⮌

Now we tended to her cravings, tried to please her with special pillows, fresh juices, and back rubs, and calmed the hyper-vigilant Chihuahua, Sweetie Pie, that I'd bought for Mother's eighty-fifth birthday when she no longer wanted to get out of bed. Sweetie Pie was an over-stimulated companion who gave Mom another five good years. No one approached her without triggering Sweetie Pie's brain-splitting, frenetic barking. Mom watched me keep busy, feed and water the dog, arrange flowers, empty and fill things around her bed.

"Are you still going for my—" Her voice was querulous, her face worldly-wise and full of weary incredulity. "Approval?" we said in unison, both of us nodding.

"Yes," I said. "Pathetic, isn't it? But I'm so glad I made it, Mom. Do you realize no one expected you to still be here? You were ready to go and then you changed your mind."

"Yes, I know I did." She smoothed the blue-and-white floral bed quilt that covered her up to her chin.

Extended family had visited one by one before I arrived. Mother had held court, handed over cash, jewelry, and practical advice, and moved her teenage great-grandson to tears. Death had been imminent. Then she'd pulled back and stalled.

Now her children surrounded her and absorbed her petulance. Her anger was easier for me than her fear—I had always felt protective. I rose from the blue recliner and moved closer. She lay against pillows with ruffled lace edging, surrounded by her cat collection. On the wall behind her bed were framed posters of giddy cartoon felines and reproductions of painted cats in repose. Shelves full of cats lined the walls—glass cats, crystal cats, sleek metallic cats. Stuffed cats sat on countertops, perched on the huge flat- screen TV, the dresser, the corner desk with her computer. Tails dangled and curled, a grumpy

Garfield winked from a corner of the room. Sweetie Pie quivered at mother's side.

"Are you no longer excited about what comes next, Mother?"

"It wasn't what I expected," she said, frowning. "It was dark, and there was *NOTHING* there."

Three

*O*n the airplane I had pictured Yohosame and I sitting on either side of Mother's bed, meditating and massaging her hands for an intimate loosening of the mortal coil. There was one such moment before Mother slid into paranoia. She turned off the television and closed her eyes. Yohosame and I joined hands across her bed and touched Mother with our other hand, completing a circuit. The dog remained quiet, and the rare moment stretched.

Later I asked her, "Do you remember going on that silent retreat with me?" She nodded, wary, as I tried to put a friendly face on nothingness.

⌐

Mother had surprised me that year with her willingness, her interest in my life. I'd met the spiritual teacher named Gangaji several years prior. She had a teaching style that was more confirmation than instruction, and she never held herself above or apart from the group, as most given guru status do. In the clarity of her presence, I'd opened, and had reconnected with the energy field of pure being I'd discovered in the sixties, and had experienced since—but it was elusive and refused to be grasped. I'd been a serious seeker, who, when my guard was down, had experienced the truth. And in a very real way I knew my search was the last barrier to realization.

The truth seemed fleeting, but it was actually my attention that was fickle. The truth had been present all along—independent of, but not separate from, all circumstance, in the only place it could be found: within myself in each present moment.

We drove to Santa Barbara and spent a silent week with Gangaji and more than two hundred other attendees we soon recognized, for beneath the veneer of learned attitudes, identifications, and behaviors, it was easy to see ourselves in each other. Mother and I analyzed our belief systems and accepted the essential nothingness revealed under direct investigation. We grew lighter as the week went on, and by the end of the retreat Mother was embraced by everyone, caught up in a love she couldn't invalidate. The powerful week gave us new tools we needed as soon as we were in my car heading back to Palm Springs. Our instructions upon leaving had been: stop; tell the truth; be still.

I pulled over onto the highway's shoulder and turned off the engine. Mom and I closed our eyes and faced the windshield. After a pause, we turned our upper bodies toward each other, and, belted in, we tried the truth and found it worked. At home, Carol and Wayne admitted something was different about Mother—she was happy.

⤸

"Well, Mother, isn't NOTHING preferable to burning hells and hierarchies of heavens?" I asked the black sheep of a devout Catholic family.

"Maybe, but it was so damned dark. It just wasn't what I expected," she said.

"Can you say that before you let go? Isn't *that* when you'll find out whether it's what you're hoping for? Remember after Grandpa died, and you had that dream where he encouraged you to join him? He said 'It's like taking off a sweater,' and he grabbed his pullover at the bottom and lifted it over his head, free of the discarded body that lay in a heap of fabric on the floor. 'There's nothing to it,' he said."

"I remember," she said. "I wasn't ready then, and I'm not ready now."

I stopped cajoling.

Our role reversal had begun early when mother suggested we live as sisters for our new life in Palm Springs, and it continued until the end. I had known I was ill-equipped to parent anyone at the age of seven, but I thought someone had to step up, and I tried—and I had continued to try.

∽

In 1990, I took Mother and Yohosame to Tahiti. My second husband had died earlier that year, and Yohosame had fallen rock-climbing six months later. He was recovering from this, his fourth teenage accident—his sixth surgery. We unpacked at Hotel Bora Bora in a thatch-roofed bungalow on stilts over the water.

"You must have been my mother in a past life," Mother said, counting out hangers. "I've learned a lot from you."

"Forget reincarnation, Mom. What about this life?" I said.

The bungalow had a deck surrounded by aquamarine water and matching sky. Mother sunbathed and read while Yohosame and I backed down the wooden steps in flippers, masks, and snorkels, and dipped at the edge of a coral reef. Schools of tiny, electric-blue fish nibbled. Eels poked out of their caves and retreated. Striped, polka-dotted, and color-blocked fish shimmied past in profusion. Stingrays coasted across the white sand bottom, and big shapes brushed by.

Chamber quartets played evening concerts before we were served French cuisine. There were no words for hunger or crime in the Tahitian language—nothing to covet, no scarcity, no front doors. Tahitians lived open-air lives.

It took time to slow to the island pace. We were accustomed to worrying, to occupying imaginary past and future events. We clung to concerns, attached to cameras recording what we couldn't yet experience—too busy changing clothes, money, and minds. Paradise softened us like pumice, a little each day.

Currents from a distant hurricane cancelled the shark-feeding expedition we'd planned, but Yohosame checked the activity board each morning and on our last day it was a go. We joined a boatload of tourists in tropical prints and neoprene and suited up, excited and nervous. Our guide, a beaming local, steered the wooden skiff to the outer reef that circled Bora Bora. He cut the motor, dropped anchor, and briefed us: "It's Pavlovian," he said. "You'll be safe as long as you stay on this side of the yellow cord. The sharks feed over there." He pointed with a straight arm away from the boat. "Line up here on this side of the cord."

He hooked one end onto a boat cleat, and stretched the coiled yellow cord into a line. He clipped the other end to a steel ring in the reef below the waterline. We dogpaddled up to the cord and lowered our masks into the water. Sharks angled into view, tails whipping back and forth. Jaws snapped at, shook, and ravaged fish flesh. We were their awkward audience, doubled over the yellow cord, pushed by the current from behind. We held our position but the current was strong. The cord bowed out close to the sharks in the middle. We strained against it, trying not to kick and cause a commotion.

Then the taut yellow cord snapped free, and we flew into the sharks, flailing, and kicking. Our masks muffled screams, as we headed for the boat, frantic. There were no casualties, just further proof that we were the sea's least graceful swimmers.

⌣

There was a panel in the floor of our bungalow that opened for night viewing. I lifted the glass and dropped a hardboiled egg I'd saved from lunch. A fuchsia-and-black-spotted eel caught it in its jaws before it landed. We were three generations hunched over the opening each night as if it were television.

Yohosame improved. Freed from months of convalescence, he bicycled around the island, swam and strengthened. Mother and I wandered, bought souvenirs at a shack in the forest, a boutique with a palm frond roof and walls, and a welcoming, open doorway.

"What was the name of that store?" Mom asked as we left and followed the crude path through the trees back to the shore.

"Did it have a name? I don't know, Mom, why?"

"Why? Well, because I want to know, that's why. And there's nothing printed on this bag."

"Nothing printed on your bag? You're lucky rats haven't chewed holes in it." I chuckled at her concern, her human need to create friction in paradise. But there was no shrugging it off. Mother clung to her point of view, more and more self-righteous about the sins of the shop owner. And I felt responsible. It didn't make sense, and my free-floating guilt made me prey to manipulation. I held out as long as I could before eventually unraveling into a familiar, reflexive crying jag. I craved Mother's approval and felt wounded when her criticism of everything in her line of sight included me.

"Oh God, Mom," I said, "I've been trying to make you happy my whole life, so you'd be nicer. And now I've brought you to Tahiti and you're complaining about something like that?"

Mother gripped my shoulders and looked into my eyes. "Honey, I've always thought you were perfect. This is just the way I am."

And I got it. The moment of clarity broke my trance, my self-defeating collusion. I was liberated and grateful.

By the end of the trip Mother was eager to separate from us, uncomfortable with Yohosame's near-nude yoga sessions and tired of French cuisine. Besides, there were eels amongst the colorful fish, spiny poisonous things disguised as coral, aspects of life to guard against, parts of oneself to encapsulate, and good reasons to worry. Carol picked her up in Los Angeles and drove her home to Palm Springs as she rehashed and trashed the trip.

Years later, however, Mother said Tahiti seemed like a lovely dream. She asked me in a letter what I thought about recurring dreams, flirting with a sequel. In this way we redesigned our memories, and reworked our lives—filling photo albums with smiling faces taken on good days.

⌐

Mother was in no pain, just a very bad mood. Stoic and sober, as always, she became difficult, and resented hospice care, refused to bathe. The hospice brochure said "People die as they lived," and I thought, *Uh oh*. Surrender was simply not one of my mother's survival skills—holding on was her specialty. Mom squeezed so expertly she made diamonds with her fists.

She held the remote, all she now controlled, and rotated through Fox News, *The Price is Right*, Hollywood gossip, and *Judge Judy*. Angry, she settled on snow, cranked up the volume, and sent us a message.

Four

Mother looked at us with suspicion, had us taste her food first, and drank only from sealed bottles. Hospice introduced haloperidol in liquid form—drops under her tongue she couldn't refuse. The drug helped us all. Wayne held her hand.

"You can trust me," he said. "You can refuse your other meds if you want to, but these drops keep you from being mean. Open your mouth." For Wayne, she was a baby bird receiving, eyes closed, mouth open, but her jaws clamped tight for the rest of us.

"You trust me, don't you, Grandma?" Yohosame asked.

"No."

"You used to trust me. Didn't you?"

"Not really, no."

I encouraged her to take the rest of her medications despite her wish for everything to stop, explaining that they wouldn't prolong her life, but could improve what remained.

"They may keep you from having another painful heart attack, Mother," I said, offering a tiny white dish of primary-colored pills—rounds, cylinders, and triangles she needed applesauce to swallow.

"How do YOU know?" she said. "You've never had one. I'll take the pills if you'll leave me alone, FOREVER."

"I can't guarantee that," I said, setting the dish in front of her. She swallowed the pills.

We had shared quiet time in the past, during Mother's

convalescence from illness and routine maintenance, and we fared
pretty well. The difference now was that she would not recover.

‿

Mother had her second hip replaced in November of 2003, and I
moved in with her while she mended. We watched *The Sopranos* and
ate Italian takeout, and I swore in a thuggish accent.

"Hey Mambo, Mambo Italiano," I sang as I sailed into her room
with something Italian on a tray. The name, Mambo, stuck, and I
used it any time I wanted to lighten the mood. She made it through
the painful recovery in good humor, and had just become ambulatory
and ready to be alone when I got the crushing news: my stepmother,
Casey, and Yusuf—George—both dead the same day.

Dad called about Casey first, and I booked flights to Carmel to be
with him, returning midweek to drive Mother to doctor's appoint-
ments. Yohosame's half-sister, Sadaf, called next. Yusuf had had a
heart attack in Asilah, and she needed to find Yohosame. I called
him, and he flew with his sisters to Morocco to bury their father.

I flew into Monterey and got a ride to the house in neighboring
Carmel. It was late when I pulled my suitcase up the footpath between
tasteful condos and immaculate landscaping. I saw Dad through the
window, a fire making patterns on the wall behind him. He sat at
the dining room table with old friends. They were loose, laughing
and crying, empty glasses in front of them. I let myself in to hugs all
around, and we resettled, the evening unwinding. The couple would
return in the morning. He and Dad would watch the game while she
and I went through Casey's closets. They rose to leave, and Dad and I
followed them to the door.

"We'll be good," he said, grinning back at me. He winked and
mugged as if we'd get it on now that Casey was gone.

"Oh Dad," I said.

"Oh Jack," the wife said, giving him a playful punch in the shoulder. She shook her head at him and gave me a look that said, "Boys
will be boys. What-are-you-going-to-do?"

Dad was in the bag, reeling from wine and loss.

We awoke early and Dad described his dream as we put break-fast on a tray and carried it to his walnut table. In his sleep he had devised a plan for rescue modules and temporary housing, fleshed out in every detail. He described how many would fit on an aircraft carrier—how they could be dropped in fours and assembled onsite anywhere. His creativity had its own momentum; his life lurched forward.

Our friends returned and spent the day. The guys watched golf for hours, while the wife and I sorted through stuff. Casey's pockets held wads of Kleenex and half-smoked packs of Benson & Hedges. We cried into the second-hand Kleenex and started smoking as we divided furs, suits, and caftans. In the afternoon Dad lowered the attic's retractable stairs, climbed up, and dropped silk gowns onto the bed. Fabrics unfurled and fell through the air, landing in soft, slippery heaps.

The Neptune Society had picked up Casey's worn out body and scattered her ashes without ceremony and without friends, family, or faith, as she and Dad had both wished. Stacked on Casey's side of the bed were scarves and jewelry, evening bags, and turbans—keepsakes I sent to loved ones.

It was easy to forget the nature of grief between losses—to forget the fatigue paired with insomnia that accompanies a hollowed-out heart, that punched-through-the-chest, emptied-out sensation. Scraps of handwriting became rare manuscripts; scraps of memory brought me to my knees.

A month or two later, my niece, Indra, and I drove to Carmel to see Dad. We walked the dog on the beach, visited the Circle Theatre, and sat on Casey's memorial bench, the bench Dad built with the engraved plaque.

Dad showed me instructions for his plaque, to be added when the time came. We stopped at the bank to put my name on his account. Alone for the first time in sixty years—the ten with Mother that segued into fifty with Casey—Dad told me he was dating.

Indra and I left carrying Dad's alabaster sculptures, and as we drove to Palm Springs we made a plan to memorialize Casey. Alvin Ailey's dance troupe was performing at McCallum Theatre—so we wrapped ourselves in Casey's style and promenaded, arm in arm, past the columns and fountains, to the entrance of the stark contemporary façade. Through the cavernous, glass-encased lobby, we strolled, drawing the attention of frail old ladies and dapper gentlemen.

"Oh, my, are those vintage?" they swooned, carried back to their less harried, more glamorous time.

⤺

Wayne stood beside me at the foot of mother's bed, ready to leave for work.

"What *ARE* you dressed for?" Mother asked me. Wayne gave me a once-over, met my eyes, and looked as confused and beaten down as I did. It was cold in the early morning. I wore pants, shoes and socks, and plain, layered sweaters in a neutral gray and black palette.

"Guatemala, where I hoped to avoid a mugging."

Sometimes she just gave me her evil eye, and said nothing. Mom's laser vision was trained to home in on imperfection. She stared until I squirmed, until I asked, "What are you thinking?"

"You know," she said, sullen.

"That I look my age?" I didn't get it, and I never would.

"Something like that. Why don't you do something with yourself?" she said, exasperated.

While she slept through the quiet mornings, I folded, boxed, and labeled her clothes. Shoes were stuck to the painted wood shelves—"Minnie Mouse" shoes, I called the little bowed flats. Dozens of handbags, all of which had waited years to be carried out the door, were lined up against the wall. On Monday, I opened the closet to finish my task and everything was back on hangers. Unboxed shoes and bags again lined the shelves. Carol wasn't ready. I felt useless and erased.

Mother switched to black-and-white classic films like *Whatever Happened to Baby Jane?* She identified with Joan Crawford, and called me Baby Jane for days. The next day, Spencer Tracy made a case for evolution as Mother plucked at the air, ducked from free-floating blobs of color, found invisible morsels in the seams of her bedding, and popped them into her mouth. I watched her sleep. Her hands moved with a plan of their own, pulling at her nightgown and her bedding, sometimes lifted and busy in the air. It was reminiscent of the week before Dad died when his hands sewed. The hospice brochure said everyone did it.

Mother waited for rare moments when she was alone to get out of bed and fall on the floor. Her legs collapsed under her diminished weight, and she was too weak to get up again. We begged her to let us help her. Wayne, Jane, Yohosame, and I met in the garage, with a baby monitor on the shelf by the phone. Wayne's wife, Jane, collected antique cow memorabilia, and we listened for the clang of the cowbell on Mother's bedside table.

"Clang, CLANG, CLANG!" We rushed to Mother's room. If she was on the floor, the guys lifted her onto the bed. Jane stretched a draw-sheet under her so that, with one of us standing on either side, we could reposition her and try to make her comfortable. Lucid moments punctuated fuzzy stretches and confused sleep. Her movements were jerky—spasms shook her awake.

I watched her when her guard was down, while she slept. I leaned in close, well within her comfort zone. She stirred, opened her eyes, and gave me a soft, rueful smile, appreciating the irony.

"I'm so busy acting out my dreams I can't get to sleep," she said.

A perfect, poignant metaphor—brilliant, I thought, loving her, my sad, tough, magnetic mother. She asked for favorite foods, more curious than hungry, and pushed them away.

"Nothing tastes like I remember it. Nothing is the same."

Wayne kissed her forehead, and left for a nap on the couch.

"He's so sweet," I said when he left her room.

"Too sweet," she said. "In this family the men are weak, and the women are worthless."

"No, Mom, remember, the men are sweet and the women are strong," I said, reminding her of her usual conclusion. We'd had this conversation many times before.

"You're not strong this month," she said.

I'd had three versions of the flu that month, unusual for me. I suspected it was a personal failing, and Mother was convinced.

"It's stress," I said.

"Stress, you think you've got stress? Anyway, that's when you show your grit," she said.

"True, but we're all showing cracks in our grit. Wayne hasn't slept in a long time," I said.

"I guess he loves me," she said. "I thought he was acting."

"You're the actress, Mother. And, for what it's worth, we all love you."

Five

*H*ospice workers scheduled visits, replaced meds, and declared our family was doing well. No one fought; we supported each other, and focused upon what we each could contribute. Hospice ignored the sweet smoke coming from the back garage, the tobacco and alcohol, as we moved through the process in relays like marathon runners. My strong-willed mother did battle with her fate. I told Wayne that if she lingered long we'd need help, and maybe I could pay for it. He made an immediate call to Beth, the hospice social worker, and we met in private later that same day.

I told Beth that Mother hated the sight of my un-dyed hair, my un-lifted face. Because I was upset, I was slow to notice Beth wore Birkenstocks and no makeup, and I doubted she'd ever considered plastic surgery. She smiled, including me in her compassionate embrace of the world, and let me vent. I told her Dad had died a year and a half earlier, and that he and Mother were both narcissists. I told her I knew how to take care of myself—that I worried about Wayne, Jane, and Carol. She explained that paid care was available, though very expensive—"but," she said, "Wayne and Jane need to do this for your mother." It was the agreement they'd struck years ago. Mother would die at home, and Wayne and Jane would inherit the house.

"It was Carol who insisted I come," I said. "I'm glad to be here, but if it goes on for months, not weeks, I may have to go." We sat at

Mother's dining room table, an army of pill bottles between us like chess pieces.

"Carol needs to orchestrate," Beth said. Beth had everyone's number, and now she had mine.

We sat vigil, tried not to worry about how long it might last, or if we'd fall apart under the pressure. Wayne and Jane slept little and ran through their vacation time. Wayne was, for the first time, openly emotional, letting his feelings flow.

"I had you all in little boxes, and you're not in those little boxes anymore," he said, enclosing me in one of his world-class hugs. We shared a natural affinity, even though Wayne was fifteen years younger, born as I wriggled free from home.

∽

I went north to San Francisco as a young woman with what I considered to be perfect timing. But a period of estrangement from Mother ensued, in which she said she cried every day. I considered the sixties to have been a lifesaving detour, and she saw them as a serious setback. Dad bragged to friends that I had emerged unscathed. Mom considered me hampered by magical thinking, and by my absurd, egalitarian worldview.

After the sixties imploded and I returned to Palm Springs with a baby, a duffel bag full of East Indian textiles, and a welfare habit to kick, Mother bought me a black skirt and white blouse, and offered to babysit while I worked as a cocktail waitress, the job I'd judged her for having when I was in high school. I worked while Yohosame wound down and slept, and I picked up his inert body at 2:00 a.m. and drove to our rented apartment. I had definite ideas about how I wanted to raise my son, uncontaminated by sugar and television for the early years I hoped to control.

When I pulled into Mother's circular driveway, she flung open the front door and greeted Yohosame with outstretched arms, baby talk, and pockets full of candy. He strained to get out of the car, eager to be inside grandma's pleasure dome, where three televisions were set on three different stations making a thrilling background cacophony.

They had bonded early in the pool, when Yohosame was a delectable fat fish to be caught in a towel, wrapped up tight, and tickled in the sun.

Yohosame loved his grandmother for life, and I was glad. His paternal grandmother refused to meet him. Ann told George to call her back when we changed his name and, years later, despite several more grandchildren with unusual names, Ann said it was just too late. Yohosame and she never met.

I tried to catch the easy affection Yohosame felt for my mother, but old bones, gnawed to splinters, wouldn't stay buried. There were shards, and ghosts singing chorus to lay to rest along with Mother. One point protruded highest and sharpest: her core belief that, as family matriarch, she alone had authentic existence. She was the one, and everyone who followed was an extension of her. All the voices and images in my head—all the imagined transgressions—spun off this central pinwheel. And of course she refused to respect my child-rearing choices. She represented mainstream values, and I was a drop-out, returned from the fringe with responsibility I needed to share.

In the early 70's, when Carol and I were single mothers raising three children under the age of five, Mother made a long-range plan to move from Palm Springs to Lake Havasu. According to the terms of our parents' divorce, half of the house we'd grown up in belonged to mother, and half belonged to Carol and me. Dad had insisted. Mother asked us to sign off on our share of the house, and offered us five thousand dollars each. It was a blatant bad deal, but Carol and I preferred being pushovers to engaging in that fight, and said yes. Mother never thanked us or apologized. She took what she considered hers and shook her head, wondering how she raised two such gullible daughters. Later she told me, "You and your sister are such nice people; I can't believe you're mine."

Around that time the Cameron business manager asked me to sign off on any future interest in George's estate. He had never been more charming, and disingenuous. He asserted the benefit to me would be in knowing I would, at least hypothetically, be loved for myself. If I had nothing, there would be nothing to exploit.

Both requests insulted my intelligence, transparent in the extreme. In compliance, I let them both think they'd put one over on me, believing that if I fought back I would be like them—crass and calculating. George wasn't to blame. Letters arrived from Afghanistan in his spidery, even script—blue ink on pale blue parchment. I read them aloud to Yohosame before putting them away for safekeeping. It was my responsibility to raise our son.

﹏

Yohosame played an unusual, saucer-shaped hand pan musical instrument that attracted the hospice workers' attention on their way in and out of Mother's room. One caregiver said to Mother, "I'd have him sit in my room and play all day." Mother snorted, and Sweetie Pie yipped.

Yohosame had night duty with the baby monitor midweek, and he stayed with me at the hotel on weekends while Carol slept on Mother's couch. One night, he and I watched a movie with familiar characters. I pointed to the screen: "There's Carol, the caretaker, and that joker is your father. Jane is the biker chick dressed all in black."

"What," Yohosame asked, "are you talking about?"

"I'm talking about archetypes. It isn't literal—it's an exaggeration sometimes—but there's Grandpa," I said, pointing to the older man leering onscreen.

"That's what Grandma was doing before you arrived, before the haloperidol," he said. "I tried to describe it to you on the phone, but you didn't understand."

"Oh—well, I get it now," I said.

The social worker said if I understood Mother in her dementia then I was her psychic link. I thought perhaps I could've been her psychic link from Guatemala, or from anywhere. My presence comforted neither of us. She shared soft moments with Carol and Wayne, but never warmed up to me. I tolerated her snide comments, and watched her welcome my sister with warmth when she arrived.

Mother didn't fake it with me: she had always said she could be herself with me, and she was proving it now. I busied myself in the

RV garage, emptied drawers of fabric, fallow projects in permanent limbo. I bagged up stuffed animals and armloads of fake flowers. And I showed up for the daily critique of my appearance, and the one positive comment about my ability to accessorize: "You brought so little jewelry," she said. "You've worn the same pieces everyday, and yet you make it work with each outfit. It takes a knack."

"Thanks, Mom."

Six

At the end of life, for the first time in her life, Mother had a circle of female friends. She much preferred men, but there were fewer left. The women met in each other's homes and played games at the Senior Center, and on Mother's ninetieth birthday they faced 120-degree heat and showed up for lunch with gifts and tributes. Mother was moved, rose from her chair, grateful and expansive, and made a speech. Ninety had been her goal; she wanted to outlive Dad and Casey. She had bested Casey by a decade, and matched Dad.

I had helped her host parties and met her friends. When they asked what I did for a living that allowed me the freedom to come and go, Mother told them I retired at age fifteen, a joke she repeated with pride steeped in resentment. A perennial student, I'd made a career of attending classes and workshops. Mother's friends called. I answered and chatted while she shook her head, eyes wide, signaling she didn't want to talk.

"Hi Barbara, no, she can't talk. She's comfortable, but no calls or visitors. I'll tell her you called," I said. "No, I haven't been to the Bead Studio. Are you still making jewelry? Oh, that's great. No, I haven't worked in a while. Okay dear, yes, I will. Nice talking to you." I hung up and returned the phone to the bedside table.

"They're just hobbies, Terry, not work," Mother said.

"Maybe, Mom, but I'm sixty-seven. I have nothing to prove. I'm certain I could support myself with my ideas and my own two hands," I said.

"And how would you know that? You've gone from one thing to another your entire life. As soon as you're good at something you drop it—never staying with anything long enough to exploit it for money—just hobbies," she said and closed her eyes.

An inner voice rose in my defense. I silently regurgitated my IQ, the admiration I inspired in strangers, the recognition I had received as an artist and as a designer. I patted myself on the back for taking risks, for finding my way in the wider world, and for developing potentials.

"The writing is work," I said.

"You've never given me anything to read," she sniffed.

"Oh sure I have, remember? I sent the chapter with Dad driving drunk in Mexico with his reading glasses on, and you said I sure couldn't write funny."

Her forehead pleated in a fan of wrinkles. "Well you can write about me when I'm gone," she said—and, eyes squinted, voice like ice, "I-really-don't-care."

"Yes, Mother, that's how it feels."

⌒

After I moved to Mexico in 2006, I visited my mother once a year, as promised. During one such visit, Yohosame gave Mother his arm and walked her across the driveway, held the rental car door while she slid into the front passenger seat. I moved to the back. Yohosame was solicitous and enjoyed the role, took the wheel, and we headed for Mother's game of Mexican Train at the Senior Center. I leaned forward between the front seats.

"Mom, I've been taking a writing workshop. I'm writing stories about my childhood in Portuguese Bend," I said.

"Then you're writing about my life," she said. She lowered her visor and looked in the mirror. I looked at her reflection as she checked her makeup. "You weren't a person yet, so you're writing about me".

I spoke to the back of Mother's blonde coiffure while she faced forward. She flipped the visor back up, and stared straight ahead.

"No, Mom," I said, "I was young, but I was alive. I'm writing from my point of view as a child."

"What point of view?" she insisted.

We pulled into the Senior Center parking lot, and Yohosame parked in the spindly shade of an ocotillo tree, and turned off the engine. Mother's attitude pushed every hot button that remained. It was useless to repeat that I wrote from my own perspective, not yet autonomous but a conscious, discrete member of the family circle and the human race.

Yohosame looked at me, apprehensive, in the rear view mirror. I bailed from the car and stormed off on foot. Zigzagging through a system of concrete washes that led to the lake, I climbed and hiked away my frustration. Many kids spent years in their parents' homes as expensive and burdensome satellites, their identities invalidated as a matter of course. I knew I would always be grateful for the sixties, for an alternative to the deep groove of my early conditioning.

༄

Mother expected I'd written a hatchet job in which she played a starring role. How could I explain that I had tried for balance and insight, and hoped to look at myself through the same critical lens? I wanted to give approval as well as to receive it. I wanted to rise above my reactions and liberate us both. Our withheld acceptance was mutual, generational, a pattern I yearned to break. I knew I could be unyielding too.

I grew up in the fifties climate that pitted women against each other and used their dependence upon men to keep them divided, competitive, and powerless. Solidarity was an as-yet-unexplored territory. I remembered Casey's discomfort when Carol and I were glad to see each other at family gatherings. We were well into our thirties before I realized *divide and conquer* had been one of Casey's strategies for maintaining control.

"Well, your gifts come from my grandmother," Mother said.

I loved the handmade life and was a repository for family artifacts no one wanted. My great-grandmother crafted a human-hair wreath I housed in a shadow box. Late in her life, with only one eye, she collected hair from family members and their monsignor, tatted it onto wire, and shaped the wire into hearts. Tiny numbers indexed our ancestors' names, which read like the last supper: Jesus, Mary, Joseph, Matthew, and John. My house was full of family art projects: Mom's painted ceramics and Dad's alabaster statues.

"Yes, and Dad," I had to say.

She grabbed the remote and pressed up the noise.

One day the ceramic lid of Don's blue urn was tilted on its side, at rest against the wall. The urn had sat undisturbed for nineteen years in its place on the entry floor. I peered at ashes and bone chips—ready to blend with my mother's, according to her plan, and to be scattered together on Lake Havasu. *Weird*, I thought, and replaced the lid.

Mother's movements became jerky and uncomfortable. It was time to introduce morphine, and time to let go. She focused on meaningless minutiae as our time ran out. On Friday our good-bye was dry, exhausted of feeling.

Yohosame drove me to Las Vegas, and we checked into the Grand, trading our London Bridge view for one of the Eiffel Tower, the Statue of Liberty, and the great pyramids. The surreal markers and the cavernous casino full of carnival sounds underscored our shared sense of shock. On Saturday, Yohosame called me in Mexico. Wayne had increased the morphine to hourly doses and rubbed mother's back for hours. Carol and Indra were on their way.

Early Sunday morning, Mother surrendered her struggle.

Seven

*W*e met at the Air Tahiti gate at LAX and flew to Papeete in French Polynesia. Indra, Yohosame, and I walked the black sand beach at sunrise, and before breakfast we swam buoyant in the warm sea. The cruise ship arrived and we boarded. For the first time, I'd made us a threesome, sprung for a port corner suite, aft, with a wraparound deck. We stood at the rail and gazed at the balm of open water—nothing but blue water, blue sky, and a navy-blue horizon line. An occasional island appeared to float by, underscoring the emptiness. I breathed in moist air, pushed past anxiety, breathed out, and dropped below melancholy.

It had been a month since Mother died. We had planned the cruise a year earlier—now it had become one more unintended memorial at sea. Carol organized a ceremony for the following month, May. We'd join the rest of the family in Lake Havasu to spread Mother's and Don's ashes then.

The ship looped through the islands surrounding Tahiti, islands like loosely strung pearls. We returned to Bora Bora, and awoke under its silhouette. A tender, one of the covered lifeboats secured to the ship's side like pods, ferried us to the dock where we found our open-air launch. A local in a wrapped loincloth, a red hibiscus anchored in black curly hair, took tickets with one hand and helped us board with the other. He straddled the boat and dock, directed us to seats on one of two facing benches. A black mesh bag mounded with rubber flippers, masks, and snorkels sat in the middle. We stashed gear under the bench and settled in as a second Tahitian boy untied the boat, fired up the motor and, rotating a wooden rudder, steered us out into open water. His sidekick stood at the bow and pointed out landmarks as we fringed the island, motored past the old Bora Bora Hotel. As we rounded a curve, Yohosame spotted the bungalow we had shared with Mother.

"There it is. That's the one. Oh my god," he said.

Once the island's jewel, the hotel had been abandoned in the economic slump of 2008. It was a shabby sight now, crumbling back into the sea in slow motion. Palm fronds blown off the thatched roof left gaping holes, and the deck was missing slats. I remembered coming up the stairs from snorkeling on the reef, describing what I'd seen to Mother as she sunbathed. Our guide spoke of vanishing coral, fewer fish; of oysters pressed into service, set free only if they survived two grafts and produced two colored pearls. But the water was still banded sapphire-to-turquoise-to-aqua, reflecting its depth over a powder-white floor.

We headed for an underwater canyon flanked by coral reefs, a snorkeling spot where the current propelled swimmers the canyon's length. Indra had never snorkeled but she'd discovered an adventurous streak in her early forties and wanted to try. As a child, Indra trailed after her older brother, Shawn, and cousin, Yohosame, an easy target for their teasing. Yet in adulthood she held her own with everyone—ran a construction company, raised a son, and tackled obstacle courses on weekends for fun. Tall, loose-limbed, and slim, with cocoa skin and long black hair, she held the undisguised attention of the two Tahitian boys. The other men on the boat cast glances her way when their wives were distracted by other scenery, and Yohosame enjoyed knowing everyone thought she was with him, just like Dad had with me on Lake Tahoe's ski slopes.

We anchored our launch in the shallow water at the canyon's mouth and walked out on a strip of sand studded with palm trees as far as we could go. Then, one by one, we entered the strong current, let go, and drifted back to where we began. Indra was thrilled, eager to go again and again.

On another day, we made a half circle of Rangiroa, anchoring on the outer reef. I sank into the water and pushed back from the stairs, surrounded by lemon sharks about a yard long, with black-tipped fins and tails. They knew the boat, anticipated reward, and both swarmed and ignored us. I stroked away from the boat and followed Yohosame and Indra over coral beds. Translucent tube fish floated ahead, just beneath the surface. Below were rippled clam mouths in fluorescent blues, greens, and purples. A riot of coral and parrot fish and squadrons of silky stingrays undulated by, their whip-like tails tapered to nothing, the stinging barbs removed. I surfaced, surprised to see how far I'd drifted.

"Lady, come back to the boat." The guide waved in the distance. I faced a school of lemon sharks—had no way out but through. Like an M. C. Escher graphic, the sharks and I moved in opposite directions and filled each other's negative spaces. In perfect symmetry we passed without touching, a hair's breadth away.

Back at the boat, the water churned with swimmers. I brushed against something and, ducking underwater, I saw it was the stingrays tipped on their sides, vertical curtains draped against bare skin, passing through the throng of swimmers like shuttles through fiber strands.

After ten days the ship returned to Papeete. Passengers disembarked and others boarded. Indra flew home, her vacation time exhausted. Another three weeks for Yohosame and me before we had to fly back to Mexico and pack for Arizona.

We were sad to lose Indra. We missed her spark and spirit. The decline of our matriarch and the deathbed vigil had brought the family closer. We told deeper truths, risked more.

Several times over the past ten days I'd awakened at five in the morning, and the door had swung open as I sipped cappuccino in our living room, the cousins just getting in, deep in animated discussion. They pushed two lounges together on our deck, pulled sheets over their heads, and snoozed until lunch. Yohosame still checked out the dance scene as I settled in for the night, but without Indra he didn't stay out until dawn.

Yohosame and I sailed on to outlying Fakarava, an atoll west of the Tuomoto island group. The beaches were a gorgeous litter of sea-shells and crushed coral, pink sand on black lava shoals. We headed for the tall landmark we spotted from the boat as we came in, hoping it wasn't a utility tower, hoping for something ancient and iconic. The goal kept us moving through blistering air as thick as water. We walked out into the shallow sea, briefly refreshed. Tracing one side of the narrow atoll, we crossed to what turned out to be an old stone lighthouse we circled but didn't climb. While we rested, a jeep full of tourists roared up and unloaded, loud and smug. We moved on and crossed through dense palms and shrubbery, and returned to the dock where natives took advantage of the cruise ship's arrival, dancing and selling precious pearls, seashell jewelry, and hand-dyed fabrics.

After the four-mile walk in heat and humidity, I revived at the tender station while I waited to return to the ship. Yohosame stayed and smoked island weed with the locals. He watched them gawk at the international crew in string bikinis, both men and women, both buff and bloated. He laughed at tourists with them, danced, and modeled for a native beauty who demonstrated how to tie the men's sarong, and he hopped on the last tender to the boat before sailing time, declaring it a perfect day.

Eight

*E*venings we headed for The Red Ginger, an Asian-fusion restaurant on the fourth deck. We traced the curves of a Lalique staircase and walked past a cascading water wall at the entrance, following our hostess past a bank of crimson ginger stalks to our table. One length of the rectangular room was Murano glass, a mosaic of repeating cone shapes in burnt orange and gold Venetian glass. The sculptured wall was backlit, and it heightened the drama of the red and black room.

"You look nice, honey," I said. Yohosame wore a white linen suit, perfect for the tropics.

"Thanks, Mom, we know how important that is," he said.

"Not just to me," I said, "it's a level of agreement in a civilized world. It isn't that it's so important; it's just nice." I smiled and nodded at the waiter presenting sushi with reverence, as if carrying trays of precious jewels.

"It's important in our family," Yohosame said. "This family is all about looking good."

"Dad designed homes and Casey decorated them." I tilted my head from side to side. "Carol and Mother in the beauty business—I guess that's arguable," I said.

"Like you weren't the worst of all, Mother? You were the one who always needed everything to be so aesthetically pleasing, so color-coordinated, and harmonious."

"You weren't happy I tried to make things nice?"

"No, I think it screwed me up," he said, calm and convinced.

"Oh, I see. Seriously, you're not glad you learned how to present yourself to the world?" I waved one arm through the air to include the room in which we sat.

"You mean how to get dressed in the morning?" he said, showing an impish smirk that reminded me of his father, one dimple deepened. "I would have figured it out."

Our waiter shook out an origami-folded black linen napkin to match my dress, and draped it across my lap. He chose a red one for Yohosame, brilliant against his white suit.

"You know, I can't believe we're still doing this. Ever since you were in second grade and I brought your lunch to school and embarrassed you, this has been an issue. I had on a black suit and you begged me to wear blue jeans and ski jackets like the rest of the mothers. Then you had *your* all-black phase."

I paused while the waiter poured fragrant tea steeped in individual iron pots. Notes of citron and vanilla exploded in the air.

"Remember when the Keystone Kops at Disneyland made you take off your black leather on Main Street?" I asked. "Right before you ditched us on Tom Sawyer's Island where they caught you smoking, and we had to pick you up at the jail?" I shook my head, remembering. This was the portal to the terrifying teens I tried not to revisit most days.

The waiter returned with a glass-topped, black-lacquered box with chopsticks on display. I pointed to ebony sticks inlaid with mother-of-pearl. He suggested cinnabar for Yohosame, a match for his red linen napkin.

"And then there was the time you were walking along the street and got hit by a car, and a witness told the police a black garbage bag flew into the air—but it was you in black leather, it was YOU," I said, breathless, leaning back against the banquette.

Our waiter placed covered bowls of delicate broth and mounds of emerald seaweed centered on white porcelain squares on the table, bowed, and backed away.

"Yeah, I remember, Mother. I took a walk with my boom box

so I wouldn't have to listen to you telling me to get busy and do something," Yohosame said, looking nineteen at forty-four, his teen persona always just beneath the surface.

"We're restless, productive California people," I said, dismissing the topic.

Yohosame clapped a hand over his mouth and guffawed.

I looked at my napkin, ran a finger over the intricate origami fold-lines impressed into the material's surface, gave in to chuckles, and said, "Okay, we're escapists, alcoholics, and drug addicts, both sides of the family, happy? And yes, I *do* judge some forms of it more harshly than others."

He laughed. "Right Mom, you make looking good and being busy core values, and then take everybody else's inventory."

I lifted my chopsticks from their miniature, pagoda-shaped ceramic stand and looked into Yohosame's intelligent blue eyes.

"Really honey, it sounds like we could've stayed in Haight-Ashbury and hung out for eighteen years, as far as you're concerned. You're not glad I was more functional than that?"

"No, I think it screwed me up," he said without irony.

"Oh, I see," I said. "It's hard to imagine I was doing my best, huh?"

"No, I'm sure you were."

Yohosame continued, over miso-glazed sea bass with steamed asparagus spears, to elaborate on his childhood trauma. I listened while savoring bites of wasabi-crusted lamb and broccoli florets. He mentioned the time, living with my second husband in the tiny A-frame with a loft we occupied while the builders finished our house, when he awakened in the night and mistook our lovemaking for mayhem.

"You were twelve by then. At least you had some idea what was going on; it was less scarring than if you'd been younger," I said, hope in my heart.

"Oh no, other things happened when I was younger," he said, grinning.

"Of course they did, and perhaps you could skip writing *your* memoirs," I said, only half joking.

I surrendered my defense and listened—stopped undermining his

position, minimizing the damage, distracting myself, and *listened*—
to what I didn't want to hear. We revisited the day on our deck in
Lake Forest, when I forced him into a chair and cut his hair—the
worst day either of us could remember. Me, furious, wielding scis-
sors, the precious locks coiled on the wood slats around the chair at
his feet. I stripped him of his early teen persona, his concert tickets,
and his long wavy hair.

"I always think of *Hallelujah*, the Leonard Cohen song," I said.

"Oh, I love that song, right, right," Yohosame nodded. He sang the
phrase and I joined in. "*She broke your throne, she cut your hair, and
from your lips she drew the Halleluljah.*"

We sang in whispers in the hushed space, over piped-in gong
and bell tones, mixed with birdsong in the background. Decades
after "the worst day," he and I could still connect over musical refer-
ences. Music was his world, his life. He listened, played, improvised,
recorded, and collected. Most complete in joyous movement, and one
with the music, he was the loosest, freest dancer I'd ever seen anywhere, the sixties included.

"And the stanza that reminds me of pregnancy. You know the
one," I said.

"*And remember when I moved in you. The holy dove was moving
too, and every breath we drew was Hallelujah.*" Yohosame enunci-
ated, sang slow, savoring the exalted words.

"YES," I said.

The freedom forgiveness brings was in the air—peace made. The
mother in me rejoiced in Yohosame's catharsis, while another aspect
marveled that I'd brought my son to the middle of nowhere to list my
shortcomings. Hadn't my mother seen to that?

A cup of clear, sweet fluid accompanied the green tea ice cream.
Our choice how sweet or bitter, or bittersweet the end of our perfect
meal was to be—it was, as usual, up to us.

I waited to write about Mother until I feared I'd lost the memories,
blocked out every one of them. As the ship creased blue water, I wrote
everything I recalled of the last five weeks of her life. The associations
rose, and I followed my feelings along convoluted tributaries—and
followed my stories until I was empty.

Maybe there's a God above.
But all I've ever learned from love
was how to shoot somebody who outdrew you.

I pictured Kitty before she was my mother—when she was young and turned toward a life with open possibilities. Listing what she loved, I wrote a piece to recite when we scattered her ashes, and each morning I read the revised version to Yohosame, polishing away any negativity he was quick to bring to my attention.

It's not a cry you can hear at night.
It's not someone who has seen the light.
It's a cold and broken Hallelujah.

Nine

Yohosame carried Don's blue urn in the joint of one arm, hugged
it to his body as he boarded the cocktail barge and sat in back next
to Indra's son. My nephew, calm at the wheel, capable, backed out of
the slip, reversed gears, and moved us into the main stream of lake
traffic. The flat-bottomed boat accommodated the entire family, its
canopy a shelter from the late May sun.

We headed out to the fringe, where fewer boats floated. Carol
sat on the side, balancing on her lap a cardboard box papered with
images of blue sky, white, puffy clouds, and seagulls soaring. Inside
were Mother's ashes. A perforated square at the top of the box gave
way to make a spout. Bone chips rattled against the inside of the box
as Carol tilted it and held it out over the water at the pontoon boat's
port side. Gray ashes poured into the outer curve as the boat made
a wide arc, blending with the gray waterfall of Don's ashes from the
tipped blue urn.

"Don, we promised to take care of Mother and we did. Now we
commend her again into your care," I said when it was my turn. Not
the most liberated sentiment, I thought, but true. We had surrounded
mother's fifth and last husband's bed as he lay near death in the VA
hospital in Tucson. Carol and I respected Don, and for Wayne he'd
been a loving, dependable father.

"Will you take care of your mother for me?" Don asked in a weak,
raspy voice, ravaged by late-stage lung cancer.

"Yes," I said. "Won't we?" I added, prompting Carol and Wayne to speak out loud.

"Yes, we will," they said in unison.

And we had. I doubted Don was around these many years later to collect his bride—and I doubted the smoke alarm was his message of immortality—but Mother had been certain, and so I acted as if he were. I imagined him a genie released from his bottle. He hovered above the surface of the lake, watching the ashes commingle in the bright air, watching the powder hang on the lake's surface a moment before drifting down on a light wind's bias descent, like snowflakes.

Five-year-olds Deagan and Zipporah animated the front of the boat, along with Zipporah's teenage brother. Zipporah had woolly black hair and shiny black eyes, and was wiry-slim and fearless. She kept a tight hold on blond-haired, blue-eyed Deagan, Indra's grandson. My other niece and her boyfriend, who owned a tattoo business, sat across from them, starboard, holding hands. They were living illustrations—custom comic book pages open to the center fold, their personal designs appearing to blend into each other's, bridging the boundaries of their arms and their clasped hands as they talked, laughed, and leaned in to kiss. Like stained glass, their bodies were covered with color fields banded by black lines, and together they looked like an enormous butterfly. Carol and Indra and I occupied the upholstered bench across from the pilot, Carol's son. His wife stood at his side as he steered. I rose and read:

Mother liked onion sandwiches with mustard and pepper; she carried butterscotch candies in her pocket. She shrugged off her clothes the minute she got through the door. She loved sunbathing, Talisman roses, small animals—rabbits and quail—and her pets: Tweeney, Scooby, Misty, JP, the toy poodles she bred, and Sweetie Pie, who she got so she wouldn't get depressed.

She danced the jitterbug all night long, combed the beach for rocks and seashells. Every summer she had the darkest tan. She loved long soaks in the tub, horror movies, a new car every three years. She loved men with good teeth, good humor, a taste for drink, her father. She liked to be right, to be private, and to be practical, unsentimental—strong enough to survive. She went blond at forty.

She loved growing up free on her grandmother's farm, disappeared for hours, and picked fruit from trees, pulled carrots out of the ground. She showed up for Parent/Teacher Night at school in cocktail dresses with cleavage, a mink stole, strappy high heeled sandals, perfumed.

She liked to water the yard, window shop, play games to win. She liked a television on in every room. She liked Hollywood gossip, Disney animation, and precious stones in traditional settings. She wore rings on her toes. She liked second chances— married until she got it right. She liked true stories, stories that rang true, reincarnation stories. She liked the idea of returning in a new disguise again and again. She was a great actress.

She loved the desert: the clean white sand, the clear night sky, the warm dry air. She loved to uncoil and brush her grandmother's waist-length hair.

"I didn't know Grandma liked horror movies!" said handsome, lanky Johnny, Indra's son.

"Oh yes, she did. She took us to the drive-in so we could scream in the privacy of our car."

"What's a jitterbug?" Zipporah asked.

"It's a very lively dance people used to do," I said. "Your Great-grandmother danced for hours without stopping, she loved it so much."

Zipporah's mother, nervous on water, rose to sing "Don't Cry For Me," a song that has nothing to do with Argentina. Her rich voice soared, and provided emotional release. Then she sobbed while my nephew comforted her with one arm and drove the pontoon boat with the other. We circled the island, passed anchored boats full of bikini-clad revelers, drinks in hand, whooping, hollering, and gyrating to music that poured from each boat and changed for us every few seconds as we motored past—a staccato roar.

Later, at lunch, Zipporah and Deagan stood before a photo collage that Carol had made, studying images from their great-grandmother's life. Floral bouquets flanked the photos: fuchsia roses, and funneled, cream-colored lilies in turquoise vases. Carol had chosen photos from our tropical trips—places I took Mother to, before the psychic told her it wasn't safe to travel on water. In the photos, Mom wore smiles, muumuus, hibiscus in her hair, flower leis, a palm-frond hat.

Wayne arrived without Jane, who was in the hospital. Jane had had a dream—of lying on her back, unable to rise, pressed down by an invisible force. She awoke struggling for breath, the first to be haunted. She was rushed to the hospital in the middle of the night—rushed to the same wing to which they had rushed Mother the final time. Wayne looked stricken, thrown back into the awful early days, a healed membrane scraped.

"The first month was hard," he said, "and slowly it got better, and now..." He trailed off and shrugged, all ground lost again. The flowers were still fresh when Carol, Wayne, and Yohosame carried them to Jane's hospital room and offered her the recycled affection.

Carol and I returned to the house the next morning, and began packing up Mom's collections: hobnail creamers, cats, paper weights, crystal.

"She just got so angry that you didn't come right away," Carol said.

"Yes, she never got over it, I guess, and she never forgave my move to Mexico."

Yohosame suggested that because I was Mother's first child that I'd been the harsh signal of new responsibilities from the beginning.

"Oh, it was all right, I guess, until the kids came along," she said to me once of her marriage to Dad. "After you kids, it was just ordinary—an ordinary marriage."

Carol and Yohosame tried to make me feel better, and I appreciated it—appreciated them. Somehow we'd learned to love and to be generous. We all bore the marks, the scars, the incised grooves of our shared experiences—our family growth rings.

⌒

At home, I missed Indra's kindness, and the way Carol and I had bypassed old friction and cooperated. I missed Wayne's hugs, and the bright and shiny five-year-olds. I even missed the mad, bristling pace of America, rife with distracting trivia and numbing intensity.

I saw myself perched on a time ladder. My birthday was coming soon, and I felt lighter-headed in this new absence of elders. It was just me now, jockeying into position at the top, next in line to go. *We'll die as we lived* is the truth we all face.

Indra and Yohosame onboard Oceania's Marina in Tahiti
Photo credit: Terry Baldwin

Six

Asilah

～

All paths are circular.

Ibn al-Arabi

George Cameron III aka Yusuf
Photo credit: Terry Baldwin

One

After our full day of travel—three flights total—Sadaf and I passed the original Olympics site en route from the airport in Athens. Pink marble grandstands, veined red, made an oval around a dirt track. At the Hotel Electra, we threw on bathing suits and bathrobes and took the elevator to the rooftop infinity pool, where we swam lazy, jet-lagged laps with the Acropolis in view on a nearby hill. After a breakfast the next morning that included dolmas and tzatziki, we boarded a small cruise ship and sailed for Turkey, Ephesus and Chisme, then back to Greece, Sicily, Italy and France.

⌣

I dreamt of dancing at the top of a bluff and of mudslides. I spotted Mother below: she shouted but I couldn't make out her words. So I snaked my way down to her, made Zs in the steep, liquid switchbacks until I stood on even ground, and I approached Mother, who appeared to be sunning. Despite a scowl on her young face, she looked soft and vulnerable. I knew her dark, arched eyebrows, the space around them tweezed to porcelain. I knew her tightly curled, dark hair and sturdy petite curves. She looked about twenty. By the time I reached her she was laid out among others lying flat on their backs, arms soldier-straight by their sides. The faces were covered now, like corpses. I thought she was expecting me, but I knew I could startle her as I lifted a corner of her facecloth.

"I sure hope this is you," I said, and we both laughed. "Well, that's better, Mom, you look so soft and pretty. Why are you so angry?"

"Too many women," she said, "just way too many women in this world."

❧

And so there was competition. It wasn't personal—more of an inbred survival instinct humming beneath the surface of our lives. Mother and daughter, we held ourselves aloof. We were miserly with our approval and chipped away at each other's confidence, conditioned not to trust.

Sadaf is complex, and I'm not easy, but our relationship is natural, full of affection and free of pettiness. She was born shortly before Yusuf's car accident in Paris—his brain injury. Her half-brother, Yohosame, was ten at the time, and he experienced an early role-reversal with his part-time father as well, but Sadaf was their father's full-time caretaker.

❧

Yusuf was riding shotgun in a Volkswagen bug when it smashed into a brick wall in Paris. He went through the windshield and was transported, comatose, from Paris to Santa Fe. His mother, Ann, was visiting Dad and Casey in Hilton Head when the accident took place, and Ann said there was nothing she could do but continue to enjoy the visit. I joined Yusuf's brother and their family friend from Pasadena, Brian, at the La Posada Hotel, where they had rented a condo.

Sadaf's mother, Mabuba, put Sadaf in my arms when she went to the hospital to visit Yusuf. The Cameron genes were dominant, and Sadaf looked like Yohosame had ten years earlier, except she had dark hair while his was blond. They shared the tiny, mature face—already stamped with character—the plump, dimpled cheeks. I fell in love for life with another of Yusuf's children. Her mother was from Afghanistan, where Yusuf had met her, and had helped her leave when it became dangerous for her after the Soviet invasion. The combination of Afghan and WASP produced in Sadaf a black-haired beauty with startling blue eyes.

⌐

The only time I left the ship was at Santorini, the tall Greek island I first visited with Dad and Carol, and then again with Indra. I was nauseous and dizzy with the heat of summer—dehydration, maybe. I slept. Two days later, the ship's diminutive Asian doctor gave me pills, but I was still nauseous. I slept and slept, woke without energy, and slept some more. After my mandatory quarantine was lifted, I searched the ship for the bland food I needed to regain my strength.

Sadaf, now thirty-three, had escapades at night, and entertained me with a pantomime of the ship's nightlife. Finally, we docked at Monte Carlo and disembarked. From there we flew into Charles de Gaulle airport, and Sadaf headed straight for Paris. I, meanwhile, was lucky to make it to my airport hotel, and I awoke eight hours later, exhausted and anxious. At checkout, I swallowed the last of the Xanax that Mother gave me years earlier, and waited for the *normal* feeling that gave me new faith in pharmaceuticals.

At Charles de Gaulle I merged with the mess of humanity, surrounded by layers of language and national costume. We surged and waited as back and forth we queued in the dense, packed room. At the gate a bus took us to the plane—still no sign of Sadaf. Onboard, a stewardess confirmed the gate was closed, but then there Sadaf was, and the door slid and sealed shut, and we were off to Morocco.

We hired a taxi in Tangiers for the thirty-minute ride south to Asilah, where sidewalk cafés lined the waterfront outside the old city, the medina. Our taxi motored by the men drinking tea and coffee, and pulled up at the entrance. We paid the driver in durhams obtained at the airport, and rolled our luggage into the heart-center where the mosques clustered. Right away I spotted Yohosame, who arrived a day earlier and didn't know when we were due. He strolled up, a welcome, smiling sight—my son in a world of staring men.

Two

We rounded a curve and came upon an oversized closet covered with blue-and-white paintings. The art celebrated a child's vision of a happy world, populated by spiky suns, seagulls, seashells and fish. I stuck my head into the small enclosure, where the artist worked like a crab in a blue-and-white shell.

"Hola, I like your work. I love your world."

I backed up out of the space and the artist followed me, saying something in Arabic that might have been about family. He pointed ahead to where Yohosame and Sadaf had stopped to watch our exchange. I was all smiles and nods, my version of universal language. He handed me a painting on a narrow rectangle of wood and pointed to Yohosame. Then another, meant for Sadaf, and a larger one for me: arrival gifts. I thought I loved Morocco, was amazed to be in Asilah, where Yusuf had lived for five years and died ten years ago. Here, I'm told, he was embraced, revered—his body carried through the streets by two hundred chanting Muslims.

Our rented house had a lacquered red door with a solid brass knocker. No one answered. We meandered around the curved chalk-white medina walls, our luggage rolling behind us like pets on leashes. Coming upon the hobbit door to Yohosame's room, the room where Yusuf died during Ramadan—just after bathing, on the holiest day of the year—Yohosame found the key and unlocked his door. Yusuf had occupied a three-story house next door that included this space that Yohosame bought after Yusuf died. I had pictured a modest room with a bath and with light—not this air-less crypt where I waited and remembered Yusuf while his children went to find the key to our sight-unseen rental for two weeks. There was only room for me and our suitcases in the tiny space. I asked that the door be left open, and black-eyed people peered in on my reverie.

The kids retrieved me, and we returned to the side of the medina that bordered the sea and stood again before the red lacquered door. I settled in the third-floor aerie with the balcony that overlooked the *krekia*, the 2,800-year-old stone wall that extended into the green shallow sea. People walked the wall, dark figures in the sherbet glow of sunset. A lone fisherman stood on the exposed ridges of red rock below. Vendors sold nuts and fruits and arts and crafts in front of the house.

Inside, my bath had a copper sink, and there were irises painted around the ceiling. Softened light streamed through painted white latticework, through transparent silk draperies, through apertures punched in brass and tin. I opened all the windows and slept with tidal sounds and smells filling my room.

I awoke early the next morning, dressed and grabbed durhams, my camera, and a key. I tiptoed down two flights and left the slumbering house. All was quiet as I walked out to the end of the *krekia*, deserted at dawn except for one sleeping figure wrapped in a brown *djellaba*, the hooded caftan both men and women wear. The tide was out and the sea bed was striated with moss-covered, red rock. The air smelled of sea and urine.

I wound around the labyrinthine curves and photographed pista-chio-colored doors, turquoise shutters, blood-red gates, lapis walls, patterned tiles against lacy latticework, and ornamental iron. Exiting the medina, I found a café open for coffee. Dark, strong roast drizzled from a silver pitcher, poured with steamed milk into a glass cup with a metal band for a handle. A slight young man asked if he could pull up a chair and join me.

"You are Yusuf's first wife, the mother of the son," he said. "I am Abdul."

Abdul covered his heart with his hand and lowered his head in a small bow. I extended my hand.

"*Mucho gusto*, Abdul. Yes, I'm here with two of Yusuf's children. You knew Yusuf?"

"Yusuf was a very good man." Abdul nodded, a serious expression subduing his lively features.

He was short, dark, and presentable in a wrinkled but clean white shirt, khaki pants, and leather sandals. He spoke enough English, Spanish, and French to sell paintings to the tourists. He riffled through a stack of ragged ovals torn from cement bags. Stylized stick figures illustrated themes of spiritual fire and women's liberation. Abdul's family painted at home, and Abdul sold on the street. I chose one and he rolled it into a tube inside a glossy magazine image of Princess Diana—her brilliant smile, her diamond tiara.

"Where is the cemetery?" I asked.

"It's through the village and up on the hill, but you will need to buy a *djellaba* to visit Yusuf, to show respect for the dead."

The Arabic around me was more guttural than German to my ears, words gargled at the back of the throat, spit out into this paradise of color and patterns. Even the municipal water hoses were bright blue. Women wore broad straw hats stippled with felt pom-poms in Day-Glo hues to sweep the streets with handmade brooms. Men walked by with plastic shoes on their feet, skullcaps, caftans bisected diagonally by woven shoulder bags. There were cats, a few dogs, and more horse-drawn carts than cars.

Asilah was home to an art and music festival that reached its peak in August, drawing tourists and participants worldwide. It began now. Pockets of music filled the village. Muralists painted the medina's walls, covering last year's imagery. A twenty-foot wall was alive with wisps of calligraphy—delicate swirls and expressive angles. The word arabesques broke out of dark teal at the bottom, and led the eye upward to where teal faded to aqua and the image became porous, became clouds, and the words were white birds, flying free.

As the air heated up, I melted down and said goodbye to Abdul. I returned to the house and pushed the kitchen window open for air, and the sounds of the street filtered in all day. At sunset, people lined the sea wall in front of the house.

I doubted I would regain my strength here, enough strength to leave. When I returned home I would learn that *E. coli* was coursing through my system. But all I knew in Asilah was an irrational fear that I could die there also.

Three

I awoke at four-thirty in the morning, and padded down the wooden stairs to the second floor, where a light shone in the back bedroom. Yohosame, still jetlagged, sifted tobacco mixed with hash through the fingers of his left hand while scrolling down a Facebook page with his right: multitasking. My son would live in the closet-of-a-room where his father died until September.

I want so much for him. It's a burden he carries, for Yohosame is happy with less. I have dubbed him the guru of R&R—the master of chill. There in Asilah, he resonated with the simplicity of the place. There was also a deep, old sadness, stitched with rivulets of ecstasy there—Asilah half enraptured, half appalled.

Yohosame followed me upstairs and we sat on the terrace which took up most of the third floor. I described the previous night's dream of Dad—older, very pale with his poor circulation, his blood-less hands. I showed him a place to rest on a hillside marked off with spaces I filled with others in need of rest and I lost track of him. Like the dream I had of Mother and others sunbathing with cloths covering their faces, this dream of communal rest on a hillside evoked the cemetery. As the sky lightened, Yohosame and I walked to the balcony to look at the new day, gazing out across the water. I looked down into the courtyard of a mosque across the street. The cement floor was paved with rectangles of old ceramic tile, their jewel tones faded. Graves, Yohosame said—green burials, bodies wrapped in shrouds.

We left Sadaf still sleeping and walked the porous, honeycombed medina where walls that were white the day before were now covered with red and gold repeating brushstrokes. Ciphers took shape and became figures. Forms evolved out of pure color and pattern, then deconstructed again into an abstract field. Trees sprouted red-lipped blooms. A bird's nest surrounded a doorknob where open-mouthed fledglings were fed by a mother bird whose wingspread covered the upper door. The highly evolved Islamic designs developed under a prohibition against depicting the human form. In modern Morocco, some rules are relaxed: there are stylized dancers with elongated limbs.

We arrived at one of the openings to the surrounding village, where cafés abounded—where Asilah woke up first, while the medina slept in. We slid into woven chairs at a table for two, ordered coffee, and took in the scene. Tall, slim glasses of mint tea, choked with leaves, sweetened to syrup, studded the tabletops alongside *cafés au lait*. A barefoot man, naked except for three blankets he had cinched around himself and anchored with one hand, offered an empty cup with the other. Beseeching eyes I did not meet. A one-legged man coasted by in a wooden wheeled chair, gravity moving him along the gradual slope. A tall, lanky Moroccan man wore a Western-style suit that folded and flapped around his frame like flags in the morning breeze. He reminded me of Abe Lincoln—his height, his dark facial hair, the seriousness of his stride. Archetypes, I smiled to remember, Mother and I finding family on the TV screen.

We reentered the medina as it, too, awakened, and merchants hung their wares on strings. Strings of shoes and strings of caps formed curtains in front of tiny shops with stacked cushions, painted ceramics, old Berber treasures, chunky coral, amber, and turquoise, engraved silver trays, and embroidered, flowing caftans.

Yohosame called out to someone he knew, and beckoned to a young man, immaculate in white, hair trimmed close around a handsome, kind face. I recognized him from photos of Yusuf carried to his rest. Hassan was in front, lifting one side of the simple litter covered with rose petals. He was a boy in the photos, now a young man. Hassan pulled up beside us on a bicycle and stopped.

Tears filled the smiling man's eyes. He shook the hand I offered with the briefest trace of eye contact, looked away, covered his heart, and launched into the story of his first meeting with itinerant Yusuf in a neighboring village, where he persuaded him to come to Asilah—a good fit: Asilah. He directed his reminiscence to Yohosame, who had heard it many times, but the recounting was for me, the emotion intense and contagious. Hassan found for Yusuf first a Sheik—a spiritual teacher—and then a place to live.

I thanked him for his role in Yusuf's life, and told him I was glad Yusuf found Asilah at the end, here where he was happy and beloved. I spoke freely, an unrepentant American woman, but with deliberately softened eyes, gaze a shade averted—my voice not too nasal or aggressive, I hoped. This tempering worked for me in Mexico.

Ten years after Yusuf's passing, Hassan's grief was fresh, the poignant memories vivid. A ghost procession surrounded us as we remembered Yusuf, the American who lived in their midst for five brief years. The men, heads tilted back, mouths open in recitation, walked the village, up through the marketplace, to the cemetery at the top of the hill. People abandoned activities to join in the procession to the hilltop where they lay the American in his grave, facing east.

⌐

We pushed Yusuf around the hospital in his wheelchair when he was well enough. His leg had a bad break and his head was bandaged. At every exit sign, his body tensed.

"Okay, let's go. Let's go now," he said, leaning forward, willing us to spring him. As we passed the door to the outside world, he collapsed in his chair. "Why aren't we going?" he whined, childlike, and grouchy.

When he was back in his hospital bed, a young physical therapist knocked on the open door of the room and asked to speak to Mr. Cameron.

"Not now," Yusuf said.

"I need to ask you some simple questions, sir." He kept his eyes on the clipboard he held.

"Not now," Yusuf said, louder this time.

The technician cleared his throat and tried again.

"I need to ask you the questions on this form for a reason, sir. I need to assess your orientation and your attitude so we can gauge your progress."

"White and rich!" Yusuf said. "My orientation is white and rich. What more do you need to know?"

The attendant gave up, put his pen in his pocket, shook his head, and scurried from the room muttering something about coming back later. We held ourselves still until he cleared the door, then we caved in to laughter. It was unlike Yusuf to claim entitlement, but a good sign his memory was returning.

It was a decades-long recovery. His marriage with Mabuba did not survive. Irritability, symptomatic of head trauma, plagued Yusuf and those around him, and escalated into angry outbursts and violent episodes. He moved to a Muslim community outside Santa Fe: Dar-al-Islam, in the community of Abiqui—Georgia O' Keefe country. Yusuf kept a pinyon fire burning in the mosque day and night while he mended. The Muslim community established a preschool during the years Yusuf was more child than adult and happiest among the students. Yusuf's siblings and friends were mostly mystified by his conversion to Islam, by his embrace of more and more fundamental precepts. But after his accident, we hoped the discipline of his practice would prove purposeful through the long years required for his brain to heal. I believed adopting a religion that forbade alcohol was a creative failsafe in light of the illness that ran in his family.

Yusuf remained, in many ways, the same character he'd always been, but much had been shaken loose, and things had gotten lost in the reshuffling. When he fell into troughs of self-pity, bemoaning the loss of what he couldn't remember having, I told him I'd known him a long time and he was the same, with one important difference: he now had a sense of humor.

"Really?" he asked, sitting up straighter.

"Yes, really."

His life arc careened from mischievous child to poor little rich boy to sixties drop-out to secretary of the Sufi Order to husband

and father to accident victim at thirty-three. Much later, he became a traveling lapis lazuli dealer, returning to Abiquiú to work with a cabinetmaker, completing a circle he began with his apprenticeship in San Francisco in 1965.

Everyone admired Yusuf's open heart and tenacious recovery. The prognosis for a dependent life was proved wrong. But we tired of his ill-timed, impromptu visits, his needy intrusions, and his embarrassing behavior. The livid scar that traversed his forehead healed and made his physical injury less obvious, but the triple-time speech and movements, the erratic and unfiltered thoughts needed explanation. I told friends he was a medical miracle, not a drug burn-out.

Yusuf wanted deeper Muslim roots, so he moved to Morocco in his fifties, traveling back to the States to bury and memorialize his brothers and his mother. There in Asilah, I had new context for the journeys home, for Yusuf's season of losses: first, his younger brother's heart attack, and short months later, the loss of his older brother also. The following year he flew to the East Coast to memorialize his mother.

Each time he returned to Asilah—to hand out candy to children, to enjoy the warmth of the people, the beauty of the place, the peace of Islam. He last returned to celebrate Ramadan, to have his heart attack in the little room after bathing. He was found when he didn't come to dinner, slumped against the door, one hand reaching for the knob, the other covering himself.

᠃

Yohosame and I returned to the house and Sadaf was awake. It was time, we thought, and we walked uphill through the open market, past pyramids of fruit and rows of clear-eyed fish, docile chickens, slaughtered cows, lamb—the carnage required to sustain human life. We crossed the highway, saw men wrapped in white seated on a bench in front of the low, white cemetery wall. At this distance it looked like a great bleached beast with many eyes. Dark faces, hands, and feet stood out in stark relief. As we neared the men rose, became three, greeted us in Arabic, and shook hands with Yohosame. They were the grave keepers. I felt naked in my short-sleeved shift and sandaled feet. Sadaf's shoulders and arms were bare.

Yohosame and Sadaf headed for their father's grave. I followed and the men fell in behind me, chanting from the Qu'ran. Yusuf's grave was lined with triangles of cobalt blue-and-white tile. His headstone was in both Arabic and English: *Yusuf Cameron,* clear amongst the symbols I couldn't decipher. It was covered in weeds and some tiles were broken. A decorative oval marker was missing: a floral design— a ceramic bouquet that disappeared long ago.

The men brought water and made a big show of pulling weeds and washing tile. Sadaf bent, scrubbed, smoothed, and rinsed. The bed was hoed and greenery placed at the head, pink flowers in a bud vase centered in green. The chanting continued. Yohosame joined in, and Sadaf added her voice now and again. Chipped pieces of tile were stacked along with seashell offerings. Four sticks of lit incense made a row down the center of the grave; a bottle of rosewater was sprinkled over the dirt, and over our hands. The empty bottle was planted upside down beside the greenery. An open bag filled with dried flowers and herbs was passed, offered. We sifted scooped-out handfuls over Yusuf's grave together, as memories and feelings flowed for the well-meaning man, flawed father, original partner—a lifetime of identities ago. Now he was decay, and radiance.

The chanting stopped. The hot sun climbed. The grave keepers left us. One of them handed me his hat as he passed by. I felt ill and emotional, joyous, sad, invisible—my personal roller coaster ride, in some way underscored by restrictions placed on women there. Sadaf cried. I fanned out to the adjacent hill, where a camel grazed with three birds lined up in a row on its hump.

Four

We three walked toward Paradise Beach, not a sip of water amongst us on a hot, dry, windy day. I turned back, questioning our survival skills, imagining what it would mean for those fasting from sunrise to sunset for thirty days of Ramadan.

A hustler with a voice so deep it could have come from an artificial voice box singled me out as I reentered the village and turned onto the busy main street.

"Here, you come with me. I have what you want." He extracted two slim wooden cylinders from a woven bag, joined them like a flute, and held the assembled pipe against the length of his inner arm. My eyes widened behind dark glasses. Maybe I'd enjoy Asilah more if I got with the program. I began to suspect kef played an equal part to Islam in Yusuf's move to Morocco.

"Come," he said, turning to cross the street.

"I'll be back later with my son," I said over my shoulder, moving away.

The man dodged a horse cart in the midday bustle and strode back to my side.

"Come on now." He leaned us toward a space in the traffic between donkeys and a Peugeot.

"I'll be back later with my son," I said, shaking my head and backing up, playing my role in the street hustler's game.

"Come on now." His arm extended toward me, cupped fingers beckoning.

I wondered why I was being so coy, as back and forth he zigzagged, moving us bit by bit toward the entrance of an open café. I folded and followed him inside, past public seating, past a counter where an ebony-eyed man watched me walk into the back room. Two wrinkled men sat smoking long pipes, surrounded by sacks of supplies, stacked crates of beverages, mops, buckets, and brooms. The gravel-voiced guy pointed me to a folding chair beside a sad-eyed man and asked for a hundred and fifty *durhams* (fourteen dollars). He disappeared from the restaurant.

The wistful one by my side passed his long, carved pipe sideways and I took it, drawing deep until I remembered how harsh kef was purported to be and stopped before I exceeded my limit. I held the smoke in my lungs and exhaled a pale stream. The universe tilted, time slowed, and colors brightened. I nodded in thanks and assessment of quality and returned the pipe.

The man we passed on the way in entered the back room and sat next to me.

"Where are you from?" he asked.

"American, living in Mexico." I smiled each time I said it. The decision to move to Mexico was a good one—the years since had been full of challenge and change.

"Why are you here?" He took me in with squinted eyes.

Good question, I thought. "Ten years ago my first husband died here and—"

"Yusuf! Yusuf was my teacher!" The shock and adulation astonished me, this transformation Yusuf inspires. "You are the mother of his son, the first wife."

"Yes, I am Terry."

"I am Moustafa." Moustafa pumped my hand. "You are in the right place," he said, opening his arms to indicate the smoky storeroom, "but with the wrong man."

"Yes, but the wrong man is gone now, and, as you say, I am in the right place," I said.

"You are a philosopher like Yusuf," Moustafa said.

"Just an observer of life. It often requires a gamble, no?"

"True, there are no guarantees," Moustafa said.

"We visited Yusuf's grave yesterday—his children and I."

"It's part of life—the passing, the dying. It's good you're close to the children, that you're with them now," Moustafa said. "Yusuf had two daughters?"

"Yes, Sadaf and Shireen, with other wives," I said.

He nodded, and I thought that the Western pattern of serial monogamy is not so different from the accumulation of partners practiced here, limited only by resources and a capacity to share. The Qu'ran endorses polygamy if the husband can support all of his wives financially and emotionally in an equitable manner. Who am I to judge what I cannot imagine?

"Yusuf and I remained friends and I feel close to his daughters. I knew them when they were young, and Yohosame loves his sisters very much. Have you met Yusuf's children?"

"No, I would like to. Yusuf spoke of them often."

"It will happen. We're here for a while. *Mucho gusto*, Moustafa." I rose, wobbled, offered Moustafa my hand, which he enclosed in both of his. We made the small bows—nodding our heads while covering our hearts with our hands, a custom I love, a grace note to every parting. I wheeled around, including the two old men in my good-bye.

⌐

The next morning I waited in front of the medina for the money changer to open, sitting on one flank of the curving cement bench that lined the entrance. Moustafa crossed the street and hurried up to me. He was taller than the other Moroccan men I'd met, and he looked more European.

"*Buenos días*," I greeted him.

"Hello, good morning." Out of breath, excited, Moustafa launched into an addendum to yesterday's conversation in the smoking den.

"I forgot to tell you there is property Yusuf helped me buy in the country, in a place like Stonehenge—you know Stonehenge?"

It takes me a second with the accent, but then I understood. "Stonehenge? The amazing rock formations in England?"

"Yes, Stonehenge, here, north of Asilah. Yusuf and I, we build cabins next to a river. Now you have a place there always, and anything else you ever want." Moustafa finished and looked expectant. His open palms held promises; his face radiated enthusiasm. I noticed he wore a Buddha pendant. I had almost worn my carved amber Buddha this morning, but hadn't in deference to approaching Ramadan. But evidently there was no rigidity here in the Asilah free zone. I was making friends with Islam in countries like Turkey and Morocco: more assimilated, less fundamental.

"*Shukram.*" What else to say to this lavish gift of future security?

"What do you do?" Moustafa asked.

"I'm writing a memoir, in part about Yusuf. And you?"

"I write also, articles for newspapers, political criticism," Moustafa said.

"Yusuf's oldest daughter is a political activist. You must meet Sadaf."

"I look forward to meeting Sadaf and your son." Moustafa waved back at me as he rejoined his friends in a sidewalk café across the street. After a few minutes, Yohosame and Sadaf strolled up, and Moustafa rushed back. I introduced them. He told them of the land Yusuf helped him buy, and the bungalows they built next to the river, near the rocks like Stonehenge. He invited us to see the land that was partly ours now. Sadaf and I handed him cards with e-mail addresses. It was cordial, but the kids had never heard of Moustafa and they were suspicious. They said they would ask Yusuf's friends Mocsin, Redouan, or Hassan if they knew him.

"Where would Yusuf have gotten four thousand dollars?" Sadaf said, dismissive.

"A special dividend? Isn't it possible that from time to time he—?" I said.

"From the letters I've read, he needed his mother's help to pay for dental work," Yohosame said, frowning and adamant. "This didn't happen."

"Moustafa didn't have to tell us this story. It certainly sounds like something Yusuf would have done. And why would he make it up?" I said.

～

Yusuf said often, of his time in Asilah, that he loved not being the craziest or the poorest man in town. One day walking by the sea, Yusuf came upon a weeping man.

"What's wrong, friend? Are you alright?" Yusuf asked.

"I can't get married. My bride's family can't afford her dowry. There will never be enough. I will never be able to marry."

"How much is the dowry?" Yusuf asked.

"Twenty goats."

"Wait here," Yusuf told the man. Some time later he returned with a herd of handsome goats in tow, and handed them over to the man who would now become groom.

～

We discussed giving according to the Qu'ran after I was dunned in the marketplace by an unhealthy young man with clouded eyes and sores on his skin. I couldn't overcome my revulsion. I ran from him rather than helping.

"It's alright, Mom. It's better to give to widows with children than to drug addicts. It says so in the Qu'ran," Yohosame said, confident in the obviousness of the rule.

"Fuck rules," said Sadaf, who heads up a donor organization that grants funds to artists and activists unable to get mainstream backing.

I let intuition guide me. I gave as I used to pick up hitchhikers in the blue bus—when it feels right, my actions having little to do with choice or charity.

Ramadan would begin soon. I was told it was festive, and I assumed it would be spiritual. Yohosame, who had been there for Ramadan before, said he liked to break his fast on the *krekia*, the old stone sea wall. He and a handful of men waited with dates, water, coffee, and joints of hashish-sprinkled tobacco, counting the minutes as the green sea swallowed the sun's glow, and turned it to a sheet of liquid silver.

An hour before sunset the marketplace buzzed with people buying food, preparing to break the fast, getting ready for all-night festivities. Ramadan follows the lunar calendar, and so takes place in different seasons. This year it would coincide with the murals, the music, the influx of tourists, and the longest, hottest days of the year. Yohosame said the deprivation and the dangerous dehydration was to remind us of the poor, of those who went without basic needs all the time.

We watched a documentary on water scarcity, *Last Call at the Oasis*, an exposé on diminishing supplies. It had already outlined future crises, already shown us the Texas-sized island of floating trash and convinced us desalination was not the answer, when we heard the voices of singing children outside the front door. Sadaf pressed pause so Yohosame could grab his camera and photograph the kids.

He was out the now-open door in a flash while Sadaf and I watched from inside. The children, who were about eight years old, finished their song, and asked Yohosame for a drink of water. He brought them a sealed liter bottle of purified water, which they declined. They'd like tap water instead, please. He returned the bottled water to the kitchen, and took them a pitcher full from the tap. The children were now happy. We missed the nuances of the exchange, but the synchronicity was stunning. We returned to the documentary, which now offered serious comic relief in the form of Jack Black endorsing brands of processed sewage water for drinking. "*Porcelain Springs.*" He sips, and smiles. "Ah, water from the most peaceful place on earth."

Five

usuf married three more times, and had a second daughter, Shireen, who received the best of her father's love and never questioned Islam. Through it all, Yusuf and I remained friends. When the mother of one of his brides came to my house for the wedding brunch, she was surprised to find that the ex-wife, not the mother of the groom-to-be, was the hostess.

Over the decades, we talked about spirituality and practice, and tried to share with one another what drew us along our respective paths. The sixties had given us common reference points for mystical experience—common vocabulary for discussing the ineffable. Talks about Islam were closed loops for me, however, more reminiscent of Catholicism than the more interesting "isms" imported from the East. But for Yusuf, his narrow path merged with legions moving toward Mecca.

Gangaji, the Mississippi-bred spiritual teacher with an East Indian name, came to Santa Fe in the nineties. Yusuf attended, curious about my interest in something called *Satsang*. He raised his hand from the front row and began talking, and continued, and wouldn't stop, until someone removed the microphone and Gangaji moved on. His words drained out without amplification. The confused supplicant sat down, rejected. At first, Gangaji had recognized in him a kindred spirit, and encouraged him by saying "Hallelujah" after his initial remarks. But the enlightened remarks turned to questions Yusuf wouldn't pause to have answered—questions about removing rust from the heart. I sat in the audience with old friends from Lake Tahoe, houseguests I had persuaded to come to *Satsang* for the first time.

"That man looks familiar. Do you know him?"

"Yes, he's my first husband, Yohosame's father," I said. "Remember, he had that accident."

"Oh yes, I remember."

⌒

I wanted to repair the broken tile on Yusuf's grave, to replace the stolen ceramic medallion, and to plant the bed with flowers and lavender. Abdul was on the street in the early morning, dressed in clean clothes to sell paintings—a smiling, helpful font of information. I'd spent as much time with Abdul as I had with the kids. Later in the day, Sadaf and Yohosame were absorbed in their computers. I scanned the rented house with restless eyes, got up and walked around, waiting for a shared activity. I needed a project. Abdul said I must take a translator to the cemetery so I could explain to the grave keepers what I wanted. Then I must go with them to the tile store to make the purchase. It was the way to get it done.

I repeated this to Yohosame and Sadaf when I got home and found them seated side by side on the L-shaped couch, still staring into tandem screens on the glass coffee table.

"So, now that I know what we need to do, I'd like to get started," I said.

"NO!" Yohosame said—or Hossam, which he had now shortened his name to—said. *Hossam* means "sword" in Arabic, and he was living up to his new name.

"What do you mean, 'No'? I want to start," I said.

"Mother, you can't go to the cemetery with anyone except Yusuf's friends, Reduoan, Mocsin, or Hassan. Why can't you trust me? I am your son," he said.

"What does trust have to do with it?" I said. "I want to fix up and plant your father's grave."

"Trust me. I'm going to hear about your behavior when you're gone. Abdul is a hustler. He doesn't love Yusuf. He's trying to sell you paintings. If he loved Yusuf he would give you paintings like your friend with his blue and white world."

Yohosame Freeborn was a Muslim. Islam was not the phase I'd been treating it as for ten years. This was a moment when I needed the reminder of his middle name. He was born free to choose, and Islam was his choice. But I feared he was adopting not only the religious tenets, but also the cultural norms.

"Honey, be realistic," I said. "I'm a morning person and Mocsin runs a club and sleeps until noon. It's too damn hot in the afternoon for me to do anything. Reduoan lives in Barcelona, and I've seen Hassan on his bicycle one time. We have no idea where he lives. I want to get started."

"No. You must leave it to me," he said.

"Okay," I acquiesced, incredulous. I wasn't up to this fight. I hadn't felt well since that dumb cruise.

&

Yusuf once relayed a dream he had of me wandering into a clearing where religious leaders convened—a holy conclave. I emerged from the forest naked, covered in the muck of the world: dripping feces, sperm, and menstrual blood. Yusuf described the image gingerly, reluctant to hurt my feelings, as if I'd see the dream as an objective judgment on my intrinsic filth, my low rung in some spiritual hierarchy.

Yohosame said, when he heard his father's dream, "It's his projection, Mom."

"Mm-hm," I said.

&

Yohosame went to the mosque to pray later in the day. Sadaf wanted to run an errand, and she jiggled the brass front doorknob. The door had been dead-bolted from the outside. My son made no conscious choice to lock us up, but Islam was insidious—it seeped in. Life on the top two floors of the houses—where the women stay, never entering the streets—began to sound okay. I took to saying Morocco was my favorite place to hate. All three of us began to have attacks of insecurity, bouts of frustration, crying jags. We were like weak teabags, over-steeped in our surroundings.

Communication was an unexpected minefield. We spent a lot of time explaining what we meant when we said whatever it was we'd said, whenever we weren't watching doomsday documentaries on a computer screen. This was one serious vacation.

"I didn't mean to lock you in, and I don't know why I said I'd hear about your behavior after you're gone. I don't know why I said that," Yohosame said, shaking his head.

"It's okay, honey. We aren't ourselves here."

The next morning Yohosame went out first and came back to invite me to Yusuf's friend Adnan's house. Adnan was a morning person, up early each day to rinse off the street. "Come in. Coffee is ready," said Adnan.

Adnan was older than most of Yusuf's friends, a contemporary. Yusuf's friends were often older father figures or kids. Adnan wore Western dress, no facial hair, a salt-and-pepper thatch on his head. His eyes nested in wrinkled pouches, lively, full of stories to tell.

He spoke without stopping of his father and Yusuf in an interchangeable and rambling discourse, handing me family photographs—sepia-toned squares with tiny figures, glimpses of his past. He invited us to visit his mother who lived in an outlying village, then he circled back in a seamless return to his father's independence in old age. How proud he was of insisting he wash his own feet before prayer—wipe his own ass. My thoughts journeyed from Dad's decline in Mexico, through the helplessness I found unbearable after back surgery, to mother's deathbed style, while Adnan relived his father's last days, sprinkled with links—mysterious links—to Yusuf, whose ghost presided over all such exchanges.

He spoke of the upper stories in the stacked houses, women's society. "Never do the men smoke with the women," said Adnan, rolling a hash-sprinkled joint to share with me. He moved on to Marx's assertion that religion is the opiate of the masses, with which he disagreed.

Religion was everything there in Asilah—separate from nothing, an endlessly fascinating topic. Adnan compared and contrasted qualities of ascension within various belief systems, analyzing subtleties: he found Buddhism soft; "awake" in Islam was stronger.

"In the garden of silence you are free; free to forget the phantasm posing as reality," he said. "Everyone is either asleep in the illusion or awake in the truth. Everyone born of woman eats, drinks, sleeps and dies. Words can be bought; books change. The Qu'ran does not change. Allah is for everyone, for all time."

Adnan described Yusuf as he walked home from the Mosque, his face shining with inner peace. He let him be, refrained from a polite good morning or good afternoon, not wishing to intrude upon Yusuf's silence.

I climbed up crude steps to admire a rooftop full of growing things; Adnan was a gardener as well as a rinser of streets. I was first to disengage, thank Adnan, and return to our nearby house. Later Yohosame said Adnan loves to practice English but probably understood very little of what I said. Yohosame spoke *some* Arabic. I have a bit of French and Spanish, but said more with eye contact, hand gestures, and body language. I enjoyed the spiritual discourse, and joined in when I could. If any organized religion had offered answers that did not require a lobotomy to embrace, I would have subscribed, but it is this spiritual communion that offers real solace, and in timeless moments, words aren't necessary—in the garden of silence, we are free.

Six

$\mathcal{M}$y world was the hollow, seamless sound of the sea. Drums sounded in the distance and blended with the waves' pulls and thrusts. A keening voice implored the faithful, broadcast from loudspeakers with competing static. I awoke in my room with the arched, white lattice door, windows open to the terrace where sunrise shimmered. A breeze stippled the mid-summer air, and fanned it, rippling sheer white curtains.

Sadaf had left for Tangiers to meet a friend flying in from Dubai for one night. So Yohosame and I were on our own for a day. Late morning we exited the medina and headed for the already crowded cafés across the street. Adnan sat alone, looking disgruntled, but stood and welcomed us to his table, and started right in on his speed-rap. I took a chair on the outside, free to look around, while Yohosame engaged our friend.

Abdul shuffled through paintings for a group of Spanish women. Moustafa nodded from another table and I nodded back. I was getting to know this cast of characters. While my eyes wandered over the lively café and street scene, I listened in to Adnan's monologue. Today he compared the vocals of Janis Joplin and Patti Smith. I imagined animated talks he had with Yusuf—Yusuf who was passionate about music. Adnan preferred Patti Smith. He tried to describe what bothered him about Janis, and stopped without completing his thought. But I knew what he was trying to say.

"Janis Joplin's voice was full of whiskey."

"What?" I had his attention now.

"Janis Joplin's voice was full of whiskey," I said.

"Oh yes," said Adnan, nodding thoughtfully.

"And," Yohosame said, "Patti Smith's voice has the aftertaste of heroin." We all nodded assent—communication.

Adnan said again he would take us to his mother's house in the country. I doubted these drives would happen. No time to meet all the mothers, to confer with the sheiks at the mosque, or to visit Morocco's version of Stonehenge. Too hellishly hot to travel by train to other towns, as Sadaf was eager to do—relaxation her biggest challenge. She lived in hyper-vigilance, the legacy of a childhood spent caring for parents. That night she would explore new Tangiers.

Yohosame and I moved through the Medina's corridors on our way home and caught snatches of song as we passed. Here Marvin Gaye's "Sexual Healing" wafted out of a bedroom window, there the ubiquitous Beatles. Live music, world music, constant music now: heavy percussion beat out rhythms, bare hands on animal skin, sticks on wood, metal on metal, cymbals, ankle bells, and drums. Wind instruments—breathy flutes and voices—played, moaned, called and responded, wove melodies through the rhythms in the village's lit-up, labyrinthine heart center.

We traced the medina's curves, stunning murals covering the tallest facades in brilliant paint. Jewel-toned shapes and flourishes—like the music—expressed movement in dynamic phrasing. Sculptured scrawls flowed into forms: figures danced, birds soared, and landscapes pulsed.

A tiny man stood in a doorway, dwarfed by a white-robed teacher from the mosque and a woman wrapped in a *djellaba*. A mad smurf: white wisps of hair stood out in tufts like meringue, bright eyes, and wet mouth with three big teeth prominent in an ecstatic smile. The man brightened further as we approached, beamed when he saw Yohosame, who remembered him from last time he was there, five years ago. We were welcomed in. Yohosame tried to back out, said he'd be there through September, another time, please—we were on our way home. But when the man learned Yohosame would be there through Ramadan, living in his closet after Sadaf and I left, he invited him to move in.

I loved this hospitality that enfolded my son in clouds of generosity. The mad smurf tried again to draw us inside, and Yohosame again demurred, but it was clear to me resistance was futile. I surrendered and entered, following the motioning arm down a long, tunneled hallway.

Out of the heat, we penetrated deep shade in the center of the house, entered a room lined with upholstered benches. Small tables were set with heavy silver, tea, and coffee services. The teacher from the mosque and the wrapped-up woman sat down too. No one spoke English—not a word. They got along in the Arabic Yohosame had mastered, and when that broke down, they quoted scriptures from the Qu'ran in unison, everyone on the same wave-length. Like reborn Christians or Jehovah's Witnesses, the tract was the tract was the tract. What else was there to talk about? What was personal existence in the face of the truth?

They recited the elevated passages, a look of rapture on their faces. Islam was for everyone, a joyous, inclusive path. Our language deficit was no barrier. Everyone joined in except me, but I was included somehow. I was the mother of Hossam. I was Yusuf's first wife. I was making my pilgrimage on the tenth anniversary of his death. Yohosame bore a strong resemblance to his father, but people were intrigued to see me around his edges. Casual encounters, charged with emotion, were delicious, disheveling falls down rabbit holes. As I walked through the medina I knew behind each door were minor miracles of connection, wordless recognitions, causes for celebration.

Yohosame and I settled in Sadaf's quarters for the afternoon. When we first arrived, I saw the red walls, the crimson satin bedspread, the heavy vermillion curtains, and kept on climbing to the cool aqua cell one more flight up. But this space was perfect for dramatic, voluptuous, young Sadaf. Her bedroom had a Juliet balcony that overlooked the ground-floor living and dining areas, the huge coffee table, the daybed stacked with pillows. Her adjoining sitting room was spacious enough for a desk, couches, and tables. A full wall of windows opened onto the sea, and the street scene below was louder, more visceral from the second floor.

◠

Sadaf's great-grandfather and great-great-grandfather were kings of Afghanistan—her grandfather, the head of the People's Party. More recently her Uncle Zalmai had made a bid to become President of Afghanistan after Karzai stepped down, the only candidate progressive enough to choose a female running mate.

Sadaf had packed a lot of living into her thirty-three years. She'd given birth to a son at fifteen, and without financial help or emotional support she had completed high school. At the commencement ceremony, her mother, Mabuba, admitted it was in spite of her and Yusuf that Sadaf was poised to achieve. And achieve she did.

Sadaf went on to receive a BA from the College of Santa Fe, then moved with her son to Costa Rica to earn an MA in conflict resolution from the United Nations' University of Peace. I traveled to the capital city, San José, in 2004, to celebrate her triumph. Sadaf was a natural, loving mother, and her son benefited from the exposures, from her strength, and from their varied, busy life; he became an A student and star athlete. I marveled at them both, and it was a privilege to keep them close.

◠

The next day I wandered late morning, and Sadaf and her friend surprised me on the street. He was a high-energy, super–buff American guy fresh from skydiving in Dubai. We sat in the only café inside the medina and talked about the one-square-mile green city outside Dubai, the progressive getaway. He described Saudi women who flew in for fun, chucked their *hijabs, burkas,* and headscarves in the airport bathroom, and emerged in revealing dress, spiked heels, full makeup, and lots of liberated hair. The women drove off in packs behind the wheels of rented red convertibles.

Ramadan began this morning, for some, with a new moon in

Saudi Arabia, where Mecca resided. Here in Morocco, however, there were hardliners who declared the new moon must first be seen. The moon was not yet visible anywhere, so they would wait until the next day to begin the month of fasting and feasting. It was a fine point of contention. Everyone seemed to realize there *was* a new moon, even though they could not see it yet. I asked Yohosame what happened if the sky is cloudy, and I was unrelieved to learn there was an allowance for postponing the start of Ramadan a few days in the event of cloud cover.

I bided my time, tried to be open to the still-unfolding experience. I was glad we'd see the beginning of Ramadan, the core of Muslim devotion. It wasn't the trip we'd planned, but when Sadaf sent me photos of the house she'd found on the Internet, and I saw the *krekia* and the sumptuous rooms, I said yes.

Now I sang "Life Is Just a Bowl of Cherries" over and over like a mantra, courting acceptance. "As Time Goes By" reminded me of fundamentals, calmed me amidst the frenetic atmosphere. My self-soothing medley climaxed in the feel-good favorite "You Are My Sunshine," crooned to our housekeeper's entranced two-year-old boy—big dreamy eyes seeking mine as I serenaded him.

Yohosame was glad we'd joined him this summer. When Yusuf was alive, he'd encouraged me to visit Asilah and I'd wanted to see him in his new environment. Then when he died, taking care of Dad, who had just lost Casey, had been a priority, and Sadaf and Yohosame had traveled to Asilah alone. Yohosame reminded me it *had* been ten years since his father died, and I'd always meant to come.

⌒

One day when I lived in Santa Fe, I rounded up a few women friends and we headed north to Abiquiu for the day to hike the mesa and explore the drip castle White Place which was close to the mosque where Yusuf lived. I had called earlier to let him know we'd stop by before returning home.

I pulled up to Yusuf's little adobe house for tea in the afternoon. He was a good-humored host, enjoyed the influx of feminine energy.

After tea I carried empty cups to the kitchen where Yusuf stood at the sink washing dishes, fastidious as usual. I spotted an open box of Super Dieters Tea on the counter. Super Dieters Tea was a powerful laxative.

"Are you doing a cleanse, Yusuf?"

Yusuf turned to me, amusement animating his face, the scar that creased his forehead a faint reminder of his accident.

"No, you are," he said.

"Oh my god, you didn't. You know we'll be lucky to get home before it hits. What were you thinking?" I said sprinting out of the kitchen, "Come on women, we have to go right now!"

As I herded my troops to the car, I glanced back at Yusuf, "Thanks honey, so thoughtful of you," I said. His grin lit up the doorway to the room full of books and music, full of toys for the kids who came to play with the joker of Dar-al-Islam.

⮌

I'm clear that when a loved one dies, it isn't their virtues we miss. It's the idiosyncratic behaviors that drove us crazy in life, that, in absence, define them. Those annoying traits give us the juiciest, most visceral reminders of what they meant to us, how they changed us, and how we carry them forward. For it is aliveness—in whatever form it takes—that is memorable, that distinguishes us as individuals within the grand promenade. Yusuf lost much in life—essential brain function—but his life illustrated the spirit which can't be lost. My memories were unleashed from any orderly passage. They swirled like Sufi dancers, and encircled my reverie.

Seven

Sirens whined through the sweltering night to announce the beginning of Ramadan. I fell into an exhausted sleep on the fourth-floor rooftop and awoke on a bare mattress under a clothesline. Laundry hung limp overhead like flags of surrender. All Muslims now agreed: the new moon was in the sky, seen by the naked eye.

Now that Ramadan was upon us, I saw firsthand that stress brought out the worst in human nature. Someone sincere—someone like Yusuf—would have been a model. Like the flying saucer attendees at Giant Rock who thought he was Jesus Christ incarnate, these men had seen their beliefs reflected in Yusuf—a stranger who hailed from the place they wish to escape to, and who chose instead their place, the place they belonged to, yet chafed against. Yusuf couldn't help but stand out. I imagined him considering his final chapter—propelled by past momentum as possible options erupted like lava and cooled into one committed magma river.

Yusuf embraced impermanence. Daily, in his interactions and in his prayers, he met harsh realities in surrender to what he believed imperishable. When my second husband, Brian, died, Yusuf and his brother came and bolstered Yohosame and me. Two years later we lost Brian's brother, Bruce, Yusuf's best friend—both casualties of the family disease of alcoholism. And it was through my marriage to Brian that I finally understood my own family. I hadn't become alcoholic—I'd married one instead, a common pattern.

⌐∩

Sadaf looked up from her computer screen, gave me the evil-genius grin that knit her eyebrows together like a blue-eyed Frida Kahlo, and coined a word for our experience:

"Drama dan. D'Ramadan."

We convulsed with laughter in the living room on the enormous, pillowed day bed, muffling our hilarity out of respect for Yohosame, who still slept. She and Yohosame had argued over Islam the previous night, angry point by angry point. Close siblings, it was the first real contention they faced.

Today, Friday, was a holy day. Men and women went to mosques and visited the graves of ancestors. Sadaf took offerings brought from home to the cemetery to lay on their father's grave. She reported she felt a strong presence when she left the flowers, sweets, tobacco, and photos. Like the Day of the Dead in Mexico, the cemeteries were in a respectful fiesta mode—families cleaning and planting the plots, arranging flowers and artifacts. So many parallels between Morocco and Mexico: the constant religious observance, the relentless hustle, the poverty. A callous and colorful realism reigns where great difficulty couples with great faith. The same things are neglected: waste disposal, conservation, health and education, birth control.

⌐∩

When Yohosame was a baby, Rodney—our honorary guru—held him upside down by his feet until he bellowed. He shook him and admired his lungs, and the strong will in charge of the brand-new body. Rodney did it while I ran errands. He did it as part of George's rigorous training. By that time George was in Rodney's thrall. The ex-marine-now-guru filled a deep need.

Jeff—who, with Drew, was one of my two sixties sidekicks—came back into my life in the summer of '86. Drew had returned to the desert to make art, while Jeff had stayed in Marin County and taken part in the seventies movement to free people from hang ups. He moved bound-up bodies from false modesty to sauna, then hot tub, then to open-air, full-body massage. When the participants were loosened into trust, Jeff guided them into a mirrored, carpeted room, where he encouraged them to discover their own rhythms—the secrets they kept from themselves. Then they danced, finally danced.

And Jeff danced, on stages with a full chorale background, wearing a silver tuxedo studded with five thousand hand-sewn rhinestones. Trixie Jarrette's Palm Springs dance studio trained both him and Gerri, who took center stage in recitals. Gerri recovered from her LSD trip the night we saw Nina Simone in North Beach, and became a regular on the Carol Burnett Show.

Yohosame was seventeen and attending a nearby boarding school in 1986. He came home to meet the Jeff he'd heard so much about. Then, in a Reno restaurant, we spotted Rodney across the room— all of us on our way to a Dylan concert, the Heartbreak Tour with Tom Petty. We planned a reunion peak climb; we'd do it once again. Yohosame flew to New Mexico and returned with his father, and we met Rodney at the trailhead in Yosemite's Tuolumne Meadows to reconfigure our sixties routine decades later.

Yohosame packed and unpacked my Mercedes sedan. Jeff and I made camp, and Yusuf came along for the ride. Rodney built our campfire as he'd done so many times before, accompanying the ritualistic gathering, stacking, and igniting with a mellow rap about synchronicity. Here we were again, around a fire assessing how the years had shaped us.

"I want to hear everything about the sixties," Yohosame said. "Mom always played the music, and I love the music, and I heard about all the camping and concerts. Hey, I hear you shook me upside down by my feet when I was a baby."

Rodney looked serious in the firelight, poking at the burning wood that hissed and sparked at the end of his stick. His voice was grave as he looked into Yohosame's eyes and said, "I did, and for that I am most deeply sorry."

"That's okay, I survived. I've just always been curious about it," Yohosame said, "about what you thought you were doing."

"I thought I knew a lot back then. I'd been a sergeant in the

Marines, and I was full of myself, and in love with my own strength," Rodney said as tears slid down his cheeks and disappeared into his full beard, salted with gray. "But life is a great leveler. It flattened me before I learned humility. We had a son, Suzy and I, a beautiful boy like you, and I did to him what I did to you. He died in my arms a long time ago, and I can't bring him back. I thought there was something to test, something to prove. I couldn't have been more wrong, and I couldn't be sorrier."

We were stunned silent, we in the circle—focused on the fire: witnesses. Rodney sobbed softly, received our pats on the back and murmured comfort—but his grief was unimaginable and permanent. Remorse was carried forward, he told us, and the marriage survived. Wiser parents produced more children. Rodney was a family man, a humbled penitent, with a raw nerve we'd touched.

We climbed, and we swam in the river in separate shifts to accommodate Yusuf, who, as a Muslim, could not bathe in the same water as women. He prayed on boulders along our ascent to Echo Peak. In camp, Yusuf grinned, and behind him, carved into the trunk of a Ponderosa Pine, was the face of a grinning man. Every one noticed it at once, riveted by the energy of the synergistic moment. I grabbed my camera.

⤺

Here in Asilah someone saw that photo, and made a painting. The canvas hung in the room where Yusuf died, now his son's room.

Yohosame wanted to be with us at the end of our visit, and would add time to the end of Ramadan. We located a midday café, aware that most locals were fasting, and pulled plastic chairs around plastic tables with metal tubing legs. We'd chosen one in a row of identical outdoor cafés, separated by plastic awnings. The menus listing items were indecipherable, but the dishes were pictured on billboards across the street. They crowned storefronts with kitchens in the back where the food was prepared. We pointed to the oversized pictures of what we wanted, and waited while the streets fill with hungry, thirsty people.

"This is all so plastic," Yohosame said, eyeing the awnings, the billboards, the tables and chairs. "Everything's made of petroleum."

"Yes, a world made of death—a constant reminder of failure," I said, sipping from a tall glass of iced coffee. "The baby boomers saw a crisis coming fifty years ago, but we failed to turn it around, I'm sorry to say."

"I wasn't there, but the hippies couldn't have imagined the current climate: corporations granted the rights of individuals—individual sociopaths, that is." Yohosame said, raking his fork across the plastic tablecloth.

It was an uncomfortable topic, not only because we believed the future was threatened, but because we received income from oil—either oil George Jr. and his brother Arthur's wildcatting days had earned, or oil pumped from Lucky Baldwin's land in California. We hated the years when the oil men occupied the White House, but we had to admit that we had benefited, and we lived with the hypocrisy.

"It's getting harder to ignore," Yohosame said. "Every time I turn a key or board a plane, I know it doesn't matter how much I recycle, it isn't enough."

"Or every time I cash an oil check," I said.

"I'll be self-supporting next year, and *that* feels good," Yohosame said.

"I hope it works out, honey. Money doesn't buy happiness, but the lack of it is measurable in degrees of misery."

The waiter brought platters of food on a huge tray from across the street, dodging horse-drawn carriages and cars, weaving through foot traffic on the busy main avenue.

Back at the house, we watched *Democracy Now*. The detention center at Guantanamo Bay would force-feed Muslim hunger strikers during Ramadan. The violation's full impact made us cry.

With the sun's slow descent there was frenzy in the marketplace. The dehydrated, hungry, strung out people invaded each other's space—yelled, shoved, fought. Some craved tobacco, kef, or hashish. The fracas crescendoed as the sun set, and then it was time to break the fast. An hour and a half before dawn, kids came through the streets banging drums to alert the faithful to their last chance to eat or drink until sunset.

Tomorrow we would leave. I entrusted the repair and care of Yusuf's grave to his son. I let go. I packed my memories: of sunrise and sunset views, of the *krekia*, the sea, the flashes of bold color and crystalline starburst patterns, the putrid odors, the seedy splendor—the burnt-out offerings of life's forgotten struggles.

Eight

Paris 2003

Christmas 2003 in Paris had seemed a good plan. No one could have foreseen November's losses: Casey and Yusuf gone the same day. Stunned, I flew in with a friend, and we headed straight for the Champs Élysées, lined with glowing goblet trees and animated *mer d' l'humanité*. We ambled with jet-lagged gait, grounding in the new cityscape and new time zone. At 1:00 a.m., I awaited Yohosame's arrival from Tangiers after a thirty-hour bus ride—coming back from his unplanned month in Asilah tying up his father's affairs.

At Notre Dame the next day, I lit candles—powerful rituals for shattering times. I breathed the air, redolent of paraffin and incense, reminiscent of my childhood. Then we left the cathedral and wandered, still saturated in French Catholicism. We entered Métro stops named for saints and hurtled beneath the City of Light, bracing for stops and starts. It was a dynamic tableau under the skin of Paris—a human throng moving toward our desires and running from our fears. The faces were full of composure, resignation, savoir-faire. One saw it all and kept moving. One filled one's time while one could— before the big sleep, before the boat slipped its moorings and slid out over a moonlit sea, free of reference, attachment, or form.

At Sacré Coeur, the magnificent white cathedral on the hill, I knelt at the end of the pew and blessed myself. My contrary, involuntary laughter burst forth amid Gregorian chants. Was it grief, frivolity, or illness, perhaps a spontaneous conversion? As a girl I'd suppressed the same bubble of mirth when sitting with my grandmother in church.

On the street we gazed at gargoyles, solid sentinels against a changing sky—the famously desirable light. Then we crossed the spangled, meandering Seine on footbridges, looking down at the reflected winter sky.

And for two freezing hours, we stood in the uncoiling line in front of the Grand Palais to be warmed by Gauguin's Tahitian paintings. I returned to my limited self, and accepted my losses—more grave than buoyant, more resigned than surrendered. I settled somewhere in the mind where deals are struck, and decisions are made about how to move forward: a calculated and counterfeit peace.

Then, when beliefs finally fled, I felt the triggers of sadness without moving. And, in stopping, I knew what can't be lost, what isn't inherited or passed on—that the clarity and aliveness of the present moment is who one truly is, and I planed complexity into something simple enough—light enough like amber—to carry home.

ഗ

Paris 2013

Sadaf and I faced off in opposite rows of molded plastic chairs at Charles de Gaulle airport. We awaited the last lap home. My chin rested on the retractable handle of my carry-on. Satisfied, ironic smiles exchanged between us, all words said, messages delivered, grave visited. Now to gaze at the international travelers—now to drift through internal waterways, images pooling into eddies, spooling out on currents of thought and memory.

The previous morning, Yohosame had walked us to the mouth of the medina. A taxi pulled up and the bearded driver opened his door and waved us over. "Aeroporte Tangiers?" Sadaf asked, shrugging off her backpack.

"You and madam? Two hundred durhams each. Thirty minutes, I get you there," he said.

Yohosame leaned in close for a parting hug. "Love you, mom, don't worry about me."

"No, I won't worry, sweetheart. I'll see you when I see you."

Yohosame opened the taxi door and I slid across the broad back seat as brother and sister said good-bye. An early flight: Tangiers to Paris. Overnight in the same hotel I found lacking after the Mediterranean, after Monte Carlo—the same room of the same hotel, now plush and accommodating after two weeks in Asilah.

Every perception is relative to another. Our big, double-lobed brain makes sense of what we see—fills in the gaps until we recognize what we already know and filter out the rest. We look at paintings up close and see color fields, shapes, and brushstrokes. A shift in perspective offers a cohesive image that mimics reality. How far back from our own lives must we stand—and in what degree of detachment—before the patterns emerge? We make the shift, and the movement shakes loose lively worlds within us, imaginary until we bring them forth in poems, songs, conversation. Our journey is to retrieve our dormant selves; our challenge, to make peace with our inherited patterns.

Our flight home was called over invisible loudspeakers, and we went through the gathering motions, shuffled in an orderly mass into numbered lines to board. Sadaf wore a street sweeper hat circled with pom-poms that jiggled as she shouldered her pack and led the way. I rolled my bag down the shabby tunnel, glad to have made this pilgrimage, grateful for the kids, and this sense of well-being that had sifted over everything.

⌒

Often I've yearned to understand life in unambiguous terms: after Debbie's suicide, at the end of the sixties when Edna O'Dowd walked into the hills and disappeared, after Mike Ellis was hit by someone who ran and left him by the highway a week before our tenth high school reunion, in the wake of Casey and Yusuf's death on the same November day, and most recently when my father said, "Wouldn't it be funny if I died from this routine procedure?" and then he did.

Naked times to slow, to stop—in new willingness to understand nothing, finally to see the possibility of surrender. My questions form a final barrier, and I have to let them go. Only then does my thrashing about on the precipice quiet. And, mid-leap into the abyss, yammering mind stills, is supple, and opens.

A teenage girl swims in the sea at night. The inky black is so frosted with starlight, she wonders where the surface is and where is the depth—which element is for breathing, and what is subject to drown.

I see Dad lurch down the hallway, chardonnay slopping over the rim of his glass, splashing onto his buttoned-down shirt sleeve, dripping a trail across the carpet. I watch him crush garden snails and fling them over the cliff, declaring, "I'm never eating escargot again. I don't care how good the sauce is."

I see Casey warming up over martinis, making strangers squirm with her inebriated getting-to-know-you style. I imagine her persuading Roger to zip her up into Dad's suitcase when he packed to leave.

I see Mother practice her evil eye. Standing before the oversized make-up mirror, she perfects her scowl, trying hard to be more intimidating than lovely.

I see Debbie's curvy grin, the beauty mark high on one cheek, as she leans over—just as the ski lift reaches the station at the top of the mountain—and slowly, with malice aforethought, unbuckles her mother's ski boot and binding.

Still I wonder what she felt as she executed her plan, how much room she left for a change of mind. I see her rolling rags she found, sealing cracks until she sat in complete darkness on the tucked-and-rolled leather seat. I imagine her hesitation in the stillness before turning the cold, cold key—before the animal roar of the engine, before the fumes began to undo her. I wonder when, and with what new urge to live, she switched off the motor before she succumbed, too late to intervene in her own act.

I was told it was a call to sobriety for the community, for those gathered that night, musicians set up after-hours in the living room, promised drinks and dancing until dawn, the boisterous pleasures stretched out as far as they would go. I was told the couples went home sobered, kissed their kids as they slept, and resolved to do better. I've heard Debbie haunts the lighthouse. If so, I wonder what drew her back, held her in limbo, and made her our family's hungry ghost.

Together in the pure and primal moment—inexhaustible and complete—we know we *are* the truth we seek. In the irony of doing nothing, we see everything. And in the imaginary landscape of memory and projection, all the ghosts dance free.

Deborah Stockham

Photo credit: Highschool photo 1962

Acknowledgments

My deep gratitude to Eva Hunter and Norman Corwin for showing me how to write from the heart. And to those at the writing table: Jim Knoch, Margaret Tallis, Cazz Roberts, Sharon Conklin, and Carol Merchasin for their patient encouragement, respect for the craft, and invaluable feedback.

My thanks to first readers: Cynthia Simmons, Laura Joseph Woods, Norman Lofthus, and Lauren Coodley; my editors, Steven Joseph, Kristin Masters, and Krissa Lagos. And my home team: Pueblito, Antonio, Mario, Margaret, and Homar for keeping me going through the long process.

And endless love and gratitude to my travel companions: Yohosame, Indra, Sadaf and Sudy, who give me specific hope for the future.

Credits

TENDERLY Lyrics by Jack Lawrence, Music by Walter Gross (c) 1946, 1947 EDWIN H. MORRIS & COMPANY, A Division of MPL Music Publishing, Inc. Copyright Renewed, extended term of Copyright deriving from Jack Lawrence assigned and effective August 7, 2002 to RANGE ROAD MUSIC INC. All Rights Reserved. *Reprinted by Permission of Hal Leonard Corporation*

HALLELUJAH © 1985 Sony/A TV Music Publishing LLC. All rights administered by Sony/A TV Music Publishing LLC, 424 Church Street, Nashville, TN 37219. All rights reserved. Used by permission.

Excerpt(s) from *THE OPEN DOOR* by Helen Keller, copyright © 1957 by Helen Keller. Used by permission of Doubleday, an imprint of the Knopf Doubleday Publishing Group, a division of Penguin Random House LLC. All rights reserved. Any third party use of this material, outside of this publication, is prohibited. Interested parties must apply directly to Penguin Random House LLC for permission.

Excerpt(s) from *PLAYER PIANO: A NOVEL* by Kurt Vonnegut, copyright © 1952, 1980 by Kurt Vonnegut, Jr. Used by permission of Dell Publishing, an imprint of Random House, a division of Penguin Random House LLC. All rights reserved. Any third party use of this material, outside of this publication, is prohibited. Interested parties must apply directly to Penguin Random House LLC for permission.

Excerpt(s) from *BRAIN DROPPINGS* by George Carlin used by permission of Hachette Book Group. All rights reserved. Any third party use of this material, outside of this publication, is prohibited. Interested parties must apply directly to Penguin Random House LLC for permission.

Leon Weiseltier quote *WHAT WE AFFIRM* used by Permission of PARS International Corp. Manages Reprint Programs.

I COULD NOT ASK FOR MORE Words and Music by Diane Warren. Copyright 1999 REALSONGS (ASCAP) All Rights Reserved. Used by Permission of ALFRED MUSIC.

About the Author

© Yohosame Cameron

*T*erry Cameron Baldwin is originally from California, where she received a BA in psychology and a BFA in painting and printmaking from Sierra Nevada College in Lake Tahoe. She has worked as a stained glass artisan, painter, printmaker, jeweler, and calligrapher. She has lived in San Miguel de Allende, Mexico since 2006. She is active on Facebook, and her website is: www.terrycameronbaldwin.com.

SELECTED TITLES FROM SHE WRITES PRESS

She Writes Press is an independent publishing company
founded to serve women writers everywhere.
Visit us at www.shewritespress.com.

The Coconut Latitudes: Secrets, Storms, and Survival in the Caribbean by
Rita Gardner $16.95, 978-1-63152-901-6
A haunting, lyrical memoir about a dysfunctional family's experiences
in a reality far from the envisioned Eden—and the terrible cost of keeping secrets.

Loveyoubye: Holding Fast, Letting Go, And Then There's The Dog by
Rossandra White $16.95, 978-1-938314-50-6
A soul-searching memoir detailing the painful, but ultimately liberat-
ing, disintegration of a twenty-five-year marriage.

Don't Leave Yet: How My Mother's Alzheimer's Opened My Heart by
Constance Hanstedt $16.95, 978-1-63152-952-8
The chronicle of Hanstedt's journey toward independence, self-assur-
ance, and connectedness as she cares for her mother, who is rapidly
losing her own identity to the early stage of Alzheimer's.

A Different Kind of Same: A Memoir by Kelley Clink
$16.95, 978-1-63152-999-3
Several years before Kelley Clink's brother hanged himself, she
attempted suicide by overdose. In the aftermath of his death, she traces
the evolution of both their illnesses, and wonders: If he couldn't make it,
what hope is there for her?

Her Beautiful Brain: A Memoir by Ann Hedreen
$16.95, 978-1-938314-92-6
The heartbreaking story of a daughter's experiences as her beauti-
ful, brainy mother begins to lose her mind to an unforgiving disease:
Alzheimer's.

*Don't Call Me Mother: A Daughter's Journey from Abandonment to
Forgiveness* by Linda Joy Myers
$16.95, 978-1-938314-02-5
Linda Joy Myers's story of how she transcended the prisons of her child-
hood by seeking—and offering—forgiveness for her family's sins